Bay of Pigs

Florida A&M University, Tallahassee
Florida Atlantic University, Boca Raton
Florida Gulf Coast University, Ft. Myers
Florida International University, Miami
Florida State University, Tallahassee
University of Central Florida, Orlando
University of Florida, Gainesville
University of North Florida, Jacksonville
University of South Florida, Tampa
University of West Florida, Pensacola

BRIGADA ASALTO 2506

BAY OF PIGS

AN ORAL HISTORY OF BRIGADE 2506

Victor Andres Triay

University Press of Florida

Gainesville · Tallahassee · Tampa · Boca Raton · Pensacola

Orlando · Miami · Jacksonville · Ft. Myers

Copyright 2001 by the Board of Regents of the State of Florida
Printed in the United States of America on acid-free paper
All rights reserved

06 05 04 03 02 01   6 5 4 3 2 1

Library of Congress Cataloging-in-Publication Data
Triay, Victor Andres, 1966–
Bay of Pigs: an oral history of Brigade 2506 / Victor Andres Triay
p. cm.
Includes bibliographical references and index.
ISBN 0-8130-2090-5 (alk. paper)
1. Cuba—History—Invasion, 1961—Personal narratives.
2. Brigada de Asalto 2506. I. Title.

F1788.T75 2001
972.9106'4—dc21 00-067816

The University Press of Florida is the scholarly publishing
agency for the State University System of Florida, comprising
Florida A&M University, Florida Atlantic University, Florida
Gulf Coast University, Florida International University, Florida
State University, University of Central Florida, University of
Florida, University of North Florida, University of South Florida,
and University of West Florida.

University Press of Florida
15 Northwest 15th Street
Gainesville, FL 32611-2079
http://www.upf.com

For Emy

CONTENTS

Preface ix

A Revolution Betrayed 1

1. A Call to Arms 7

The Students: Jorge Silveira, 16; Mario A. Martínez-Malo, 18; Juan "Johnny" Clark, 19

The Rebel: Higinio "Nino" Diaz, 21

The Cadets: Hugo Sueiro, 23; Esteban Bovo, 26

Civilians and Working Men: Jorge Giró, 27; Andrés Manso, 28; Jorge Marquet, 29; Antonio González de León, 32; Rolando Martínez, 33; Mario Girbau, 35

2. Training and Preparation 37

Hugo Sueiro, 46; Sergio Carrillo, 48; Mario Abril, 50; Francisco "Pepe" Hernández, 51; Francisco Molina, 53; Eduardo Zayas-Bazán, 54; Néstor Carbonell, 58

The Infiltrators: Javier Souto, 61; José "Pepe" Regalado, 62

3. The Battle 68

April 16 and 17 72

April 18 78

Apriol 19 80

D-2: Gustavo Ponzoa, 83; José Flores, 85

The Invasion, Blue Beach, Girón: Grayston Lynch, 87; Jorge Herrera, 89; Tulio Díaz Suárez, 91; Ricardo "Ricky" Sánchez, 93

The Invasion, Red Beach, Playa Larga: Francisco "Pepe" Hernández, 98;

Rafael Montalvo, 99; Luis Morse, 103; Jorge Marquet, 104; Juan
  Figueras, 105; Juan Sordo, 107; Luis León, 108
The Invasion: Air War: Esteban Bovo, 109; Gustavo Ponzoa, 110
The Invasion: Infiltration Teams/Underground: José Basulto, 110; Rogelio
  González Corzo, "Francisco," 112

4. Retreat and Capture   114

Humberto Cortina, 115; Luis Morse, 118; Pedro Encinosa, 119; Fernando
  Martínez Reyna, 121; Julio Sánchez de Cárdenas, 122; Sergio Carrillo, 124;
  Tomás Macho, S.J., 125; José "Pepe" Regalado, 127; Alberto Sánchez de
  Bustamante, 127; Jorge Giró, 130

5. Prison and Liberation   131

Jorge Silveira, 138; Mario A. Martínez-Malo, 142; Eduardo Zayas-Bazán,
  144; Sergio Carrillo, 146
Sports Palace: José Basulto, 148; Rafael Montalvo, 148; Andrés Manso, 148;
  Julio Sánchez de Cárdenas, 148; Jorge Herrera, 149
Injured Prisoner: Fernando Martínez Reyna, 149
Naval Hospital: Juan "Johnny" Clark, 149
Negotiations for Release: Néstor Carbonell, 150; Hugo Sueiro, 150;
  Humberto Cortina, 151
Castillo del Príncipe: Mario Abril, 151
The Trial: Antonio González de León, 152; Rafael Montalvo, 152; Jorge
  Marquet, 153
Isla de Pinos: Tulio Díaz Suárez, 153; Tomás Macho, S.J., 153
Reunion: Jorge Marquet, 154; Pedro Encinosa, 154
The Orange Bowl: Juan Sordo, 155; Fernando Martínez Reyna, 155; Grayston
  Lynch, 155; Andrés Manso, 155; Alberto Sánchez de Bustamante, 155

6. Those Left Behind   156

Myrna Pardo Millán, 157; Rosa María "Ia" Freyre, 163; María Leonor
  Portela, 165; María "Mary" Wilrycx Allen, 168; Josefina Encinosa, 172;
  Dulce Carrera Jústiz, 174; Esperanza Díaz Suárez, 176; Isabel
  Quiñones, 177

7. The Aftermath   179

Appendix   185
Notes   187
Bibliography   193
Index   197

PREFACE

The failure of the Bay of Pigs invasion had profound consequences for the United States and Cuba alike. For the U.S. government, the event represented both a foreign policy failure and the beginning of an era of mutual distrust between different sectors of the government. It also brought with it a Soviet-backed base in the Americas, from which numerous Marxist guerrilla movements in the hemisphere would be sponsored. The Bay of Pigs invasion had even greater significance, however, for the people of Cuba. Those who supported the Castro regime at the time saw in it a great victory, a validation of their faith in Cuba's new order. For Cubans opposed to Communist rule, the failed invasion represented the end of Cuba's hope for democracy and the initiation of a period of totalitarian, Marxist rule on the island. It also marked the beginning of a mass migration of Cubans to the United States which, to date, has lasted over four decades.

This book is an oral history of Brigade 2506, the unit of Cuban exile volunteers who were recruited, trained, and landed at the Bay of Pigs by the United States on April 17, 1961. With the exception of certain elements of the leaders' story written by Haynes Johnson in the early 1960s, the story of the Brigade largely has been ignored in most English-language writings about the Bay of Pigs invasion. While discussing the invasion mostly from the point of view of its significance to the United States, the works largely have portrayed the men of the Brigade as secondary characters or, at worst, irrelevant, nameless, faceless pawns. It is the goal of this work to present these men, in their own words, to the public. A chapter on the women they left behind is also included.

Because so many veterans of Brigade 2506 were alive at the time this book was started, there seemed no better way highlight their stories than in an oral history format. Although the Brigade members' testimonies make up the bulk of the work, each chapter contains an introduction designed to give context to the veterans' words. More specifically, each introduction provides the history behind the personal experiences related by the veterans in that chapter.

The interviews all occurred in 1999, mostly in Florida. The majority of them were conducted in Spanish and translated into English by the author. The idiosyncrasies of language and culture are such that some things inevitably are lost in translation; therefore, every effort was made to retain the true feelings and perceptions of each interviewee's experience as expressed to the author. Needless to say, the material presented, whether spoken in English or in Spanish, was not transcribed verbatim. Like most oral histories, the interviews were done in a question-and-answer format, and they have been edited, compiled, and rearranged into a coherent narrative for ease of reading. With that goal in mind, expressions sometimes were rephrased to provide greater fluidity, as well as to replace physical gestures, half sentences, colloquialisms, or any other communication not easily converted into a written narrative. Whenever editing was done, it was with a solid commitment to convey the true intention, emotion, and meaning expressed in the interviews. On occasion, corrections were made on dates and other details—sometimes resulting from a follow-up inquiry to an interviewee. Also, the names of persons mentioned by the interviewees were left out if they were unintelligible.

I owe an enormous debt to the many people who assisted me in the completion of this book. My wife, Emy, deserves a medal for her infinite patience and understanding. Without her support (not to mention her computer skills) not even the first page of the book ever would have been written. With this in mind, I dedicate the book to her. I would like also to thank my parents and the rest of my family for their never-ending love and support. My father deserves special thanks for patiently answering my many questions about the translations and about Spanish grammar in general and for his willingness to proofread the manuscript. I would also like to thank Dr. William Rogers, my former major professor at Florida State and my mentor since graduation, for his constant willingness to offer wise counsel at a moment's notice.

I am also indebted to the library staff of Middlesex Community College as well as that of Wesleyan University in Middletown, Connecticut. I would like to thank specifically Randy Wilson, Howard Einsohn, Gayle Esidore, Lan

Liu, Carol Nelson, Alma Zyko, and Anne Paluck. A debt of gratitude is owed also to the various friends as well as interviewees who helped me link up with the people who became part of this book. In particular, I thank Carlos Espinosa, Juan Clark, Eduardo Zayas-Bazán, Jorge Marquet, Ricardo Sánchez, María Allen, Mario Martínez Malo, Felipe Basulto, Grayston Lynch, Migdalia Garí, María Elena Triay, Tania Goyanes, Jorge Triay, Clara Triay, Hugo Sueiro, Tulio Díaz Suárez, Esteban Bovo, Dulce Carrera Jústiz, José Flores, Antonio Varona, and Beatriz, Alvaro, and Benito Larin. I am indebted also to my good friends Frank and Rachel Izquierdo as well as to Peter and Carolyn Caprioglio for volunteering so generously to proofread chapters of the final manuscript. A special thanks also goes to Randeane Tetu for all her encouragement.

The book, however, had a secret weapon in Roberto N. Allen. Roberto and I have enjoyed a rare and valued friendship since early childhood. We met in kindergarten, attended school together through the twelfth grade, and have stayed closely in touch ever since. Roberto's father, Carlos Allen Dosal, died tragically in 1973, when we were in the second grade. A Brigade veteran who lost his right arm during the invasion, Carlos remained a powerful figure in Roberto's life in spite of his untimely death. When Roberto, now a Baltimore attorney, heard I was writing an oral history on the Brigade (and especially when he heard some excerpts from the interviews), he became completely absorbed. He immediately volunteered to do whatever he could to assist me. Throwing himself into the project with zeal and energy, he conducted four of the interviews, proofread chapters, suggested changes, and conducted useful research for me on the Internet—all with a high degree of professionalism and objectivity. At times he stepped up and completed certain critical tasks for me when other work and deadlines would have made them almost impossible to accomplish. Thus, on Roberto's behalf, I would like to dedicate his efforts in this book to the memory of his father, Carlos.

We come in the name of God, Justice and Democracy. . . . We do not come out of hatred, but out of life. . . . The Assault Brigade is composed of thousands [*sic*] of Cubans who are completely Catholic and Christian. . . . Catholics of Cuba: our military might is crushing and invincible and even greater is our moral strength, our faith in God and in His protection and His help. Cuban Catholics: I embrace you on behalf of the soldiers of the liberating Army. Families, friends and relatives . . . soon you shall be re-united. Have faith, for victory is ours because God is with us and the Virgin of Charity cannot abandon her children. Catholics! Long live Cuba, free, democratic and Catholic. Long live Christ the King!

Manifesto, found in the baggage of Father Ismael de Lugo, Brigade 2506, April 1961, as quoted in Cuba, *by Hugh Thomas*

A REVOLUTION BETRAYED

The Caribbean nation of Cuba entered 1959 in a state of relief, hope, and festivity. Fulgencio Batista, the former military man and president who had disrupted the constitutional order when he launched his successful coup d'état in March 1952 and subsequently established a political dictatorship, had fled the country on New Year's Eve. Numerous groups, ranging from Cuba's democratic political parties to student organizations, had played a major role in his ouster. Of all the groups, however, the 26th of July Movement was the largest and most popular. Led by Fidel Castro, a dynamic former student radical and lawyer, the 26th of July had launched a campaign that included guerrilla warfare and urban sabotage. Castro and his rebels, wearing their trademark beards and military fatigues, arrived in Havana in early January and assumed control.

Cuba had achieved a relatively high standard of living by 1959. It consistently ranked at or near the top among American nations in all standard-of-living indicators. It had a large middle class, which comprised one-fourth to one-third of the population. Cuba's tight economic ties to the United States translated into equally strong cultural ones. Yet the political corruption that had become commonplace in Cuba caused a deep sense of frustration among many in the population. It was commonly believed that the country had not

yet reached its social and economic potential because of its political difficulties. The level of poverty—especially in the countryside and certain parts of
the cities—was viewed likewise as a major problem, as was the gap between
black and white. The revolution, in large measure composed of people from
the professional and middle classes and supported by all classes, promised to
remedy the island's woes. A number of leaders who shared power with the 26th
of July in Castro's early governments held democratic, liberal principles;
many of them had fought dictatorship in Cuba even before Batista.

Fidel Castro's true intentions, however, started to become clear as early as
1959. Whether he was a genuine Communist or a political opportunist is an
open question, but even before Batista's ouster the 26th of July Movement had
started cooperating with the island's Communist Party—although the Communists earlier had dismissed Castro's movement. Ernesto "Ché" Guevara
and Raul Castro, Fidel's brother, had close contacts with the Communists and
may have been responsible for the early ties. Whatever the circumstances,
both supporters and opponents of the revolution began taking notice of the
large number of Communists assigned to powerful, high-level positions
within the first few months after Castro took over. A number of Cubans, including revolutionaries, condemned this. As the trend continued, people
whose reformist ideals included an adherence to constitutional democracy
turned against Castro, and many entered the opposition.

Besides the rise of Communists, other key events in 1959 alerted many
Cubans to the totalitarianism that was to come. Among the numerous trials of
Batista officials during the revolution's first few months (many of which were
carried out in front of boisterous crowds and were devoid of all legality and
procedure), forty-four former air force pilots stood accused of war crimes in
the city of Santiago. The court acquitted them, but they were not released.
Castro then ordered a new trial with a court composed of committed follow-
ers; this court, not surprisingly, found the pilots guilty.[1] Such an undermining
of the rule of law—whatever the truth behind the pilots' actions—soured
many people on Castro. Later that year, Huber Matos, a 26th of July commander and the military governor of Camagüey Province, was arrested for
his criticism of Castro's inclusion of Communists in the government. Meanwhile, the liberals were purged systematically from the cabinet. The most
prominent was Manuel Urrutia, the provisional government's president, who
was ousted in July for publicly criticizing Communism.

aimed at ousting Castro. Although the first rapprochement effort failed, another attempt was made in March through the last liberal minister on Castro's cabinet, Finance Minister Rufo López Fresquet. It was rejected by Castro, and López Fresquet resigned.[6] On the same day, Eisenhower approved the CIA's plan. Still searching for a nonmilitary solution, however, the president suspended Cuba's sugar quota in July 1960, in an attempt to pressure Castro. This act often has been identified as one of the most pivotal events that helped drive Castro into the Soviet camp. However, the die had been cast: Castro's intention of making Cuba a Communist state aligned to the Soviet Union, as evidenced by his actions, was clear to many in Cuba and the United States long before the cut in the sugar quota was even contemplated. Historian and Kennedy advisor Arthur Schlesinger did not subscribe to the idea that the United States somehow pushed Castro into the arms of Moscow: "It was not until July 1960, long after Castro had effected the substantial communization of the government, army, and labor movement and had negotiated economic agreements with Russia and China, that the United States took public retaliatory action of a major sort. The suspension of the balance of Cuba's 1960 sugar quota (that same quota which Guevara had already denounced in March as 'economic slavery') was the conclusion, and not the cause, of Castro's hostility."[7] In January 1961, the United States broke off diplomatic relations with Cuba.

In Cuba, life had become impossible for Castro opponents. The very act of organizing a dissenting political organization was unlawful, and being caught meant facing a very real threat of imprisonment or execution. Because there were no legal, constitutional outlets for the opposition, any group pitting itself against Castro had to do so clandestinely and at great risk. As the regime increased its control over the population and launched effective counterintelligence efforts, any likelihood that such groups would succeed diminished. As a result, many Castro opponents went overseas to continue the fight from abroad. The majority found themselves in neighboring Miami, Florida.

At the same time, large numbers of Cuban refugees began arriving in Miami. Unlike the relatively small wave in early 1959, this group was fleeing not because of Batista's ouster but because of Castro's imposition of a Marxist state. The composition of the Cuban exile community was severely altered; it now consisted overwhelmingly of people with no ties to the former dictator. A disproportionate number were part of Cuba's educated middle and upper classes. Among the exiled political leaders who arrived in Miami in late 1959 and 1960 were men who had been opponents of Batista and later, after his true motives were revealed, Fidel Castro. A number of them were well-known statesmen who had left organizations in Cuba that were secretly conspiring against the government. In 1960 the U.S. government entered into a partnership with a coalition created from those leaders, who were later organized as the provisional Cuban government that was to be landed in Cuba and recognized by the United States.

An exile army, made up largely of young idealistic men from the exile community, likewise was assembled. Its objective ultimately became to seize and protect a beachhead from which the provisional democratic government could operate. The overall goal was to overthrow Castro and to reinstate the popular, progressive, and democratic constitution of 1940. The exile army was mostly recruited in Miami, trained in Central America, and landed on April 17, 1961, in the Bay of Pigs area on Cuba's southern shore. The small force, which took the name Brigade 2506, was a diverse group comprising all sectors of Cuban society. Students, workers, former Castro supporters, former army personnel, professionals, the rich, the poor, and the middle class all came together with the single unifying goal of ridding Cuba of Communist rule. Due in large part to decisions made in Washington shortly before the invasion, the Brigade was routed, captured, and imprisoned by Castro forces.

The invasion was nevertheless pivotal for the history of Cuba and its people, as it helped Fidel Castro consolidate his power and marked the true beginning of Communist rule on the island. And, as a result of the invasion's failure, the United States was faced not only with a Soviet base in the Caribbean but with over four decades of having Cuban refugees arrive on its shores. Among the approximately two million people in the Cuban exile community in the United States, the small group of men who made up Brigade 2506— although largely ignored by Americans—have always enjoyed the highest levels of respect and reverence.

It was my turn to do something for Cuba.
Probably the purest thing I have ever done
in my life was to make the decision to go.

Rafael Montalvo, Second Battalion

1

A CALL TO ARMS

The initial U.S. decision to develop a contingency plan against Castro occurred in January 1960 during a meeting between CIA director Allen Dulles
and President Dwight Eisenhower. The president, after listening to Dulles
outline a plan to sabotage Cuban sugar refineries, asked the director to come
back with an enlarged program. It clearly was time to move beyond a mere
harassment of Castro.[1] Consequently, the CIA established a special task force
called WH/4 (Branch 4 of the Western Hemisphere) to come up with such a
"program." Jack Esterline, the CIA chief in Venezuela, was recalled to lead
the team. Meanwhile, the agency enlarged its contingent in Havana and
opened a branch station in Miami.[2] Overseeing the entire Cuba operation
was Richard Mervin Bissell Jr., the CIA's deputy director for plans and the
American whose name is most closely associated with the Bay of Pigs invasion.
A Connecticut aristocrat and former Yale professor, he was renowned within
the agency for his leadership skills and intellect. He had coordinated the program that produced the U-2 spy plane and was a rising star at the agency and
the top candidate to replace the aging Allen Dulles.

Immediately following Eisenhower's January 1960 directive, WH/4 prepared an ambitious plan designed to overthrow the Cuban government; it was titled "A Program of Covert Action against the Castro Regime." It was approved several weeks later by the Special Group (a secret committee composed of the CIA director, representatives from the Departments of State and Defense, and the White House). A broad outline, it provided a blueprint for the planning that occurred over the next several months. The plan proposed to create a united Cuban political front in exile to serve as a visible opposition to Castro and as a body to which disaffected Cubans on the island could be loyal,[3] to establish a broadcasting facility for a powerful propaganda offensive, to organize a "covert intelligence and action organization within Cuba,"[4] and to bring together a paramilitary force outside Cuba. The plan also called for "a small air supply capability under deep cover."[5] On another front, the United States hoped to pressure Castro through economic sanctions imposed by the Organization of American States.[6]

On March 17, the same day Castro rejected the attempted rapprochement through Finance Minister Rufo López Fresquet, President Eisenhower approved WH/4's program, now code-named Operation Pluto. At the meeting, which was attended by top administration officials, the president, according to Bissell, demonstrated his usual desire for "plausible deniability."[7] He also insisted that, among the Cubans with whom the U.S. government was going to enter a partnership, both *Batistianos* (supporters of ousted dictator Fulgencio Batista) and Communists be excluded. In the late summer, President Eisenhower approved a $13 million budget as well as the use of Department of Defense personnel and equipment for the covert military effort.[8]

To carry out the propaganda offensive, the CIA set up Cuban exiles to broadcast from Radio Swan, a powerful radio station on Greater Swan Island off the coast of Honduras which formerly had been used by the agency.[9] The timing of the broadcast initiative was opportune, as the Castro regime already had shut down nearly all means of free expression in Cuba.

A far more daunting challenge for the United States was creating a unified political front from among the more politically astute—and often divided—exiles. By June 1960, the *Frente Revolucionario Democrático* [Democratic Revolutionary Front] was formed from among the leaders of different non-*Batistiano*, democratic Cuban groups represented in Miami. The original members included Manuel Antonio "Tony" de Varona, a former prime minister, senate president, and leader of the underground group Rescate. Varona also had been an active opponent of the Batista dictatorship, a leader in the *Auténtico* Party, and an early critic of Castro's failure to hold promised elections.[10] Frente members Justo Carrillo and Manuel Artime once had been part of the Castro government but were alienated by the leader's turn to Communism. For his part, Artime became the leader of the exile faction of the *Movimiento de Recuperación Revolucionaria* [Revolutionary Recovery Movement, or MRR], the most significant underground movement on the island. He later became the Frente's representative with the military arm of the operation and the CIA's main link with the Cuban exiles.[11] Former foreign minister Aureliano Sánchez Arango and Christian Democratic Movement leader José Ignacio Rasco rounded out the original group. Col. Martín Elena, a high-ranking officer in the Cuban Army, popular among democratic politicians for having given up his command to protest Batista's coup, was originally the Frente's head of military affairs. He resigned in February 1961 because of tensions over the level of American control over the operation. Sánchez Arango later resigned. In time, new members joined the ranks of the Frente.

Months later, Manuel Ray, a former Castro supporter who headed the formidable underground organization called the *Movimiento Revolucionario del Pueblo* [Peoples' Revolutionary Movement, or MRP], joined the group after a good deal of bickering with other Cuban political leaders in Miami who were quick to brand him a Communist.[12] Also included was José Miró Cardona, a well-known liberal lawyer and Castro's first prime minister in 1959. Weeks before the April 17 invasion, Miró Cardona was chosen as Cuba's provisional president. At that point, the group changed its name to the Cuban Revolutionary Council; according to plan, it would act as Cuba's provisional government after Castro's ouster.[13] In the weeks before the invasion, they were moved out of Miami's frenzied atmosphere and into New York City's Lexington Hotel.[14]

The Americans found their Cuban partners to be contentious and fragmented—although some believe this may have been the result of deliberate U.S. efforts to keep them divided and thus easier to control. By the same token, Frente members were frustrated over the heavy-handedness of the United States in the operation designed to free their homeland. Some resented that their relationship with the United States was kept clandestine and that they had to work with an agent named Gerry Droller (code-named Frank Bender) who did not speak Spanish and knew nothing about Latin America. The CIA later sent Howard Hunt (code-named Eduardo), who was fluent in Spanish and more amiable, to help with the Cubans.[15] Another source of tension was that the CIA managed all the finances; Frente leaders would have preferred a war loan and a formal alliance.[16] Nevertheless, the Frente, composed of men who were well known on the island, in exile, and throughout Latin America, maintained its own intelligence network. All possessed impeccable democratic credentials and actively promoted Cuban democracy in international conferences throughout this period. The Frente's reliance on the U.S. government should not be misconstrued as a lack of will or of a sense of independence by its members but simply an unfortunate reality they had to tolerate in the short run.

One of the Frente's main tasks was to recruit men for the exile army and air force. Among the first recruits for the CIA's anti-Castro army were former Cuban military officers with no political connections to Batista. One group of young officers, approached by Manuel Artime in Miami, had been training in Florida and planning an expedition of their own in the spring of 1960.[17] Some were suspicious at first because of Artime's former ties with the rebel army. Their misgivings also sprang in part from an earlier incident in which anti-Castro conspirators had approached two army majors, Eloy Gutiérrez Menoyo and the U.S.-born William Morgan, to seek their support for a plot against the regime. The conspiracy was betrayed, and the counterrevolutionaries were delivered to Castro. Despite their initial skepticism, the officers went along with Artime after they confirmed that what he said was true. The young soldiers believed that anything backed by the U.S. government was certain to succeed.[18]

The officers were taken to Useppa Island, off Florida's west coast. At Useppa, they met other early volunteers, many of whom were students from the *Agrupación Católica Universitaria*, a university Catholic student union that had opposed Batista and now was fighting actively against Castro. A devout Catholic himself, Artime was closely associated with the *Agrupación*. Other early recruits were from different student organizations as well as the various anti-Castro groups in Florida. Together, these clusters of men formed the cornerstone of the exile army that later would invade Cuba as Brigade 2506.

Tensions ran high at Useppa between the soldiers and students, as the latter were quick to brand any former military personnel as *Batistianos*. Such resentments, left over from the Batista era, continued later in the training camps. After extensive testing, a part of the Useppa group was sent to a training base in the Panama Canal Zone to receive guerrilla instruction and to be trained as a cadre for the liberation army. The rest remained on Useppa for a radio communications course.[19] The military plan, as it stood at the time, called for the training of a small guerrilla force schooled in the finer points of sabotage, communications, and infiltration. The group would train others and eventually ignite a guerrilla war in Cuba. Cuban pilots, both military and civilian, were likewise recruited for the exile air force.

The CIA also busied itself with establishing links to democratic underground groups in Cuba. The most important of these was Artime's MRR.[20] Having been composed originally of former rebel army officers, it had expanded and developed important links to other resistance groups throughout Cuba. By the spring of 1960, it was the best organized Castro opposition. In Cuba itself, the MRR was headed by Rogelio González Corzo, code-named Francisco, a twenty-seven-year-old who had served as director of agriculture in 1959. The organization remained the CIA's "chief hope" for a long while.[21] During this period, Cuban exiles also were actively running guns to their partners on the island in daring maritime operations.[22]

The CIA, meanwhile, because of State Department opposition to using U.S. territory for training the Cubans, secured the use of a 5,000-acre coffee plantation in the mountains near the Pacific coast of Guatemala. Named Helvetia and owned by Roberto Alejos, the brother of Guatemala's ambassador to the United States, it began receiving Cuban liberation fighters during the summer of 1960. Soon afterward, plans were laid out for a more expansive camp near Helvetia called Base Trax. By that time, an airport designed to train Cuban exile pilots was nearing completion in neighboring Retalhuleu.[23] The first Cuban commander at Trax was a young officer named Oscar Alfonso Carol.

Throughout the fall of 1960, tensions between Havana and Washington increased. News of the "secret" training bases in Central America had hit the press. As Cuba's mission at the United Nations blasted the United States for conspiring against the island nation's government, CIA-trained exile pilots flew missions over Cuba (mostly unsuccessful) to drop supplies for the guerrilla fighters in the Escambray Mountains. The U.S. presidential campaign was also in full swing. Facing each other were Vice President Richard M. Nixon, Republican, and Senator John F. Kennedy, Democrat. Kennedy seized on the Cuba issue in an effort to dispel the notion that he was weak on Communism. Accusing the Eisenhower administration, and thereby Nixon, of ignoring the Castro threat, the Kennedy camp released a statement to the press: "We must attempt to strengthen the non-Batista democratic anti-Castro forces in exile, and in Cuba itself, who offer eventual hope of overthrowing Castro. . . . Thus far, these fighters for freedom have had virtually no support from our government."[24] Little did Kennedy's people know just how involved the government, including his opponent, had been in helping the "fighters for freedom." During a speech in Tennessee, Kennedy stated, "Those who say they will stand up to Khrushchev have not demonstrated any ability to stand up to Mr. Castro."[25] In part to protect the operation, Nixon accused Kennedy of recklessness and publicly advocated a "quarantine" of the island.

Just prior to the presidential election, Operation Pluto's military plan underwent a fundamental change. The CIA shifted away from the idea of a guerrilla infiltration to that of a large-scale amphibious assault. The immediate goal became the capture of a beachhead on the island from which further operations could be launched. Various reasons for the change included the difficulties the effort already had encountered with infiltration and resupply, the capture and execution of key members of the underground, and the obstacles inherent in maintaining an underground network because of the Castro regime's growing control over the civilian population through the use of informants and block-by-block vigilance groups. The most important reason, however, was the need for an immediate and devastating blow against the Castro regime to counteract the amount of weaponry it began receiving from East Bloc countries. Soviet MiGs were expected within months.[26]

Recruiting for the exile army was interrupted temporarily in November 1960. A revolt by the Guatemalan army, which was brought down in part by strafing Brigade planes, forced the CIA to consider alternative training sites.[27] In the end, they chose to stay. In December, a group of the Brigade's leaders visited Miami to stimulate enlistment and to eliminate the delays that potential recruits had been encountering. In addition, more men would be necessary for a frontal assault.[28]

As the basic structure of the operation was put into place, Cuban men arrived in Miami with the determination to join the effort against Castro. Most of them had supported Batista's ouster but felt the revolution had been betrayed by Castro's establishment of yet another dictatorship—this one even more oppressive and with a totalitarian, Communist orientation. Feeling a duty to prevent a Communist takeover and spurred on by patriotism and religious zeal, many chose to fight, often seeking out organizations such as the

MRR, the Christian Democrats, the Auténtico Organization (OA), Rescate, and numerous other groups of all shapes and sizes. Many were encouraged by their organizations to join the "camps" (nobody referred to it as the Brigade at the time) where the liberation army, the military arm of the Frente, was being trained. Many others, perhaps most, were inspired to join as a result of the Frente's recruiting efforts or because of encouragement from friends. That the Frente was composed of men with unquestionable democratic track records and not *Batistianos* was a source of comfort for many—especially some of the more idealistic students. Solid assurances of U.S. backing also played a major role in overcoming any doubts the recruits may have had, since the United States never had lost a war. With the memory of World War II still fresh, the United States was perceived as a strong and loyal ally. Most had come to the conclusion that outright military action was the only way Castro could be ousted—as no legal means for opposition existed on the island. In addition, the need for military action was seen as becoming even greater because Castro was bolstering his grip on power and protecting his dictatorship with military aid from the Communist bloc.

The enlistment process for many of the recruits began with a visit to the offices of the Frente, where they were registered and processed. They later were run through psychological and physical exams. On the day they were assigned to leave for the training camps, most of the men were dropped off at one of the Frente's offices by family or friends. Some came alone. After saying their good-byes, they were checked in, given some gear, and taken to Opa-Locka airport, near Miami. The trucks in which they traveled were sealed to prevent them from seeing where they were being taken. Then they were put aboard airplanes with windows covered with tape for the same reason. Most of the men took the process in stride, as the Americans seemed to know what they were doing. At some point in the process, each man received his Brigade serial number. The numbers began at 2501 in order to give possible Castro informants the impression that the group was much larger than it actually was. The members of the Brigade air force were assigned numbers counting backward from 2500.

The exile army eventually chose the name Brigade 2506, in commemoration of a young man named Carlos Rodriguez Santana, nicknamed Carlyle, who had died in an accident during the early training period and whose serial number had been 2506. The approximately 1,700 men who ultimately passed through the Frente's offices and joined the Brigade represented a cross section of Cuba. University students made up the largest single group, accounting for 240 of the men. Only about 135 men had ever been soldiers before joining the Brigade, and very few were true *Batistianos* before the revolution. Although blue-collar workers, fishermen, and small farmers were among its ranks, the Brigade contained a disproportionate number of educated middle-class men and even a handful from the upper class.[29] It included the sons of the Frente's José Miró Cardona, Tony Varona, and Antonio Maceo (the physician designated to be health minister after the invasion and the grandson of Cuba's great Afro-Cuban independence leader of the same name).[30] It included four Catholic priests, a Protestant minister, numerous professionals, and Cuba's former ambassador to Japan. Fifty Brigade men were Afro-Cubans, and many more were mulatto; the majority, however, were white. Their ages ranged from sixteen to sixty-one, but most were in their twenties and thirties. A large number had children, and there were even siblings and some father-and-son pairs among the men.[31]

Consistent with the characteristics of the island's middle to upper classes, many of the Brigade's men felt a tight kinship to the United States. It was not uncommon for some to have gone to American schools — Catholic and otherwise — in Cuba or the United States or to have studied at U.S. colleges or universities. A number of them spoke English in addition to their native Spanish. Some, however, especially the students, were angry because they suspected that their American allies were calling all the shots and bypassing the authority of the Frente, which they considered the leader of the military component and the representative of democratic ideals. Yet whatever tension may have existed, accepting help from the Americans to overthrow the Havana government did not conflict with the Brigade members' own strong sense of Cuban independence and nationalism. They and other exiles saw the war as being waged against a puppet regime of international Communism which had manipulated the political upheaval in their country to establish a base in the Americas. Despite their occasional chagrin over the Americans' authority over the enterprise as well as the secrecy that surrounded their mission, they viewed themselves as allies of the greatest democratic power on earth in the most important struggle of their day.

Whatever the political tensions, the men of the Brigade embraced their cause with fervor and a great sense of bravado. It was both significant and unusual that the rank-and-file soldier was so politically astute and that so many were highly educated — often more so than their American trainers. All were volunteers and well aware of the cause for which they risked their lives. The depth of their patriotism and love for Cuba, as well as their democratic principles, served as their primary motivation. Moreover, the anti-Castro and anti-Communist ideology of the time had a profound religious component. Although the Brigade and other anti-Castro elements in Cuba and in exile certainly included Protestants and Jews (many of whom were fairly prominent), they were, for the most part, Roman Catholics. Many of the Brigade's earliest members were associated with activist Catholic movements, especially organizations like the *Agrupación Católica Universitaria*. The regime's anti-Catholic rhetoric and actions, as well as the prospect of a totalitarian Communist society characterized by state-mandated atheism, was enough to spur such people, as well as any liberal who valued religious freedom, to action.

The aura of the Roman Catholic Church and its open opposition to Communism clearly emboldened even those anti-Castro fighters and Brigade members who may have been only nominally Catholic before the revolution. Among those sentenced to die by firing squad at the execution wall, what the Cubans called *paredón*, it became customary to declare "¡Viva Cristo Rey!" (Long live Christ the King!) just before being riddled with the executioners' bullets. The slogan became associated with the anti-Castro cause for years to come. In the preamble to the *MRR's "Ideario: Puntos Basicos"* [Body of Ideas: Basic Points], Artime wrote that the purpose of the organization was "not only to overthrow Fidel Castro, but to permanently fight for an ideology of Christ; and for a reality of liberating our nation treacherously sold to the Communist International."[32] The Brigade's emblem contained both a Cuban flag and a Christian cross, along with the number 2506.

Because they possessed such a sense of purpose, it is easy to understand why members of the Cuban Brigade resented the view that they were "assets" or "instruments" of the U.S. government. To this day they remain adamant that their war was for Cuba and view their participation primarily within the context of Cuban politics and history. One veteran summed it up in 1996: "I think that the feeling among the people in the Brigade was that we were using the CIA, not the CIA using us; that we had a purpose and the purpose was going back to Cuba, to try to change our country and to bring about a democratic movement."[33]

The opening chapter traces the experiences of Brigade veterans from their lives prior to the revolution to their departure to the Guatemalan training camps. Included are their feelings about the revolution at its inception, their entry—philosophical and otherwise—into the Castro opposition, their arrival in Miami and subsequent enlistment in the Brigade, as well as their departure to the "secret" training bases. In order to represent a cross section of the Brigade, I have chosen to highlight the stories of men from four broad categories: three university students, a former high-ranking Castro rebel, two young military officers, and six men who were mainstream citizens when the revolution occurred. Most of them shared in the national euphoria of Batista's overthrow and the democratic promises of the revolution. Like other Cubans, however, they were horrified when they realized their country was entering the Communist bloc. They went into exile and heeded the call to arms by joining the Brigade.

The Students

Jorge Silveira, Third Battalion

Born in Havana in 1938, Jorge Silveira was the son of an attorney and important judicial functionary, Silvio Silveira Cartañá. Jorge graduated from Havana's private Añorga School and was in law school at the Catholic University of Villanueva in Havana when Castro came to power. Assigned to the Brigade's Third

Battalion as a radio operator, Silveira saw action on the San Blas front and upon his capture was imprisoned with most of the Brigade until December 1962. He later graduated from the University of Florida. After having spent many years in the private sector, he is presently the procurement manager for Miami-Dade County in Miami, Florida.

Like almost all students at the time I was against the Batista regime, and I had joined an anti-Batista group at the

Jorge Silveira, Third Battalion, in his Miami office, 1999. Photograph by author.

university known as SAC, *Salvar a Cuba* [Save Cuba]. When Castro came to power, I had the misfortune of having to address his *ley once* [law number eleven], which threatened private and religious education in Cuba. (The law invalidated all university study completed at other institutions while the University of Havana was closed during the struggle against Batista, as completing coursework during the war was seen as unpatriotic.) I was part of a committee of five students and a professor who were given an audience with the new education minister, Armando Hart. It was still very early, perhaps during the first three months after Castro took power. We wanted them to remove the sanctions, especially against the University of Villanueva, whose students were for the most part affluent and had raised money for Castro and had cooperated with the revolution. In fact, there was a letter that Fidel Castro had written to one of the high-ranking clergy saying that the University of Villanueva should remain open, unlike the University of Havana, because it was a great financial resource for them.

At the meeting, Armando Hart and Fidel Castro told us that we shouldn't worry because, since we had been part of revolutionary actions, our studies at Villanueva would be accepted at the University of Havana. The overall plan, they explained, was to bring an end to religious and private education in Cuba. I began to conspire against Fidel Castro when I left the meeting that night.

SAC, in a sense, was reactivated to fight Castro. A few original members, however, remained with the government. Seeing how anti-Castro groups were so easily penetrated, it was kept small. We worked closely with the MRR and other organizations. Eventually, some in the group had to leave Cuba, and others were imprisoned.

When Mikoyan came to Cuba, we took part in the protest at Havana's Central Park. When the police came and put down the demonstration, some protesters were arrested, including the law school student president. Since I was the law school's student vice president, I became acting president. Of course, holding such a position at a Catholic university, I was also pursued. One day, the G.2 went to pick me up at my home. Luckily for me, the pharmacist at the nearby drug store was a friend of my mother, and she called to warn her. I went into hiding and left Cuba on September 8, 1960.

While in Miami, we tried to enter the frogman units but were never able to. So we were left with the alternatives of going back to Cuba or joining the training camps. I wasn't in Miami to hide or to be in exile; I had come to fight against Castro. Thus, the only viable option was to go to the camps. Mario Martínez Malo, who was with SAC, had left for the camps before I did, and we agreed that he would send a coded letter indicating whether or not we should go. His letter said the camps were great, which really meant things there were not good. I chose to go anyhow. I felt that if things were really so bad, I had an even greater obligation to go. I left for the camps in Guatemala in early February, 1961.

Mario A. Martínez-Malo, Second Battalion

Born in Havana in 1938, Mario A. Martínez-Malo was a graduate of the Jesuit Colegio de Belén, one of Cuba's premier boys' schools and the alma mater of Fidel Castro himself. The son of an attorney, Martínez-Malo attended the University of Havana's law school. He was incorporated into the Brigade's Second Battalion as part of the forward observer group and was captured and imprisoned until December 1962. He later graduated from the University of Florida, where he received an M.A. in economics and finance. He currently owns an insurance business in Miami

Mario A. Martínez-Malo, Second Battalion, in Coral Gables, 1999. Photograph by author.

I was the founder of a group called SAC, which mainly worked from the University of Havana law school. We were anti-Batista but never pro-Castro. When Fidel Castro arrived in Havana on January 8, 1959, and spoke on television, my father asked me, "What did you think?" I said, "I didn't like it. I think this guy is going to be very dangerous." My father, who was always apolitical, said, "I hope I am wrong, but I think this guy is the worst person who could take control of Cuba." I agreed with him, and in January 1959, SAC became an anti-Castro group.

SAC mostly engaged in propaganda, but we also did some minor sabotage. I didn't believe in using dynamite and all that because it could kill innocent people. We often pooled resources with other underground political groups like the MRR, who was the main leader and with whom we were connected through the University of Havana. I knew about the training camps because I had been educated at Belén. Most *Belemitas* [Belén graduates] at the university were closely associated with the Agrupación Católica Universitaria, and the Agrupación provided many of the original Brigade members.

Since things were getting tighter and tighter in Cuba, it was difficult to organize a comprehensive fight against Castro. The pressure was becoming terrible. So, after a brief meeting, we decided that the people who were most "burned"—those we were afraid would get caught—would come over to the United States. I was one of them. Unfortunately, many of the people who remained in Havana were later executed, most of them because of the Bay of Pigs.

When I got to Miami in August 1960, I came with the idea of joining the camps. But we first had to get some people out of Cuba, to whom we had been supplying weapons through a small airline that used to fly to Havana. I would say that 100 percent of the original SAC guys who came to Miami joined the camps, and I was the first one who joined. I enlisted at the Frente office, where I knew my way around because I was the head of a small political movement. I left for the camps January 6, 1961.

Juan "Johnny" Clark, Paratrooper

Juan Clark, paratrooper, in Miami in 1999, shows a microscopic letter he smuggled to his family from prison. Photograph by author.

The son of a sugar mill administrator, Juan Clark was a 1955 graduate of El Colegio de La Salle, a prominent Havana boys' school run by the Christian Brothers. He entered the University of Havana the same year. The descendent of mostly Spaniards, he is also the great-grandson of a nineteenth-century English settler—hence his Anglo surname. After joining the Brigade, he was put in the First Paratrooper Battalion and headed a squad that parachuted into San Blas. He subsequently was captured and imprisoned until December 1962 with most of the Brigade. Upon his release, he became involved with humanitarian projects in Latin America and then attended the University of Florida, where he received a Ph.D. in sociology. He is currently a professor of sociology at Miami-Dade Community College and a noted researcher and author.

I was in high school when Cuba's constitutional order was broken by Batista on March 10, 1952. I was very much opposed to that arbitrary and unjustified act, and I started acting against Batista as a high school student. I got involved in one particular plot in which I printed manuals for the use of .45 caliber pistols and hand grenades. Fortunately, it never materialized, because I would have never made it here today [he laughs].

At the University, I joined a group called the AAA (*Amigos de Aureliano Arango,* or Friends of Aureliano Arango) headed by Aureliano Sánchez Arango. I was also deeply involved in the Catholic Action movement, as I had been the president of the Young Catholic Students in Cuba at the end of high school. I became active against Batista, as was my brother, who was captured and tortured and had to leave the country.

When Castro came to power we were, like most people, sympathetic toward the revolution. But I was never really pro-Castro, because I had doubts about the person himself. I had heard about his gangsterlike activities at the University of Havana years earlier and about his murder of a University police sergeant. Despite my strong reservations, I nevertheless admired his actions to an extent. Pretty soon, though, I realized things were not going as they had promised. The trials of the aviators in March 1959 opened my eyes, as did President Urrutia's overthrow and the Huber Matos incident. Castro then practically began saying that the promises of the revolution would be betrayed—such as his "¿Elecciones para qué?" campaign. It became obvious that we were definitely moving in the direction of another dictatorship and most likely a Communist one.

I began sharing my doubts with other people, and I had a talk with Bishop Martín Villaverde of Matanzas; eventually, I decided that something had to be done. Some people had alerted me that what was going on was very much along the lines of what Lenin had outlined in his book *The State and the Revolution.* We were by now very concerned with Communist infiltration, and we realized that even if Castro was not a Communist himself, he was betraying his promises.

We began organizing with the students at the university, and I also had some contact with the MRR and the Christian Democrats. My activities got me to the point where I was what was called "burned." In June of 1960, I left Cuba with the idea of joining something militarily, along with my brother who had left earlier, because it was obvious Castro was not going to allow any sort of political process to occur. Unfortunately, force was the only way to get rid of him. By the time I left Cuba, my brother had already left for the training camps.

At first I thought it was important to do some type of propaganda outside the mainland United States, so I went to Puerto Rico on my own for that purpose. When I was told the camps were developing fast, I decided to join formally. I had friends in the Frente office, and I enlisted in December 1960. I arrived in Guatemala on December 8.

The Rebel

Higinio "Nino" Díaz, Commander, Special Group

Higinio "Nino" Díaz, Special Group commander, as rebel in Oriente Province, 1958. Photograph by permission of Higinio Díaz.

Higinio "Nino" Díaz was born in 1925 in the city of Guantánamo, Oriente Province, in the easternmost part of Cuba. Raised and educated in Santiago de Cuba, also in Oriente, he entered his father's coffee business upon completing secondary school. A former chief in the 26th of July Movement, Díaz was one of the MRR's founders, and he eventually joined the effort to oust Castro as the head of the Special Group, whose mission it was to land in Oriente as a diversionary maneuver shortly before the Bay of Pigs invasion. He is currently a businessman in Miami and heads the group called Ejército Libertador Cubano [Cuban Liberation Army].

Nino Díaz at his home in Key Biscayne, Florida, 1999. Photograph by author.

Because of Batista's dictatorial government, there was a great deal of pressure at the time, and all the merchants were suffering from government extortion. By the time Fidel attacked the Moncada Barracks, I was part of *Joven Cuba* [Young Cuba], and we had also formed the *Movimiento Acción Libertadora* [Liberation Action Movement], which included many men who were later part of the 26th of July Movement.

I participated in the subversive wars inside the cities until the situation in Cuba had become intolerable and I went to the United States, from which I sent arms into Cuba. I returned to Cuba in 1958 and joined the 26th of July's guerrillas. The first combat we had was at the Boniato Barracks; I was a captain then. After another battle we were transferred, by an order from Raúl Castro, to the second front. I told my commander that we shouldn't go to the second front but instead concentrate our forces between Guantánamo and Santiago, to create a strong column there, and not subordinate ourselves 100 percent to Raúl Castro—about whom I already had my doubts. But he gave the final orders, and he chose to transfer us to the second front.

We had many successful battles against the army, but in September I began noticing Communist infiltration. I heard a conversation between Raúl Castro and his wife about Communism. There were also Communists infiltrated in Mayarí, with whom Raúl Castro would spend two and three hours in a *bohío* [country hut] talking and planning everything they were doing with them.

Soon afterward, I was sent to the area between Guantánamo and Santiago, where I took eighty kilometers of territory in a month and ten days. Raúl sent me there with the expectation that I would be killed. As I was not killed—and, in fact, I was very successful—Raúl Castro decided to have me arrested and executed.

I was called to a meeting at Mayarí, supposedly to plan the final capture of the province. But it was a trick: I was there to be tried and executed. They accused me of numerous things, all of which were lies, and ended up sentencing me to death. The next day I was transferred to another place to be executed. However, the country people of the area learned of it, and more than a thousand of them went on horseback to the headquarters. Leading them was one named Francisco who knew me well. He told Raúl that if they killed me, there would be a machete war right there and then. Raúl gave in to cowardice and ordered them not to execute me. I made him look bad because I insulted all of them and they were scared.

I was under arrest until December 28, 1958, when I escaped into Santiago de Cuba. When I learned Castro's people were truly Communists, I formed the *Movimiento de Recuperación Revolucionaria* (the MRR) and began committing sabotage all over Cuba in 1959. Later, the Americans gave the MRR to Artime—who at the time of its formation was still with Fidel.

[Nino Díaz explains how he believed Artime sold out the MRR to the Americans. He also told of how he was offered to head the Brigade while in Panama but told the Americans he would accept only on the condition that the operation remain under Cuban control; he was reportedly rejected.]

The Americans went to my house a few days after I returned from Panama and offered me a plan in which they would give me all that I had asked of them. They gave me troops to take to Louisiana to train them there.

The Cadets

Hugo Sueiro, Second Battalion Commander

One of the best known and most highly respected veterans of Brigade 2506, Hugo Sueiro was a 1956 graduate of El Instituto de Marianao, a public school. He entered Cuba's Cadet School upon graduation and served as an officer in the Cuban army until he went into exile. He eventually was named commander of the Brigade's Second Battalion. Called a "tough little fighter" by the American CIA case officer Grayston Lynch, Sueiro served in the U.S. military after his release from prison in Cuba. He later was seriously wounded in Vietnam.

I came from a poor family and went to the Instituto de Marianao. I then attended the Cadet School, and upon graduation we were sent to the Sierra to fight the Castro guerrillas. On December 31, 1958, we were at our post all day awaiting an attack that never came. The next day, we learned that Batista had left the country. For us, the news was really something. We were almost glad of it, in the sense that the never-ending fight was finally over.

We stayed at our post and decided that if the rebels came and shot at us, we would shoot back; but if they came peacefully, we would let them pass through and into the town. We were in that position for a few days until one of Fidel Castro's most important subordinates arrived at the airport—a guy who later turned against Fidel and was executed. We received instructions from Havana to cooperate. We let him pass, and then Fidel came. He wanted us disarmed.

I served with the new government in the rebel army. I still have a letter saying I had not committed any war crimes or anything else during the Batista era. The new government offered a group of us the opportunity to teach classes, and we became instructors at the Columbia military base for a time. It was at Columbia where we saw the barbarism and abuses of the new government as well as the movement toward tyranny. Some of our friends who had done nothing were executed. Then the indoctrination of the troops began, and Communist leaders started coming in and giving classes on capitalism, etc.—in many cases to people who barely had a fourth-grade education. We began to distance ourselves, but we couldn't just come out and resign, because we would be arrested. They would ask you why you wanted to resign and whether it was because you were against the system.

I was invited to join the William Morgan conspiracy. Many of my friends were arrested, but by some miracle, I wasn't caught as I hid all over the place. I sought asylum at the Mexican embassy and arrived in Mexico in October 1959. When I got my passport in the mail from Cuba three months later, I went to Miami.

One of my great motivations to go fight in Cuba was the responsibility I felt for those friends I had left in jail there. Our little group of former cadets who were in Miami started going out into the Everglades to shoot and to do light training. We also went to train at some lakes near Orlando, where for the first time I saw coral snakes. At this time some other guys from our group arrived, like Manolito Blanco, Oscar Carol (who headed the Brigade for a while), Roberto San Román, and Alejandro del Valle.

Del Valle went to Mexico to find a farm where we could train, imitating exactly what Fidel had done. With the support of wealthy Cubans in Miami, we bought equipment and guns. Then one day we were invited to a meeting.

At the meeting, Manuel Artime, who had made contact through Manolito Blanco, spoke to us about an operation. Pepe San Román was at that meeting. The Americans needed military people who were clean; that is, they were not implicated criminally or anything like that with Batista's government. We were offered something that we were led to believe was large, well organized, and had support. They never told us directly that it was the U.S. government, even though it was understood more or less that it was.

We were somewhat nervous because Artime had come from the rebel army. Because of our experience with the William Morgan conspiracy, we decided to keep training on our own just in case what Artime said wasn't true. Nevertheless, we decided to send one individual, Manolito Blanco, to Artime's people, who would let us know by code if Artime's story was true or not. One day, after hearing a positive review from Blanco, the Americans came and told us we were leaving.

Before leaving, one of our companions named Céspedes said, "What if this is another trick?" I remember we went to Southwest Sixth Street to a friend's house to borrow a gun—just in case. Another companion, Miguel Orozco, was also doubtful and got guns for my little group of three. In the end, all ten of us in the group carried guns. That night, we went to a home on Brickell Avenue that belonged to a Cuban air force commander who had once been with Fidel Castro. We waited until after midnight, and we were finally put into two cars and headed west on Route 41.

Halfway through the trip, they asked us if we were armed. They said, "If you have a gun, you cannot have a gun." They repeated it later. Orozco told him he was armed and gave the American his weapon. Céspedes had two guns and gave him one. We arrived on Pine Island, north of Fort Myers, at dawn, and we were taken to a boat. We were scared, as they could have boarded us and then blown up the boat. When we boarded, everyone got into a corner just in case a gunfight broke out.

We finally arrived on Useppa Island at five in the morning, and we were taken to a room. The same person as before told us again, "If you have a gun, you cannot have guns here." We positioned ourselves into the corners again in case we had to shoot our way out. The same guy said, "If you have a gun, you have to turn it in." Roberto finally said, "Well, everyone here is armed, but until we see Manolito Blanco we won't turn them in." So they went and got Manolito Blanco, who had been sleeping, and then we turned in our weapons.

At Useppa we underwent all sorts of exams. We had psychological tests, polygraph tests, and some training. Then more groups came. I turned twenty-one there. Then a group of us was sent to Panama to be trained as a cadre.

Esteban Bovo, B-26 Pilot

Born in Havana in 1938, Esteban Bovo's paternal grandfather was an immigrant from northern Italy. Esteban studied at the Catholic Escuelas Pías and graduated from El Instituto de la Habana, a public school, in 1956. He thereupon entered the Cadet School. Obsessed with flying from a young age, he trained extensively in the United States while a cadet. During the invasion, he was part of the group of B-26 pilots who ran sorties from Nicaragua to the combat zone. After the invasion, Bovo settled in the United States, where he worked as a retail executive. He is currently a senior field representative for the U.S. Census Bureau.

In late 1957, I came to study in the United States. We went to Graham Air Force Base in Florida and then to Texas to learn to fly B-25s in order to fly B-26s in Cuba. When I got back to Cuba, the revolution had already triumphed. All of us who returned were arrested. I was in prison only for about a week, because they could not charge us with things we had not done because we had been overseas. They had even wanted to put us on trial with the aviators in March, who were companions of ours in the air force.

I got involved in various conspiracies against Castro with military people and aviators, including Blanco Navarro and Hugo Sueiro. I left Cuba in January 1960, at twenty-one years of age, and went to Mexico. At the time, those of us who had been in the military were very unpopular in exile. The Frente was controlled by Tony Varona, Justo Carrillo, and a group of people who were of a very anti-Batista tendency. They accused us of being *Batistianos*, and a group of us were ignored for some time.

Those of us in Mexico were trying to buy some P-51s. We almost had them when the Americans called upon us to go prepare for the invasion—but before that, we had planned on setting the place (Cuba) ablaze. The Americans had made contact very subtly, through other people. Manuel Artime then came to Mexico, and we all went to the camps.

Civilians and Working Men

Jorge Giró, Aviation Ground Crew

Born in Havana in 1933, Jorge Giró graduated from La Salle and subsequently attended law school. Upon completing his studies in 1957, he went to work for a prominent Havana law firm. After joining the Brigade, he was made part of the crew that outfitted the exile aircraft that journeyed between Central America and Cuba, both before and during the Bay of Pigs invasion. He is currently a professor of Spanish at Towson University in Baltimore, Maryland.

Jorge Giró, 1999. By permission of Jorge Giró.

Like my family, I was not involved in politics. Yet when Castro took power I saw what his intentions were. So I began to associate with some subversive anti-Castro groups in order to act against the government. I was associated with the people in the William Morgan and Menoyo conspiracy, but I was not completely part of it. They were discovered, and the majority were condemned to twenty years in prison. After that, I was part of another group that was organized into cells, with the central cell at the beach of Jaimanitas-Santa Fe, a place situated past the Biltmore district in Havana. The group tried to bring guns into Cuba for the underground rebel army hiding in the mountains. After a few months of operation, we were discovered.

One day, I was at the law firm where I worked and a group of Castro's people came in asking for Jorge Giró. Luckily, the secretary went to my office and told me, "There are eight to ten persons who would like to see you. I don't know who they are and I haven't asked, but I don't think you have any appointment with them." I immediately became aware of the situation. Because there was no way out of the office except through the front door, I took the chance to walk right past those people and pretend that I was an ordinary customer of the office. Thank God, it seems they had no information or photographs of me, and I was able to leave without any suspicions from their part.

Later I had to make contacts to see if I could receive asylum in an embassy. My brother was working for the Castro government, and he soon learned I was in hiding. He sent me the message that I should turn myself in, and that he could guarantee that I could leave Cuba. I paid no attention. After three months of fleeing and hiding in different houses throughout Havana, I was able to find refuge in the Peruvian embassy in August 1960, thanks to my wife's grandfather, who was close friends with Peru's president. I was there for about four months with fifteen to twenty other Cubans who had also sought refuge.

From the Peruvian embassy, a group of us went to Lima, Peru. In Lima, we worked with the CIA, which gave us training in guerrilla tactics, subversive action, etc. We were there for about thirty days. My wife, who was actually my fiancée then, had left Cuba with her family for Miami. In December 1960 we were reunited in Miami.

In Miami I frequented the Frente's offices on Biscayne Boulevard to receive information on Cuba. It was there I learned of the Brigade and the camps, and I decided to enlist. I went to a small house on Southwest Twenty-seventh Avenue in Miami where people would sign up. A couple of weeks passed and I was called, and we were taken to Opa-Locka at night and put aboard an airplane for our flight to the Guatemalan camps.

Andrés Manso, Sixth Battalion

Born in Camagüey Province in 1935, Andrés Manso was the son of a sawmill operator. After moving to Havana at the age of fifteen, he received his secondary education at the Instituto del Vedado, a public school. He then became a salesman in Havana. After joining the Brigade, he was assigned to the Sixth Battalion and saw action near Girón. Released with most of the Brigade in December 1962, he remained active for some time in anti-Castro missions.

Andrés Manso, Sixth Battalion, at the Brigade Museum, Miami, 1999. Photograph by author.

My life in Cuba was more or less normal, and you could say I was middle class. I had relatives in Batista's government, but I never really had any problems with the government; Batista had his own ideas, and I believe he had made a mistake when he launched his coup in March 1952. But I did not fight against him, nor did I do anything for him. They never did anything against me either.

When Fidel came into power, I was totally opposed within six months, as I became suspicious that he was a Communist. My views were influenced by my brother-in-law, a naval officer, who was an older man and a great intellect. We began sending money to the anti-Castro fighters in the Escambray in 1960, and I participated in the MRR.

Later, when we began to conspire on a grander scale, someone informed on us. Since I did not want to enter clandestine work and I did not want to engage in terrorist activities—I never liked that sort of thing—I decided it was best to travel to the United States. Fortunately, I was a member of a racing-boat federation in Cuba and had an indefinite visa. I left for Miami in September 1960.

I had a brother in New Jersey who had come during the mid-1950s to find new horizons. He helped me financially, as I had left Cuba with only five dollars in my pocket. For the next six months, I worked at different jobs to support myself. During that time, I began hearing about the Frente over the radio and in the newspapers. Then the rumors began about people training in Guatemala, etc., and without thinking much about it, I made contact.

I went to New York City with a friend to sign up for the camps. The office had a sign that read "Frente Revolucionario." My friend was rejected because he had something wrong with his hands. They asked me many questions about where I was from and about my family. Everyone there was Cuban; there were no Americans. I was then given a transfer order to Miami along with a ticket on National Airlines.

I had to present myself in an office on Twenty-seventh Avenue in Miami, where they put me through another series of questions and had me fill out more forms. They then gave me a uniform and boots and took a group of us to Opa-Locka airport, where we were put on an airplane at dawn bound for Guatemala.

Jorge Marquet, Fifth Battalion

Born in 1930, Jorge Marquet was one of numerous married men with children who joined the Brigade. After working for several years in the business his grand-

father had established, he left Cuba in 1960. He joined the Brigade and was assigned to the Fifth Battalion; he was trained to use a bazooka. Upon his release from prison, he settled in Los Angeles, where he worked as a cargo agent with American Airlines. He settled later in Miami and is currently the secretary of the Brigade 2506 museum in Little Havana.

Jorge Marquet, Fifth Battalion, Brigade Museum secretary, Miami, 1999. Photograph by author.

I worked as a customs broker in Havana. It was a family business for many years, and it had passed from my grandfather to my father and from my father to me. We worked independently and acted as the intermediary between the merchant and the government.

Although I was not a *Batistiano*, I never did anything against Batista, because my father—even though he worked in the business—was also a member of the House of Representatives as a member of the Liberal Party, which was then in a coalition with the government party. Certainly, everyone in Cuba wanted a change of government, a different sort of politics than Batista's. But just as I was never in favor of Batista, I was against Fidel Castro. I never liked him. I remember in one of his first speeches, he had a white dove land on his shoulder and all the press made him look like some sort of a messiah. I never believed any of it. Yet I did nothing about it. Like I said, my family was marked and under constant pressure from the government, especially my father. In one week, we endured more than twenty-one home searches. Even though they could not find anything against my father except that he had been a politician, he had to leave Cuba. He went to Mexico, not as an exile but as an honored guest of the embassy.

At the time, we still had the business, and I stayed in Cuba principally to make sure my parents had the economic means to survive—first in Mexico and then Miami. I had two children from my first marriage, and I was able to get them and my former wife out of the country. During that time, I learned that I was being watched. I had many friends who had fought against Batista, and they informed me that in spite of never having been involved in politics I was being scrutinized because of my father. Eventually the new government did away with independent customs brokers, and I left Cuba in November 1960. Before leaving, however, I had made contact with the Christian Democratic Movement. I was not affiliated at that moment because I was still under government scrutiny. When I came to Miami I joined up with them immediately.

I also began working when I arrived in Miami. My first job was as a "house man" at a Miami Beach hotel called the Sans-Souci. It just so happened that when I married the first time and came to Miami for my honeymoon, I had stayed at that very hotel. When I applied for a job, the person who interviewed me asked how it was possible that I was applying for work there. I said, well, that I was now a refugee with no money. After that job, I worked at a mattress factory in Hialeah.

My cousin, who worked with the Christian Democrat Movement and was our contact with the Frente, had already gone to the camps. I went to the Frente office and signed up for the camps in mid-March. I already knew, thanks to the letters I received from my cousin, what the camps were like. I told the people at the Frente that if they were going to mobilize me, it had to be during a certain week. I already had two children, and my current wife was seven months pregnant with my daughter—who was born later while I was in prison. I told my family, "This is a decision I have already made. I feel I have a duty to try to do something for the fatherland, and I feel it is the opportune moment."

It was a difficult decision to leave the family and run the risk of what I was going to do. Although they supported me, my wife once asked me, "How is it possible you are not thinking of your child?" I told her, "No. It is precisely because of that child and the two others I have here that I am going. I plan to return to my fatherland, and I don't want a Communist fatherland with Fidel's dictatorship." My older daughter was eight years old, and my son was six. On March 15, I left for Guatemala.

Antonio González de León, Second Battalion

Born in 1941 in the city of Morón, Camagüey Province, Antonio González de León was educated at local public schools. The son of a restaurant owner, he was still in high school at the time of the struggle against Batista. After joining the Brigade in Miami, he was made a rifleman with the Second Battalion and fought on the Playa Larga front as well as at Girón. After his release from prison in 1962, he went to Los Angeles, where he worked as a salesman. He later settled in Miami.

My father was a businessman in Morón. I never sympathized with Batista, because I believed in having a free country without dictatorship and Batista was a dictator. When Fidel came to power, like everyone else, I imagine, I had

Antonio González de León, Second Battalion, stands before a picture of Manuel Artime at the Brigade Museum, Miami, 1999. Photograph by author.

hoped that things would change—that Cuba would become a free and democratic republic.

Very early, however, I saw certain injustices that I did not like. I started to think differently—especially because of the violence, the executions, the arbitrary acts of the government, and the type of mentality that was emerging. I saw it was not what I had thought it was going to be.

Then my father started to have problems. They confiscated his properties. He was a modest man of limited means and a hard worker. In 1960 he said, "I think the best thing would be to leave." I had an uncle in New York, so he sent me, my mother, and my sister there. My mother and sister went back to Cuba, but I decided to stay in New York.

Another uncle, Luis Oria Finalés—who later was killed as part of the Brigade's infiltration teams—called me while he was receiving training in Florida. He was one of the Brigade's founders and had a very low Brigade number. He said, "Why don't you come to Miami and you'll be closer to us?" So I came, and he got me a job through a friend of his. One night, he came and told me that he was going to Cuba. I asked him, "Don't you think I should go, too?" He said, "No, no. You shouldn't get involved in this; you're too young."

With a mutual friend who also wanted to go, we enrolled at the Frente's office for the camps in January. We were called in March, and we went. We were put into a small barracks somewhere in Miami and then taken to the airport and the camps. My family was still in Cuba, and they did not know what I had done—though my uncle may have had an idea that I would get involved in something.

Rolando Martínez, MRR

Rolando Martínez was born in 1922 in Pinar del Río Province, where his family was involved in agricultural enterprises, especially pineapple, and owned several businesses. Although he never aspired to political office in the years prior to Batista and Castro, he describes himself as always having been concerned with the problems that plagued Cuba. It was that concern that led him to be an active participant in the Auténtico Party. Even though he was never officially part of Brigade 2506, he was a key member of the political-military opposition to Castro and was responsible for running hundreds of covert maritime missions between the United States and Cuba—including the transport of Brigade infil-

Rolando Martínez (*left*), anti-Castro operative, in Miami with life-long friend and colleague Armando Ortega, 1999. Photograph by author.

tration units. He was a central figure in later attacks on Castro's Cuba. In 1972, Rolando Martínez was among the men arrested during the Watergate break-in.

My political association was with the Auténtico Organization. I fought against Fulgencio Batista, and my involvement was enough that I had to leave Cuba. I came to Miami, and I helped smuggle many arms into Cuba.

When Batista left Cuba, I was in Mexico with Lomberto Díaz, a former senator. Our original intention was to land in Pinar del Río and join a group awaiting us there; when we heard Batista had fallen, we returned to Cuba immediately. I had few illusions about Castro, although we were happy Batista was gone

It was a great surprise to all of us that Castro took power the way he did. Although the 26th of July Movement had men of talent supporting them, they were individuals of no popular significance in Cuba. And nobody thought Castro, who had failed at everything he had ever attempted, could have reached the top of the government structure. I had known Fidel years earlier, and I had once accused him of murder.

By April 1959, we felt the government was heading toward Communism. Then Communists began to participate in the government more actively and touted the revolution as being *their* victory. When I came back to the United

States as a Castro opponent in December 1959, I came as a member of Artime's MRR. I had met "Francisco," Rogelio González Corzo, in Cuba. In 1960, we began running guns to the guerrillas in the Escambray Mountains. The Americans helped us. But, for us, it wasn't the CIA; the word CIA has been so abused and misused. The money came, and it could have come from Defense, the FBI. The Americans helped, but I did it as a member of the MRR, and I did it for Cuba. In all, I made 354 missions to Cuba before and after the invasion.

Mario Girbau, CPA

Born in 1916, Mario Girbau was from Matanzas Province. His father, a sugar cane plantation owner, sent him to Mount St. Joseph's College in Baltimore, Maryland, from where he graduated high school. Upon his return to Cuba, Girbau entered the University of Havana and received a degree in business administration in 1943. He then worked as an inspector in the government's Ministry of Finance until going into exile in 1960. He joined the Brigade in Miami and was made its financial manager by the CIA.

Mario Girbau, CPA, Miami, Florida, 2000. By permission of Mario Girbau.

When the revolution took over, they fired all the inspectors at the ministry. Coincidentally, though, during the Batista years an inspector friend had once asked me for one hundred pesos. He said he couldn't return it or tell me what it was for; but he was a friend, so I gave it to him. When Batista fell, they gave control of the ministry to a person who had been a fellow student of mine at the university. He knew I had given one hundred pesos—which, as it turned out, was to get him (the new minister) out of Cuba while Batista was in power because he was about to be arrested. So, he thanked me and recommended me for a job at the division of rents. I was one of two or three inspectors who stayed after Fidel came to power.

I never sympathized with Fidel Castro. A conspiracy was initiated by the American embassy, headed by a Cuban who had been a CIA agent in Cuba. I will not mention his name, even though he is already deceased. It was through him that I got involved in this thing. I left Cuba on April 25, 1960. I was forty-four years old.

I arrived with the idea of going straight to the camps. But because I was a certified public accountant and spoke English, they removed me from all that and put me in charge of the money that was used by the delegations, the recruitment offices, and all other local expenses. Along with another certified public accountant, whose name I will not mention either, I handled all of that. Since I was the one who spoke English, I was the one who went to the interviews, the one who received calls from Washington, D.C., and all that.

Most of the money was for the dependents of the boys who were going to the camps and later to the families of those who had died. The checks initially came from an account under my name and that of the other certified public accountant. Later a corporation was opened, and then the checks were sent from the corporation. We made it seem like the two of us would leave that business completely, even though we kept administering it. I was never told from where the money came. It came through bank transfer—sometimes from Switzerland, sometimes from New York, and sometimes from other places. The bank would only send me a paper that told me how much had been deposited. It was my understanding that the CIA handled everything, but we reported to certain individuals who never mentioned the name CIA. It never came up in all those conversations, and I never dared mention it.

After a few years, the government came to do an audit. They took two rooms in a hotel on South Bayshore Drive. I had to take all the books there in a truck because they would not go to the office—it had to be there in the hotel, all very secretly. We spent seventeen days answering questions, and when they finished the audit, luckily (and it's something I should not say because it would seem I am giving myself credit) they shook my hand and told me, "Thanks to you, the Bay of Pigs was a military disaster and not an economic one also."

On September 1, 1978, we finally closed the office. The government spent years trying to bring about an official solution to the business of the payments to the widows—which had been guaranteed in writing. Then it was made to seem that it was the Department of Labor that was paying from that moment on. I think that is what actually happened.

We felt that in fighting for the right cause, God was with us, and with the United States backing us in this operation, it increased our faith in the war for Liberation.

Alberto Sánchez Bustamante, M.D., surgical team aboard the Lake Charles

2

TRAINING AND PREPARATION

John F. Kennedy's first official briefings on the Cuba plan as president occurred in late January and early February 1961. The plan called for establishing a beachhead in southern Cuba from which further attacks could be launched and a provisional democratic government could be established. Although told by the Defense Department that the plan had a "fair" chance of success, the new president was concerned nonetheless about such a bold move so obviously supported by the United States.[1] It would make the U.S. hand hard to hide, and the diplomatic price of being branded an aggressor would be high. There was also the fear of a Soviet reaction. Yet he knew that any scaling down of the operation would be detrimental to its success. Of course, President Kennedy's greatest dilemma was the corner into which his own campaign rhetoric had placed him weeks earlier. Having repeatedly blasted the Eisenhower administration for its alleged soft stance on Cuba and his own open support for the Cuban "fighters for freedom," he could not simply dismantle the Brigade and scrap the invasion. To be branded a liar and a coward by his political enemies, not to mention the prospect of Cuban exile leaders and Brigade members exposing his withdrawal of support, would be politically detrimental to him. Thus, Kennedy was faced with what Allen Dulles called a "disposal problem" if the Brigade were disassembled.[2]

On March 11, Kennedy was presented with the invasion's details. According to plan, the Brigade's infantry and paratrooper units would land and establish a perimeter around the southern cities of Trinidad and Casilda. Meanwhile, the Brigade air force would launch surprise D-day attacks and destroy Castro's air force while it was on the ground. Having established total air supremacy, the Brigade pilots later would land and be stationed permanently at Trinidad's airfield, from where they would protect the beachhead and launch continuous raids on Castro military targets. Meanwhile, the Frente—later renamed the Cuban Revolutionary Council—would be flown in to establish a provisional government dedicated to democracy and the progressive 1940 constitution. Trinidad was an ideal location, as it was flanked by natural terrain and had only one access bridge, which easily could be destroyed. Its neighboring mountains were well suited for guerrilla operations if such became necessary. Trinidad's landing sites were along sandy beaches, and its population was known for its opposition to Castro. Casilda, a few miles away, had excellent deep-water ports, which would be used by the Brigade's naval arm to resupply the beachhead.[3]

Kennedy rejected the plan, calling it "too spectacular," and made known his desire for a "quiet landing" and, astonishingly, "preferably at night." Kennedy was obviously swayed by State Department fears about a Soviet response. Thus, the president asked the Cuba task force to come back with an alternative plan. Four days later, in what Johns Hopkins scholar Piero Gleijeses called a "clumsy compromise," the president approved the change in landing sites to the sparsely populated area around the Bay of Pigs.[4] Years later, Marine colonel Jack Hawkins, the lead military planner for the invasion, stated that the change in landing sites was, "the first fatal error made by President Kennedy: rejecting a plan [Trinidad] that offered a good chance of success and placing 'plausible deniability' ahead of military viability."[5]

The Bay of Pigs—in Spanish, *Bahía de Cochinos*—was located ninety miles west of Trinidad on Cuba's southern coast. From its ten-mile-wide mouth, it runs like a funnel about eighteen miles north to its tip at Playa Larga. Twenty miles southeast of Playa Larga and connected by a coastal road that ran along the Bay's eastern rim was the seaside town of Girón, where Castro recently had started constructing a beach resort. Girón, a few miles from the bay's mouth, had an airstrip capable of accommodating B-26s. The road that ran from Playa Larga to Girón continued along the island's southern coast to the city of Cienfuegos. A few miles northeast of Girón and connected by a different road was the tiny village of San Blas. The area's shoreline is made up of rocky soil that, moving inland, soon gives way to soft, smooth land. Beyond that immediate coastal area lies the Ciénaga de Zapata, a large swamp several miles wide and deep.[6] The area that contained Girón, Playa Larga, and San Blas—what was to become the approximately forty-mile-long beachhead area seized by the Brigade—was virtually insulated by the swamp. Aside from the coastal road, the only way to the beachhead area was across three narrow causeways, each of which ran directly through the swamp for several miles.

The new plan called for the Brigade to land, set up its headquarters at Girón, and guard the three narrow roads to the beachhead. One of the roads went north seventeen miles from Playa Larga to Jagüey Grande, near the Central Australia sugar mill. Five of the seventeen miles cut directly across the swamp. This road would be taken initially by a company of paratroopers, who would be supported by the Fifth and Second Battalions after their amphibious landings at Playa Larga, now code-named Red Beach. The other two roads, which likewise ran directly through the swamp for several miles, forked off from San Blas and also would be seized initially by a paratrooper company. On this front, the paratrooper units would be dropped at three points: The two advance units would land along the roads in front of San Blas, near the villages of Covadonga and Yaguaramas, twelve and twenty-two miles from San Blas, respectively; the bulk of the company would land at the main paratrooper command center at San Blas. The paratroopers here would be joined by part of the Fourth Armored Battalion, which would move up after landing at Girón, now code-named Blue Beach. Meanwhile, the Third Battalion would land twenty miles east of Girón, at a site code-named Green Beach, to protect the coastal road from Cienfuegos. The Sixth Battalion, the last to be formed, would land at Girón and would be held in reserve. Also slated to land at Girón were the headquarters staff; the Heavy Weapons Battalion; a tank unit; and the group that made up Operation Forty, whose mission it was to administer occupied areas. The Brigade's battalions (whose numbers the planners hoped would swell in Cuba) were actually the size of regular companies, and the companies were the size of platoons.

The primary goal of defending the beachhead was to protect the Girón airfield for the Brigade's twenty-two B-26 bombers. As in Trinidad, the overall objective of the ground units was to prepare the way for the execution of an air war. The basic air plan still called for a surprise D-day raid by Brigade planes on Castro's small air force while it was on the ground, thus gaining air superiority at the outset. U.S. reconnaissance photographs could pinpoint the Castro planes' exact locations at H-hour. According to plan, the exile air force would set out from Puerto Cabezas, Nicaragua, and would land later that day at the Girón airstrip. From Girón, enjoying complete air supremacy, the Brigade planes would land and take off freely. With their .50 caliber machine guns, five-inch rockets, and heavy bomb capacity, the B-26s, supported by the infantry, would be the main protectors of the roads to the beachhead. Because the roads were built on causeways, the enemy could not pull its forces off of them, bringing about what David R. Mets called in *Land-Based Air Power in Third World Crises* "an ideal interdiction situation."[7] Mets observed, "It seems that the planners had a clear grasp of air doctrine and tried to apply it in a logical way."[8] The pilots appropriately dubbed areas where the roads cut directly through the swamp as "shooting galleries."[9] Once established, the Brigade B-26s also would attack the enemy's military targets, particularly highly exposed enemy troops and equipment moving along Cuba's highways.[10] Under such circumstances, it was believed that the beachhead could be held indefinitely and that new recruits could be brought in from exile, from other parts of Cuba, and from Castro's demoralized troops.

At that point, the new government could be flown in to the beachhead and declare itself a government-in-arms. Being a democratic, constitutional government, the United States (and, it was hoped, other American nations) could recognize the new administration and send aid, military and otherwise. It was at that point that any internal developments the planners anticipated—such as an uprising—would occur. Although plans for Phase II were not as well developed, it was assumed things were "bound to happen" if the Brigade and the provisional government could not be dislodged from the beachhead.[11] In any event, the entire operation hinged on Castro's air force being destroyed on the ground. Otherwise, his T-33s and Sea Furies easily could shoot down the slower B-26 bombers or at the very least prevent them from landing at Girón. Thus, the Brigade would lose its air support and the ability to defend the critical roads. Moreover, the Brigade's ships would be either sunk or forced to evacuate. In such a scenario, the Brigade would be totally cut off and routed.

The CIA decided not to inform anyone in the underground about the time and place of the invasion, including the Brigade's infiltration units which they had trained and sent into the island. Because the invasion's time and place were the only secrets left and since the underground was so riddled with informants, it was decided to activate the underground after the landings.[12] Moreover, any overt, popular support for the invaders was expected only after the beachhead was established, the Brigade was clearly winning, and Castro was seen to be on the run.[13] U.S. planners and exile leaders were not as delusional on this point as some have made them appear.

Two diversionary landings were also worked into the scheme. One, led by Higinio "Nino" Díaz, was to take place in Oriente Province, in eastern Cuba, a couple of days before the invasion. The other diversion was to come at Pinar del Río, in western Cuba, and was to consist of CIA electronic equipment that gave the appearance of a major battle.[14]

The new landing site, while meeting the president's political requirements, was clearly strategically inferior to Trinidad: The distance from Havana (and thus Castro's military concentrations) was cut; there were no deep water ports, thus requiring the Brigade to be supplied by landing craft going back and forth between the ships and the beach; and the local population was small and not necessarily sympathetic. In addition, coral rock lined the shore, a fact that the CIA became aware of only during the landings. (A photo interpreter had concluded that certain dark spots were seaweed, and the agency accepted this conclusion despite warnings to the contrary.) The president's insistence on a night landing—attempted only once during World War II, by a highly experienced U.S. force—complicated things even more. Nevertheless, the Joint Chiefs of Staff, while preferring Trinidad, believed the operation could still be successful if carried out as planned.[15] There were no Castro troops nearby, and the Girón airstrip could accommodate the B-26s.

One of the plan's greatest flaws was that the area was totally unsuited for guerrilla operations. Hence, there was no alternative plan if things went poorly. Bissell did not tell the president that the guerrilla contingency was now dead, and thus he assumed it was still an option. Bissell admitted that "we either encouraged or allowed the president and his advisers to believe that in the event of uncontainable pressure at the beachhead the brigade could retire and thereby protect the guerrilla option."[16] The agency nevertheless believed that the guerrilla option would be unnecessary. If in fact the Brigade could not hold the beachhead, and the alternative was defeat, they thought the president would send help. Having grown accustomed to Eisenhower, they felt it was impossible that a president of the United States would allow such a venture to fail. In "The Confessions of Allen Dulles," Lucien Vandenbroucke commented on Eisenhower: "If during a covert operation it became necessary to choose between making the American will prevail and preserving the fiction of U.S. noninvolvement, he had few hesitations. As he explained during the CIA's intervention in Guatemala: 'When you commit the flag, you commit to win'."[17]

Kennedy's first dilution of the operation came as a result of fear by the State Department and its secretary, Dean Rusk, that such massive air strikes designed to destroy Castro's airforce would make it difficult to hide U.S. involvement. If the strikes were smaller, the claim would be more convincing that they had been carried out by defecting Castro pilots (instead of U.S.–sponsored ones). Also, they wanted the first strikes to occur on D-2 instead of on D-Day to make the story more credible. So the first strikes were moved to D-2, and the number of B-26s was reduced from twenty-two to sixteen. A phony defector scheme was developed, in which a Brigade pilot would land in Miami on D-2 claiming that he was one of the Castro pilots who had bombed the airfields that day.[18] Other strikes would follow, with the main one coming on D-Day to destroy any remaining Castro planes. In the end, the effect of the D-2 strikes was to undermine the element of surprise and to allow Castro to round up thousands of real and suspected opponents before the Brigade even arrived in Cuba.

When plans for a guerrilla war were scrapped in favor of an amphibious landing in late 1960, the training in Guatemala was transformed. Training now as a conventional unit, the Brigade was divided into the aforementioned battalions and units. Efforts such as choosing the Brigade's name and symbol were made to foster high morale.[19]

Meanwhile, the Brigade's air force came together, now containing the B-26s in addition to the transport planes. Its Cuban pilots, a collection of former civilian and military fliers, were trained by members of the Alabama Air National Guard. Four guardsmen later lost their lives over the Bay of Pigs.[20] Although the use of B-26s has been criticized, they were more than adequate for the mission at hand, especially since Castro was to have no air combat capability whatsoever.

The naval component also came together. The CIA hired a Cuban company, the Garcia Line, to supply ships to transport the men from the embarkation point at Puerto Cabezas, Nicaragua, to the waters off the Bay of Pigs. The cargo vessels included the *Río Escondido*, the *Houston*, the *Caribe*, the *Atlántico*, and the *Lake Charles*. All but the *Lake Charles*, which was ordered to the beaches two days later and carried part of Operation Forty and a surgical team, were used on D-Day. Although the use of the nonmilitary Garcia cargo ships also has been criticized, they were adequate for their mission: to take the Brigade and its supplies to the beachhead.[21] At no time were the ships supposed to be involved in combat. The CIA also brought two converted LCIs (landing craft infantry), the *Blagar* and the *Barbara J*, to act as command ships.

In the meantime, frogman units under the command of Andy Pruna and José Alonso were trained at Vieques Island, Puerto Rico, and later in Louisiana. Their mission was to lead the Brigade on to the beaches and later, among other things, to carry out underwater demolition. Also at Vieques was Silvio Pérez, a Cuban Navy veteran, who was training a team to pilot the landing craft.[22] A U.S. naval force consisting of five destroyers led by the carrier *Essex* would lead the Brigade ships to the Cuban coast. According to plan, each Garcia Line ship would sail in a different direction from Nicaragua and would be escorted by a destroyer to a rendezvous point code-named Point Zulu near the Cuban shore. With A4 Skyhawk jet attack fighters slated just for this mission, many U.S. personnel came away with the impression that the United States would help the Cubans if they got into trouble.[23]

Assigned to coordinate the beach landings were two CIA agents, Grayston Lynch and William "Rip" Robertson. Lynch, a native Texan, former army captain, and veteran of World War II and Korea, was what writer Peter Wyden called "the closest thing to an on-the-spot military commander that the Cuban operation ever had."[24] He trained the frogmen in Louisiana and later joined Robertson at the CIA's secret base in Key West, Florida; from there they were sent to Central America to join the Brigade shortly before the invasion.

In January 1961, a political crisis developed in Guatemala when the recruits heard rumors about a possible coup d'état against the Frente by the some of the Brigade's military commanders. Angry soldiers, especially the highly idealistic students, had no contact with the Frente in Miami and assumed the Americans at the training camps were supporting the attempt to undermine the Cuban civilian leadership. Existing animosity between the students and career soldiers made the situation even worse: As mentioned earlier, the students had always distrusted the career soldiers and had branded them all *Batistianos* (a charge that was probably unfair for the vast majority of former cadets). They were also upset about the appointment of José "Pepe" San Román as Brigade commander. San Román, a twenty-eight-year-old former officer, had been educated at Cuba's cadet school and at U.S. bases in Georgia and Virginia; he was chosen primarily because of his experience and training.

His appointment was at first seen as a symbol of total submission to the Americans, who by then seemed to be calling all the shots and usurping the authority of the Frente.[25] Ultimately San Román was greatly respected, even among those men who had opposed him during the incident at the training camps.

At the time of the shift of power in the camps, 230 of the 500 men then in training resigned. Those who remained were motivated more by a desire to get the mission moving and a general indifference to what they considered political infighting than by any sense of loyalty to either side. After his own short-lived resignation, the open backing of an American official, and an impassioned patriotic speech, San Román remained Brigade commander and persuaded all but 100 of the men who had resigned to resume training. They returned to the Brigade after Frente officials were allowed to visit the camps to hear their grievances.[26] Shortly thereafter, the Brigade was returned temporarily to their base in the plains near San José for further training; the base was nicknamed Garrapatanango (loosely, Tick City or Tick Base) because of the many ticks (in Spanish, *garrapatas*) present there. The change in location and the round-the-clock focus on military training helped ease much of the political tension.[27]

By mid-February the Brigade had undergone something of a transformation. Although political tensions remained, they were consciously set aside in the spirit of liberating Cuba. Most of the men who eventually made up the 2506 arrived at the camps after the crisis and thus added new life to the operation. Great camaraderie developed, devoid of class or racial tensions despite the diversity that existed. The greatest problem the men faced was an overwhelming impatience to land in Cuba; some had been in the dreary camps since the previous summer. Spurred on by a great sense of patriotism—and, for many, religious zeal—their enthusiasm was underscored by the confidence of their American instructors, who assured them of success. The morale surge was timely, as the invasion was only weeks away.

In February 1961, the first members of Brigade 2506 landed in Cuba as part of the infiltration units. Having trained in Panama, Guatemala, and different parts of the United States, they had the enormously dangerous job of assisting and training anti-Castro groups on the island. They were also to organize uprisings and establish positions at which to receive supplies. Before it was all over, a number of infiltrators were caught and executed.

The resistance inside Cuba suffered numerous setbacks shortly before the invasion. In February, MRR leader Lino Fernández and five hundred others were rounded up and jailed.[28] In March, guerrilla resistance in the Escambray Mountains was all but broken. Also in March, in perhaps the greatest blow to the internal resistance, Rogelio González Corzo (code-named Francisco), the devoutly Catholic head of the MRR in Cuba, was arrested. He was executed shortly after the invasion.[29]

At the State Department in Washington, on April 4, Kennedy held a meeting about the invasion. In this poorly conducted meeting, the president asked those present, including low-ranking advisers, to vote yea or nay on the invasion. Although they agreed to proceed, Kennedy was still apprehensive. A few days before D-Day, he commented that if they had to get rid of the Brigade, it was "much better to dump them in Cuba than in the United States, especially if that is where they want to go."[30] Clearly, the "disposal problem" still dominated the president's thinking. On April 12, he gave a press conference in which he unequivocally stated that no U.S. forces would intervene in Cuba.

The president's words were confusing to the Cuban exile leadership, as they had been promised an "umbrella" of protection for the troops.[31] According to Néstor Carbonell, a young adviser to the Frente who later joined the Brigade, Miró's notes state that he had been assured on April 6 by the State Department's Adolf Berle that "the invasion forces would have 'control of the air' (he didn't use the term 'air cover') and that they would be supported by fifteen thousand additional troops."[32] Carbonell later stated, "Miró was aware of the responsibility he was assuming and asked for a more explicit guarantee. Berle understood his concern but pointed out that the United States could not enter into a formal alliance. He gave the Cuban exile leader, however, his word of honor (*parole d'honneur* was the expression he used)."[33] After the president's April 12 statements, Miró, Berle, presidential advisor Arthur Schlesinger, and Harvard professor John Plank met for lunch at New York's Century Club. Schlesinger, the only one at the meeting not fluent in Spanish, reported that Miró was told that the U.S. would only back the invaders once they had established themselves on the beachhead. For his part, Miró left the luncheon reassured by Berle's statement that their agreements still stood.[34] One can only wonder how the two men left the same meeting with such divergent impressions on such a critical point.

Oblivious to all the events taking place in Washington and New York, the Brigade was given word of their upcoming departure. The men were ecstatic; with encouragement from their American trainers, the men of Brigade 2506 were supremely confident that they would succeed. Brigade leaders, moreover, were assured they would land under complete air superiority. The men remembered words such as "the skies over Cuba will be blotted out"[35] and "we will be over you, under you, and beside you."[36]

As the men broke camp in Guatemala and were transported to the embarkation point in Puerto Cabezas, Nicaragua, their enthusiasm had reached a fever pitch. Seeing with their own eyes the B-26s and P-51 fighters at Puerto Cabezas, they believed they could not lose.[37] They sang patriotic songs and issued numerous "*vivas*" as they embarked on the historic journey to liberate their homeland.[38] Shortly before leaving, the officers were briefed on the battle plan. The Brigade soldiers, meanwhile, boarded the ships and anxiously awaited their departure. For many, the adrenaline was intoxicating.

In the sections that follow, Brigade veterans share their experiences from the training period through their arrival in Nicaragua. Included are the testimonies of one battalion commander, a paratrooper, three infantrymen, a frogman, and Néstor Carbonell, quoted above. Two of the men discuss the political crisis at the camp. Other themes include the religious life at the camps, the training regimen, and the men's reaction to being told of their imminent departure for Cuba. The stories of two Brigade infiltrators are also included.

Hugo Sueiro, Second Battalion Commander

A group of us who had certain military expertise were sent to Panama to be trained as a cadre. They took us there in the same mysterious fashion in which they had taken us to Useppa. We left at dawn to a to a field near Ft. Myers and, after waiting all day, they took us at dusk to an abandoned airport where they put us aboard a plane and took off.

At Useppa they had told us that it was not really an army that was being formed, but that we were going to go in as guerrillas. At that point, people were given the opportunity to separate themselves from the operation, and there were some doubts among those people who had little children. But in the end, we all figured, "How are we not going to go? We are going to fight for Cuba. Maybe they'll kill us, but we're doing the right thing. We are also going to help our friends in prison." In the end, the whole group went; none chose to stay behind.

In Panama, we began to receive our training as guerrillas. Besides the soldiers, many Agrupación Católica people were there. During that time, we had certain difficulties because the rivalries were still fresh between former Rebels and what they called *Batistianos*. A lot of comments were made back and forth, as those of us who had been in the armed forces were all considered *Batistianos*—whether we had been or not. There was also a difference in ability. Many of the lessons they taught us in Panama were in things we as soldiers had already mastered at the academy. Perhaps that was why the Americans liked us: We shot and hit the target; the others shot and missed. After that, we went back to Guatemala, where we joined the people from the original groups at Useppa and some new ones who had arrived.

During that time, we never doubted the Americans. Our view of them was deeply embedded: They had won World War II and all the wars they had ever fought. We had all seen the movies, and we viewed the Americans as supermen and men of conviction. But in Guatemala there were already doubts: We were subordinating ourselves completely to the Americans.

Another big problem was that the command staff in Miami was putting the recruits through a filtering process and, as a result, too few people were getting to the camps. So the Americans sent a group of us to Miami on a two-week recruiting trip at Christmastime to help speed things along, especially after the change to a brigade concept. For an invasion, we needed more people than for a guerrilla war. I really didn't know any of the important people in Miami, as I was just a kid and I didn't come from a world of important contacts in Cuba. Carol and Pepe San Román, who did know them, nevertheless had trouble with them over the processing issue. We also had trouble with our own career military people. We would say, "We need you guys to go." They would ask, "Well, what position would I hold? I'm an officer." We would explain that there were no officers. Some chose never to go.

Back in Guatemala, after some political turmoil at the camp, we were sent to Garrapatanango. It was the best thing that could have happened to us, because we got away from all the problems at Trax. My battalion really came together solidly at Garrapatanango, and I could compare it to any unit in the world at that moment. Not long after we were sent back to Trax, more men began arriving from Miami, and I told those under my command, "Look for people among the arriving recruits. If you see somebody and you know he is good, bring me his name." Many of the men in my battalion were students, and many others were from Oriente. There were never any conflicts or cliques based on social class.

When the news came that we were finally leaving for the invasion, it was very emotional. The heads of the units were brought together for the briefing.

I had an argument with the Americans because they only wanted to give us eighty bullets apiece. They explained to us how they had experience in these things and that we didn't need more bullets. However, I knew from personal experience that inexperienced soldiers get nervous and have a tendency to shoot a great deal. So later, while aboard the *Houston* on the way to Cuba, I went into the hold of the ship to look for ammunition. I found some and gave it to my people.

At our briefing at Puerto Cabezas, we were given several promises. The American told us, and I remember this like it happened today, "Don't worry. If they have fighter planes, you will have fighter planes; if they have jet planes, you will have jet planes." Of course, the Brigade air force didn't have fighters or jets. They obviously were referring to American aircraft.

Sergio Carrillo, Paratrooper

Father Sergio Carrillo, paratrooper, in his Miami office, 1999. Photograph by author.

Born in Havana to poor, working-class parents in 1934, Sergio Carrillo was one of over fifty Afro-Cubans in the Brigade. As a boy, he and his friends were brought closely into the Catholic faith due to the imaginative evangelical efforts of a priest at a local Catholic school. As a teenager, Carrillo and fellow Boy Scouts at his parish organized resistance cells to oppose Batista. Through his Boy Scout organization he also became associated with Manuel Artime, with whom he joined the revolution's early efforts to help the rural poor and later entered the Castro opposition. He came to Miami in late 1959 and went to the Guatemala camps in the summer of 1960. Ironically, his father and brother —not knowing Sergio was in the Brigade—fought at the Bay of Pigs on Castro's side. Exactly twenty years after the invasion, Carrillo was ordained into the priesthood. He currently serves as a Catholic chaplain at Miami's Jackson Memorial Hospital.

My family had no idea what I was up to when I left Cuba. The only thing I could think of was to tell them that I was going to a Boy Scout jamboree in the United States. They all believed me.

The camps in Guatemala were always hard. We would wake up early and have breakfast and immediately begin training in the mountains. Afterward, we had lunch, rested a little, and trained more in the afternoon. At night we had classes. The training was very hard; and when I became part of the paratroopers, it was even worse, as we would have to wake up at two, three, or four in the morning.

At the camps I was often called the *heladero* [ice cream vendor], because I was the sacristan and I would call people to mass by going around ringing a bell; the image is the most remembered of me at the camps. The religious efforts were in some ways similar to those of a parish church. We had daily mass, gave catechism classes, and prepared some men for their first Holy Communion. Some men were even baptized at the camps. There were also Protestant ceremonies, but 90 percent of the men were Roman Catholic. There were many young men who received counseling from the priests, as a number of them had problems because of the situation; that is, they were in a military environment for the first time, and they were separated from their families. A large group of us, including those from the Catholic schools and from the Agrupación Católica, helped the priests a great deal. During that whole time, there were no conflicts in the camps between people of different social classes, nor did we experience any racial problems.

One day we were suddenly told that we had to break camp. We suspected what was going on and spent most of the day dismantling the camp. We went down to Retalhuleu, slept there, and had breakfast there the next morning. That night we boarded an airplane and went to Nicaragua and spent the next day at a military airport. It was there that they told us that the next day we would be in Cuba. That day we spent receiving information, looking over maps, preparing ammunition, and all that. We had hardly anything for lunch and had a light dinner of about three pieces of meat and some salad. At dawn, we boarded the airplanes bound for Cuba.

Mario Abril, Second Battalion

The Second Battalion's Mario Abril, renowned musician, poses with guitar, ca. 1999. Photograph by permission of Mario Abril.

Born in 1942 in Las Villas Province, Mario Abril attended the local public schools and then went to the University of Santa Clara. His father, who had worked for the Ministry of Education, suspected the direction the revolution was taking and sent Mario to a military academy in the United States in January 1960. The next summer, Mario went to Miami to rejoin his family when they went into exile, and he subsequently joined the Brigade. As a member of the Second Battalion, he saw action at Playa Larga and Girón. After his release from prison, he went on to receive his Ph.D. in music theory. Today, he is a professor of music at the University of Tennessee at Chattanooga and an internationally renowned classical guitarist.

They put us in trucks in Miami, and we drove and drove until we finally arrived at an empty airfield. They flew us in an old army transport that had its windows taped, so we couldn't see outside. After flying all night, we got out of the plane and we were put into a food line. I saw a guy from my hometown, and I asked him, "Where the hell are we?" He said, "Guatemala." I had an idea where Retalhuleu was. We were put into trucks and went up the hill to Trax.

At the very moment we arrived at Trax, we began our training. There was a sergeant there, the kind that yelled—only this one did it in Spanish. When you were assigned your weapon, that was your baby. I was assigned the Garand, the same one I thought was so old-fashioned at the military academy, but it turned out to be a terrific weapon. It's a little clumsy, but it makes up for it in ruggedness.

Our typical day started with an early reveille over a megaphone, which the guard on duty would shout into your tent. We usually had a quick breakfast and then a jogging session in combat attire, without guns—but sometimes with the damned gun, too. They marched us up and down and made us do push-ups, and our arms hurt because they also gave us what seemed like eighty-two shots for every God-damned disease you could think of. We then had fifteen minutes rest before having to go up the hill to the bunker where we did all the shooting. It really was a good hill, and you had to work to get to the top. Every day there was also something special. For example, one evening at eight we had a lecture on how to put together and operate a .30 caliber machine gun; the next day certain squads went up to the bunker to use it. It was a pretty full day.

The spirit of the camps was very high. People there bonded relatively well; there were some differences, but all in all we operated very well together. The morale was high, and so were the skills. When the politicians came to visit, among them Miró Cardona, I remember the whole Brigade assembled up in the shooting bunkers. It was a very impressive sight. I felt so good: I remember jogging not too long before we left, and I felt like I could jog on and on and on. When we were given instructions to dismantle the camp, we knew it was a "go."

In Nicaragua we arrived at the airfields and boarded a train. We were then carried to a commercial pier. I remember the net effect the crossing to Cuba had on me: It was extremely pleasant and placid. It was really a beautiful crossing.

Francisco "Pepe" Hernández, Second Battalion

Born in Havana in 1939, Pepe Hernández was the son of a lieutenant colonel in the Cuban Army who was not connected politically to Batista. A graduate of El Instituto del Vedado, a public school, Pepe entered the university and became active in the engineering school's student union and in the Juventud Estudiantil Católica [Catholic Student Youth]. Hernández was a supporter of the revolution until early 1959, when his father, after having retired from the army, was tried and executed when he refused to give false testimony at the trial of fellow officer. Pepe then became involved with Rescate, the underground group headed by Tony Varona, and later departed for the camps. He is currently a Miami businessman and the best known director of the Cuban American National Foundation, the largest and most powerful Cuban exile lobby in the United States.

The camps were totally different from what I thought they would be. We got there with the idea that we were going to be sent into different parts of Cuba in small groups to conduct guerrilla warfare. When we arrived, I recognized that this was not the case and that the group was now organized into battalions, companies, and platoons which were training for a conventional attack. We also saw that all the power was in the hands of some military men, and we didn't know if they were following the Frente's instructions from Miami. My impression was that they were not and that they were basically following instructions from the CIA. When we arrived at the camps, we had done so as civilians and students, not as military people. We felt that whatever happened in Cuba had to remain under civilian control.

I was in the Second Battalion, and we were sent to Garrapatanango for two or three weeks, where we heard several rumors. When we got back to Trax, we were called one morning to the parade ground. We formed by unit, and San Román and several officers of his staff were there. San Román told us that we were soldiers and that we had to obey our superiors. Then he said something that seemed very stupid to me: He said, "Those who want to go with me to Cuba, stay in your place. Those who do not want to go with me, step to your right." I thought, "I never thought that my struggle and my fighting for my country had anything to do with accompanying you to Cuba. I'll go with whoever represents the ideals and convictions I do."

I stepped to the right with a number of other people in my battalion, including Miró Cardona's son, who was in my same company. Tony Varona's son was also there. The rest of the Brigade was dismissed, but we had our weapons taken away and separated from our units. We were put into tents near the edge of a cliff and stayed there for a couple of weeks. It rained all the time, and I thought the tent would go down the cliff because the mud there was so terrible. We told them that we would not participate in anything until we received a visit from the leaders of the Frente. So they came, and we had the opportunity to talk to both Miró Cardona and Tony Varona. They told us that everything had been arranged, that we shouldn't have any more problems, and that we should continue training. We did just that. During their visit, there was a parade, and they addressed the Brigade.

After the controversy—and especially after the visit—the spirit improved. Even though we recognized things were not exactly as we had expected, we were exhausted by the situation and by the fact that the conditions there were fairly poor. The spirit was higher also because people started to hear rumors and see signs that we were going to go. The Sunday before the invasion, I remember Father Lugo gave mass and told us that the next Sunday was going to change the history of Cuba. He prayed that everything was going to be all right.

We were taken to Puerto Cabezas on a C-54. We were then taken on trucks to a long pier where the ships were. Our ship, the *Houston*, was one of the furthest out. I was a little bit concerned that we were not going on military ships, but rumor had it that we were supposed to transfer to other ships at sea. To tell the truth, though, I was really not very concerned about that. I felt that we had enough with what I could see. From what I was told, we weren't going to have any concern with Castro's air force; to me that was perhaps the main concern, even though I still did not know where we were going to land.

Francisco Molina, Second Battalion

A native of Oriente Province, Francisco Molina worked in a travel agency at the time Fidel Castro came to power in Cuba. His father was an inspector in the Ministry of Public Works. Immediately suspecting Communist infiltration, Molina began working against the government by helping individuals in the underground leave the island. He left for Miami in November 1960, with the intention of going to the camps. He left for Guatemala in late January 1961. After being released from prison in Cuba, he lived in New Jersey for several years and is currently retired in Miami.

Francisco Molina, Second Battalion, at his Miami home, 1999. Photograph by author.

On the night we left, we went to a house on Twenty-seventh Avenue in Miami. We ate there and were then taken to Opa-Locka airport, which we left at about 12:30 A.M.. The windows of the airplane were covered so that we wouldn't know where we were being taken. Of course, we all knew.

We had some problems in Guatemala. One day, some people came from Miami with rumors about a coup d'état against the Frente. We then rebelled right there and told them, "If we came to combat dictatorship, how is it that you want to establish a dictatorship from here?" We had guns but no bullets, and a group of us barricaded ourselves in a barracks. When the instructors came, we said, "Those of us in here know how to use guns. If you want to form a war here, we'll do it right now and nobody will be left standing." Later some people from the Frente came. Things were cleared, and Artime became the coordinator between the Frente and the military unit.

The principal problem of the camps was that the food they fed us was not what we were used to eating. They would give us Spam in the morning and hot dogs in the afternoon, blue rice, green rice, yellow rice. But there were no black beans and rice; there was no steak, no chicken. When there *was* chicken, it was already breaded, and they would stick it in the oven with "Shake and Bake," and that's it. Some of us volunteered to cook; I know how to cook, so I started cooking. People's spirits lifted after that. Before that, we were on Kool-aid, hot dogs, and cheeseburgers. They then started bringing meat, fish, fresh chicken, and pork.

My battalion, the Second, was called the Battalion of the Rebels and the Spoiled Kids, because two companies were from Oriente and had battle experience from the guerrilla war and the others were young sons of wealthy people from Havana. People got along well, though, and they started to become friends in the camps as soon as they started getting to know one another. There were no conflicts between the rich and the others or anyone else. Plus, the training was such that there was no time to lose looking for trouble. Our typical day, Jesus Christ, would start at five in the morning to march double-time and to train. We would have lunch outdoors. When you went back at the end of the day, you were ready to sleep already.

We learned that we were leaving when they came and told us, "You have two hours to get ready, we are going down." We were very happy and enthusiastic. We were taken to Nicaragua on airplanes, and when we arrived, we saw a line of B-26 bombers and C-54s, and some P-51s. When you see that, you say, "¡Coño!" [damn!] This isn't Mickey Mouse. This for real!"

Eduardo Zayas-Bazán, Frogman

Eduardo Zayas-Bazán was twenty-five years old at the time of the invasion. His highly respected family, from Camagüey Province, was one of Cuba's oldest and

most aristocratic. It had provided a number of independence-era heroes as well as statesmen during the republican era. After graduating from the Georgia Military Academy in 1953, Eduardo returned to Cuba to study law. Initially enthusiastic about the revolution, he soon became disillusioned and joined the MRR in 1959. In August of 1960, he was tipped off by a friend who was an officer in Castro's army that he was being watched; knowing an invasion was being planned, he decided to come to the United States. During the invasion, Eduardo was wounded in the right knee. After his release from prison in Cuba with other wounded Brigade members in April 1962, Eduardo became a professor of Spanish. He taught at East Tennessee State University for over thirty years, wrote Spanish textbooks, and became a national leader

Above: Frogman Eduardo Zayas-Bazán in Key Biscayne, Florida, 1999. Photograph by author. *Below*: Eduardo Zayas-Bazán (fourth from left and shirtless), flanked by fellow frogmen Andrés Pruna, Jorge Silva, and Amado Cantillo (*left*) and Jesús Soto and Carlos Fonts (*right*). Photograph by permission of Eduardo Zayas-Bazán.

in foreign-language education. He is now retired and lives in Key Biscayne, Florida.

We had high hopes for the revolution and applauded Castro upon his magnificent entrance in January 1959. I had been fed up with corruption in Cuba. Corruption is one of the traditional evils that have ruined the possibilities of our countries in Latin America. I turned against the revolution when the trial of the aviators took place—when they were declared innocent and then Castro forced another trial. It was very clear to me that this guy did not respect the law. Then other events took place that made me suspect the path the revolution was taking. By the end of 1959, I knew democracy was in trouble, and I joined the MRR.

One of the sad things that has happened over this period in the history of Cuba is that historians have not given credit to the idealism of those who turned against the revolution. We really were full of good will, and we wanted to make Cuba better. We all felt that Castro had wasted a tremendous opportunity, because psychologically he came to power at the right time to make all types of major changes. He could have said, "What happened before is ended. From now on we are going to have honest politicians, we are going to respect the law, we are going to pay our taxes." There were many of us who believed very strongly that this could have taken place, that we could have built a better Cuba.

When I left Cuba on September 26, 1960, it was to join an invasion force. My wife, Elena, followed me in October, and on November 1, 1960, our son was born. When I left to train for the Bay of Pigs invasion, my son was only two months old. During that time, my wife had ambivalent feelings, but she knew that I was doing the right thing. I remember during the training, they let us loose in New Orleans for two days; I called Elena, and that was the first time she actually said, "I don't want you to go."

When I arrived in Miami from Cuba, the first thing I did was to go to the offices of the Frente, where I knew Tony Varona, who was also from Camagüey and had been a senator with my father. I had been an all-American swimmer at the military academy in Georgia (as a matter of fact, I had been offered a swimming scholarship to the University of Georgia), so when I learned there was a need for frogmen, I said, "This is for me, this is where I really fit." They put me in contact with a former naval officer named Renato Díaz, who was the head of the naval effort. The eleven frogmen selected were among the Bay of Pigs invasion's most educated people. All of us had either finished college or were college students in the United States, and we all spoke English fluently.

We went to Vieques Island in January 1961, to a military training area, where we were totally isolated. We were on a wonderful white beach on kind of a semicircle, and we slept there in tents. The training was fairly intense. We would wake up in the morning and swim for a couple of hours, and then we would have different types of training, such as underwater demolition and underwater navigation. The idea was for us not only to secure the beach at the time of the landing but later to attack naval ships at night and to do other missions as needed. At Vieques, we had no contact with the outside world, except when the CIA would bring supplies to us every so often. One time, Father Cavero, one of the Brigade chaplains, arrived on a supply ship, and we celebrated mass with him.

After being at Vieques for about a month and a half, we were flown one night to a small naval base in Puerto Rico proper. We were there for more than a week, passing the days waiting for the transport plane to take us to wherever it was we were going next. When we left, we had no idea where it was we were flying to, and the windows of the plane were covered. We finally got to a military airport close to New Orleans.

We were trained near New Orleans for about a month in an army depot a few miles from the entrance of the Mississippi River. It was there we met Gray Lynch and Rip Robertson, who were the last of our instructors. The training was a little bit different, as we did a lot of firing with different guns and practiced more demolition. We also did a lot of underwater swimming in the pool. Some of the guys who were being infiltrated into Cuba were there, as well as the Nino Díaz group.

We left New Orleans aboard the *Río Escondido*. At the mouth of the Mississippi River, we had to get into the water to inspect the propeller after a log got caught in it; we found it all bent, and nothing could be done. Because of the broken propeller, it took us about five days to get to Puerto Cabezas in Nicaragua. Until that time, we had no idea whatsoever about the rest of the Brigade. We hadn't even known they had been in Guatemala. It was only when we got to Puerto Cabezas that we were even told we were in Nicaragua!

Puerto Cabezas was a desolate and miserable place. We were there for several days. The frogmen had much more freedom than the rest of the Brigade, because we had our rubber rafts and got to go around. We visited the air force base and got to see some of our friends. I also saw my brother Rogerio and my old friend Néstor Carbonell, who were with Operation Forty. After about a week or so, we departed for Cuba.

Néstor Carbonell, Operation Forty, Frente Advisor

Néstor Carbonell, Operation Forty and Frente advisor, Greenwich, Connecticut, 2000. By permission of Néstor Carbonell.

Born in Havana in 1936, Néstor Carbonell came from a family that was deeply involved in Cuba's wars of independence, in the foundation of the republic, in politics, in diplomacy, and in the private sector. After attending Havana's Ruston Academy, an American school, Carbonell graduated from a private high school in Florida and then went on to receive his law degree from the University of Villanueva and his L.L.M. from Harvard. Before leaving Cuba for Miami in 1960, he wrote articles opposing Castro's communization of the island. After serving as a Frente advisor for several months, Carbonell joined the Brigade. He sailed for Cuba aboard the Lake Charles *as part of the Operation Forty group that was not able to land and was forced back to Nicaragua. He is currently a vice president of Pepsico, Inc., and resides in Connecticut. The following contains parts of his oral testimony as well as excerpts from his book* And the Russians Stayed.

After my speeches and writings against Castro's totalitarian design, my life became somewhat impossible in Cuba. Tony Varona, who was among the first to organize an opposition outside the island, left Cuba in early 1960, and I contacted him through secret channels. I had sent him the text of a manifesto I had written; it was a statement of principles about why we should break with Castro. He incorporated part of that manifesto into his writings. I left Cuba in June 1960, having made the decision not to go into exile simply to emigrate and rebuild my life but to fight for Cuba's liberation. So I became part of the Frente as an advisor to Tony Varona.

I was with Varona throughout 1960. With other colleagues from the Frente, we attended the OAS meeting of foreign ministers convened in San José, Costa Rica, in late 1960, to discuss the Cuban situation. There, we represented the voice of a democratic Cuba. We issued statements that were published in the newspapers, and we tried to persuade the foreign delegates to take a more direct anti-Castro stand. Throughout this period, I was very active overall in the areas of diplomacy and public affairs. I also joined the planning committee of the Frente that was to develop the legal framework for a democratic transition following Castro's fall. All of the principal exile groups were represented. It was like a mini-parliament which conducted studies and prepared reports and interim legislative drafts for eventual consideration.

[The following material is from Carbonell's book *And the Russians Stayed*.]

By mid-March 1961 I had completed my assignments at the front's [Frente's] planning committee, which included the drafting of communiqués to be issued by the government-in-arms requesting diplomatic recognition and military support. Realizing the Brigade would soon depart for Cuba, I decided to enlist as a private. My parents and friends, including Varona, tried to persuade me to remain at the front headquarters, arguing that my intellectual skills would be more useful to the cause than my insignificant military abilities. I felt, however, a sense of moral commitment. Having called for a war of liberation, how could I, at the moment of truth, fail to practice what I preached? I thought of my paternal grandfather, who at the tender age of fifteen fought for the independence of Cuba. What counted in his case—and perhaps mine, I thought—was not the experience that he lacked, but the passion that he gave and the example that he set.

Just before leaving for Guatemala, some of my colleagues persuaded me to join a newly formed unit—"Operation Forty"—which was to be integrated into the Brigade and charged with the occupation and temporary administration of liberated territories. (I later heard bizarre stories, echoed by noted reporters and historians, about the purported sinister task of this unit: that of eliminating "leftist" leaders, including Miró, who might stand in the way of reactionary plans!) This unit was composed of about eighty men, most of them young professionals known to me, and was headed by an amiable colonel of the Cuban army, Vicente León, who had honored his uniform throughout his career.

Phase one of our brief training was conducted in Miami, where we were subjected to polygraph tests and apprised of our mission as guardians of public order and custodians of human rights. Then one evening we were asked to board army trucks with rear canvas flaps pulled down. We rode in total darkness to an abandoned airbase in Florida, Opa-Locka. Soon we were airborne inside an old C-54 military transport with metal seats placed along the fuselage, and windows painted black and covered with masking tape. We felt claustrophobic—enclosed in what seemed a long, narrow vault piercing the night. We were naturally apprehensive about many unknowns. But we had faith. We believed in the righteousness of our cause and had confidence in our staunch ally.

My short stay at Trax base in Guatemala—about three weeks—was an unforgettable experience. By the time I arrived there, all of the rustic training facilities had been completed in the heights of cloud-shrouded mountains. I was extremely happy to see my nineteen-year-old cousin Humberto Cortina displaying his usual zest and effervescence. He had become a deft radio operator, and was fit and keyed for action. I also met many old friends and made new acquaintances—Cubans of all ages and from all social classes. I saw proud fathers with their young sons preparing for battle. I saw political adversaries burying their differences for the good of the common cause. The feuds that had initially marred the Brigade were gone; a spirit of kinship and a sense of mission pervaded the ranks. I saw the commingling of races without any sign of discrimination. Nepotism and corruption had not surfaced their ugly heads. Sons and relatives of exile leaders were not accorded any special privileges. Scions of families that used to be symbols of wealth and power marched side by side with men of humble origin.

San Román assembled the Brigade [April 10] and told us that the invasion was imminent. He used no oratorical flourishes, yet his voice carried the vibrance of a military leader about to embark on an epochal mission. He said, "Fight fiercely, but protect the civilians and respect the prisoners. . . ." "On to victory," was his rousing finale, "freedom is our goal; Cuba is our cause; God is on our side!" We clapped and cheered wildly.

We left Trax in a joyful mood, singing popular songs and shouting *vivas*. Were it not for the camouflage uniforms that we were wearing and the deadly weapons that we were carrying, we could have been mistaken for a throng of college students on their way to a football game.

The Infiltrators

Javier Souto, Infiltration Unit

Former Florida state representative, senator, and current Miami-Dade county commissioner Javier Souto, Infiltration Unit. Photograph by permission of Javier Souto.

Born in Sancti Spíritus, Las Villas Province, Javier Souto was the son of a local businessman. Educated at La Salle in Havana, he went on to the University of Villanueva, where he majored in economics and was part of the anti-Batista resistance. Although he mistrusted Castro, he worked for the new government following Batista's ouster as part of the Ministry of Economics and helped with agrarian reform. He entered the Castro opposition within a few months, however, and left Cuba in March 1960. After the invasion, he stayed busy in anti-Castro activities and graduated from the University of Miami. After several years in the private sector, Souto served in Florida's house of representatives from 1984 to 1988, and in Florida's senate from 1988 to 1992. He has served as a Miami–Dade County commissioner since 1993.

I left Cuba on March 25, 1960. We stayed at the Sands Hotel that night and got in touch with Manuel Artime's people the next day through a nun called Sister Miriam; she had been in Cuba with the American Dominicans and was then at Gesu Parish. We then went to an old frame house where Artime lived on Brickell Avenue, where thirty or forty of the original recruits lived. Of course, we had come with the intention of contacting Artime; he was like our big brother.

We were the Brigade's first members. We went on the first trip to Useppa Island, and I was given the number 2504. We believed that we would be trained as guerrillas and that someone—we were not sure exactly who—was going to help us here in the United States. Since Artime had contacts at the

U.S. embassy in Havana, we thought we would be trained at some American military bases.

We left Useppa on July 4 and were taken to the Florida mainland. We were put on closed trucks and taken to an airport, where we boarded an old cargo plane with just jump seats; its motors were already running. We flew all night and landed at dawn. I remember how much the flowers smelled and thinking that we were in Central or South America. Then, I saw a car with a license plate that said "Guatemala." We later took some buses to a farm called Helvetia.

At that time, there was no camp or anything, so we lived in an old wood-frame house there on the farm. They then separated people: Some went to be trained in telegraphy; others were chosen as a cadre. I was chosen to be trained with the cadre, but there were a few things going on that I didn't like, so I stayed with the radio operators. We left Guatemala around December 15 and went to Panama, where we trained until January 1961. From there, I was taken to a military base near Norfolk, Virginia.

In Virginia, Jorge Gutiérrez, another radio operator, and I were called out one day and put on an airplane to Washington, D.C., where two Americans who had just arrived from Havana briefed us about the situation in Cuba. They then put us on a commercial flight for Miami, where we checked into a hotel. The next day we were taken to a big, comfortable house near Homestead (south of Miami), which we later nicknamed the Golden Cage. One day in February, we were told a group of us was going to Cuba.

We were taken to Key West, put aboard a small yacht, and taken to Cuba. We landed at a place we code-named Punto Fundora, after the man who organized the landings and who was later executed by Castro. From there, the man with whom I had landed and I went to a beach near Havana and stayed at the home of a family. The next morning, a man came to make contact with us from the underground. In the afternoon, Rogelio González Corzo, the head of the underground who was code-named "Francisco," came to see us. He told me to go to Yaguasay, Las Villas Province, to prepare a guerrilla plan to take the pressure off the people in the Escambray. So, I went with a member of my team and some people from the underground.

José "Pepe" Regalado, Infiltration Unit

Born in Havana in 1937, José "Pepe" Regalado graduated from La Salle and subsequently attended the University of Villanueva and received his degree in

1959. Married to the daughter of an assassinated high-ranking Batista officer, he was immediately targeted by the new government. After surviving a violent encounter with a Revolutionary unit that demanded a ransom from him, he came to Miami in April 1959 and later joined the "Anti-Communist Revolutionary Crusade," one of the early exile groups. He left for Guatemala in the summer of 1960, and was later chosen for the infiltration team when the brigade concept replaced the guerrilla plan.

José Regalado, Infiltration Unit, in his Miami office. Photograph by author.

On January 16, 1961, those of us being trained as infiltrators in Panama were awakened and told, "There is a group that passed its training and will be taken to Cuba. The rest will not go and will be reintegrated into the Brigade." My name was among the forty or so chosen not to go to Cuba at that moment. When we were put on the airplane, we were informed that in fact *we* were the ones going to Cuba and *not* the others.

So, we went back to the Guatemala air base. We were upset because we thought nobody there cared that we would soon be in Cuba. But, the people there gave us a great surprise later at night: when we were leaving, the air force marched out with the Cuban flag and all of that. They stood in formation along our airplane at the top of the runway. The air force chaplain was there, and he blessed us and gave us each a small medallion. Many beautiful words were spoken about us being the first going to Cuba. It lifted our morale greatly.

We were taken to the United States to a farmhouse near Homestead, Florida, that was surrounded by tomato fields. Our cover story was that we were young Cuban doctors learning English in order to pass the exams to practice medicine. We were told the first team to go into Cuba would be the one going to Matanzas. It included: team leader Jorge Rojas; telegraphy operator Jorge Gutiérrez Izaguirre, who was nicknamed El Sheriff; Jorge Recarey in armaments; Antonio Abel Pérez Martín in psychological warfare and propaganda; and myself in intelligence.

We left Key West aboard two boats: one was called the *Wasp*, and it was painted all black and was about thirty-four feet long. It was captained by Kikío Llansó. Also aboard was Rolando Martínez, the most courageous Cuban I have ever known. The other ship was commanded by Captain Villa, a Spaniard. We had to make four trips to Cuba before we finally landed on February 14.

After our landing, we made our way to the Vía Blanca, the road that connected Varadero Beach and Havana. Soon, a Studebaker pulled up with Patricio Fundora and a woman. El Sheriff and I got in with him and the others got into another car. Our cover was that we were coming from a Mr. Rodríguez's funeral in Matanzas. My false identity was Juan Rodríguez, and my assumed address put me at a home two houses from where I had grown up and of which I knew every detail. I also had a fake identification card from the Communist Youth.

We were taken to a doctor's home who was in the MRR with Artime. The next day, we had lunch with the doctor and his family. Although he knew who we were, he had to tell his family that we were relatives of the overseer at his father's farm in Camagüey and that we had come to Havana because we had won scholarships to study at the Agrarian Reform Institute; he told them we were Communists, sympathizers of the Revolution. His sister-in-law was there, and she was a practicing and super fanatical Catholic. She looked at us with such a look of hatred. El Sheriff, who loved to tease people, began talking bad about the priests at Belén. Of course, in reality, he was a million times more Catholic than she was [he laughs]!

That day Rogelio González Corzo, "Francisco," came to see us, and later some others. On the third day Pérez Martín, El Sheriff, and I were picked up to join a guerrilla group in Matanzas, which we would help train. The MRR coordinator in Matanzas joined us. On the way, the car flipped over, and we had to hitch a ride—equipment and all—to Colón. We got transportation and eventually went to a place near Jagüey Grande. Yeyo Peña, the head of the guerrillas there, was present and had about sixteen boys with him. We spent several days there and had some differences with the local MRR leader because our mission was to help *all* anti-Castro groups and not just his. A trip to Havana did not resolve the issue.

Several days later, Pérez Martín and I received orders to go to another guerrilla front in Manguito, which was also in Matanzas. The guerrillas were on land there that was flat, and where the vegetation was filled with thorns. During the time we were there, we knew our situation was precarious. Whenever the government wanted to, it could wipe us out. I remember the young guerrilla leader's father—his name was Sotolongo—took me in his pick-up truck and asked me please to take care of his boy. It was his only son.

The little guerrilla camp was in a small island forest surrounded by cane fields. All day people walked by the small woods, and the boys—none of whom was over twenty years of age—had to spend all day crouched down and camouflaged hoping nobody came into the little forest. The only thing I could teach them was evasion and escape. One night I got to talking to one of them, who was only sixteen years old. I said that the Revolutionaries were supposed to help people like him, the children of poor country people. "No," he said, "I fight because I don't accept their teaching me that Fidel is God. . . and I want the freedom to do whatever I want with my life, not what they tell me." He had written a hymn called, "The Traitor who Sold our Fatherland to the Soviet Union." This young boy, knowing he was going to die, asked me to prepare him for death. So, that night I taught him how to prepare to go "up there." I taught him the Act of Contrition and how to talk to the Lord. Soon after, I told Pérez Martín that we had to tell Sotolongo to disband his guerrillas and to get out, because they were dead men there.

The guide who would bring us food took Pérez Martín and me to his country hut. We changed clothes and went to the town of Colón on the night of March 10, 1961, in a taxi. It seemed as if it was daytime from all the fires in the cane fields and factories, set ablaze by saboteurs. Pérez Martín and I agreed to meet in two weeks at the Varadero bowling alley.

I stayed in a Colón hotel that night near the bus stop. The buses were filled with *milicianos* coming back from battles in the Escambray Mountains, so it was impossible to get one to Havana. I couldn't stay any longer at the hotel because I was burned, in tattered clothes, and all my belongings—one pair of underwear, a shaver, a toothbrush, and a hand grenade—were in a paper sack. I had only five hundred pesos, and I had to be in Havana before daybreak. There in Colón I met a young girl who liked me. She was traveling with her aunt and they were likewise trying to get a bus to Havana. I began to flirt with her and decided to use them to get to Havana. I hired a cab across the street and took them with me. I told them I was on my way to study agrarian reform and that some friends were throwing a going away party for me. I spoke in favor of the government the whole trip.

After I dropped off the two women, I had to figure out what to do. I decided to see if my grandmother was still in the country. I arrived at her house at two in the morning. An aunt of mine who opened the door nearly had a heart attack when she saw me. She was extremely nervous. She took me to another aunt's house, since my grandmother was no longer in Cuba. I had three first cousins at the other aunt's house, one of whom was making his first communion the next day at La Salle. So, I sent a message to the brothers at La Salle telling them that I was in Cuba as an infiltrator and to please send someone to get me out of my aunt's house. That afternoon they sent a very brave girl named María Antonia from Manolo Ray's movement, *Movimiento Revolucionario del Pueblo* (MRP). She sent me to the man who owned the buses from La Salle School, and he took me to an apartment in the middle of Havana.

In the apartment lived a woman called Nicolasa, who was part of the MRP and had retired from the Cuban Telephone Company. When she saw me so thin and with cuts all over, she began to feed me yogurt with sugar cane syrup and little cans of Libby's peach juice she had hidden away. She treated me like a son. It was at that time that I began to train saboteurs.

Since I was not safe in the apartment anymore, I was moved to a new home. This time I ended up in the same building, and on the same third floor, as Cuba's cultural attaché in Czechoslovakia, who was also a member of the Communist Party. All the paintings in his apartment were anti-clerical, depicting nuns and priests engaged in pornographic acts. He also had a collection of articles from Soviet magazines. Yet, he wore Florsheim shoes and took American medicines. He was also the brother-in-law of Drs. Alfredo and Lily Reboredo, who lived on the second floor. Alfredo was part of the MRP and Lily was part of the Auténtico Organization (OA).

I ate breakfast and dinner daily at the Reboredos' home. I told Mrs. Reboredo one day to take down the sign she had on her front door that read "Everything with God; nothing without God" and to replace it with "Fidel, this is your home." I also told her to put up a picture of Fidel in the office. Meanwhile, in that home we had a mimeograph operator from OA working out of the balcony, and in the sofa bed—where bed clothes were usually stored—I hid four pounds of explosives without detonators. Soon afterward, I began to receive and train people there from the OA and the MRP.

On March 19th, Fidel sent 5,000 soldiers to wipe out the guerrillas in Matanzas. El Sheriff, who had remained to destroy the mimeograph equipment, was captured there and had his thorax blown away. After escaping later, he was ultimately caught and sent to the Isle of Pines with a thirty-year sentence, of which he served around seventeen. Jorge Rojas, meanwhile, was not caught, and he went to Havana, where he stayed with me.

On April 15, the bombings preceding the invasion began. Jorge and I woke up and opened a bottle of wine and toasted the freedom of Cuba. From there, I went to the Marist School to take communion, so that I could be in a state of grace in case something happened to me in the days ahead.

For the first time in my thirty-seven years, I was ashamed
of my country.

Grayston Lynch, CIA case officer, Bay of Pigs invasion

THE BATTLE

No compromises were more destructive to the Bay of Pigs invasion than those
involving air power. All other obstacles—placed in the interest of plausible
deniability either by the CIA or the White House—by and large were surmounted. Despite being told repeatedly of the importance of air superiority,
political considerations nevertheless caused the administration to scale back
the critical air operations, upon whose success the invasion depended. First
came the inclusion of D-2 strikes, which were later reduced from twenty-two
to sixteen airplanes. Then, on April 14, the night before the strikes, Bissell
again was asked to reduce the number of sorties. In the end, only eight Brigade
planes flew to Cuba from Puerto Cabezas on D-2.[1] Planners nevertheless still
hoped the now-reduced D-2 strikes, when combined with the D-Day attacks,
would be enough to fulfill the indispensable requirement of knocking out
Castro's small air force on the ground. Such hopes would be frustrated in the
hours and days to come.

The Cuban B-26 pilots took off for their targets over Cuba before dawn on
April 15. The mission, given that it had been so weakened in Washington,
could be considered a success for eight unprotected B-26s. In all, the mission
left Castro with approximately three Sea Furies, two T-33 jets, and two or three
B-26s.[2] One Brigade plane was shot down, and two others had to make unex-

pected landings on Grand Cayman Island and at the Naval Air Station in Key West before returning to Puerto Cabezas.[3]

Meanwhile, the Brigade had shipped out from Nicaragua. Unaware of the developments in Washington, there was "wild cheering" among the Brigade staff when news came of the first air attacks.[4] The liberation of Cuba now within their reach, the men's morale soared. One Brigade member claimed that, as they approached Cuba, even those among them with selfish motives began to feel the patriotism and sense of crusade shared by the others.[5] With the United States behind them, they felt they could not lose. It was now time to demonstrate their worthiness to their compatriots.

April 15, however, proved to be a fateful day. As the Brigade planes made their way to Cuba, Nino Díaz's diversionary landing in Oriente was aborted. The 164-man group canceled the landing at the last moment when they reportedly spotted militia on shore. They planned on landing the next night but in the end never made it to Cuban shores.[6]

In Miami, the phony defector pilot, Mario Zúñiga, landed his B-26. The press immediately was told the prearranged story. The farce lasted only briefly, as it was pointed out that the noses of Castro's B-26s were different from the plane flown by Zúñiga. Nevertheless, Adlai Stevenson, the prominent Democrat serving as U.S. ambassador to the United Nations, was told nothing of the scheme. When Cuban UN ambassador Raúl Roa protested and denounced the U.S.-backed bombings, Stevenson flatly denied U.S. involvement and gave the version presented in the press: The bombings were carried out by rebelling Castro pilots. Assured of the story's authenticity, he displayed before the United Nations photographs of Zúñiga's plane bearing Cuban air force insignia. When the story began to unravel under press scrutiny and the truth emerged later that day, Stevenson was furious. The embarrassment caused nervousness in Washington over international repercussions and impacted the decisions that were made over the next hours and days.

Meanwhile, in Cuba, Castro mobilized. The relative peace following the D-2 strikes gave him plenty of time to prepare for the invasion. One can only imagine what would have occurred if Castro had been faced unexpectedly with a twenty-two-plane strike at different points across Cuba, a landing on Cuban soil, and uncontested Brigade B-26 sorties across the island from the Girón airfield. Instead, Castro was faced with a minimal strike and was then given two days to recover and mobilize his army, militia, and internal security forces. Among his first moves was to round up anyone even suspected of counterrevolutionary activities. Security forces worked from lists put together over the months preceding the invasion and moved with great speed against the opposition. In two days, over 100,000 people (including Cuba's Roman Catholic bishops) were detained in jails, movie theaters, stadiums, makeshift camps, and any other structure that could hold prisoners.[7]

In Washington, things had gone from bad to worse. Just hours before the invasion, President Kennedy completely cancelled the D-Day air strikes designed to finish off Castro's air force. No decision concerning the Bay of Pigs invasion has been more controversial than this one. The president's critics believe it was the final act dooming the already emasculated invasion to certain failure. Some believe the CIA had failed to advise him properly throughout and had led the president to believe that such a move would not be so devastating. Some think that if Allen Dulles had been in Washington (instead of in Puerto Rico), he could have impressed more forcefully on the inexperienced president the one factor that persons closely connected with the invasion regarded as most crucial to its success: Castro's air force had to be completely destroyed before the liberators landed on the beaches. Thus, the net effect of the dilutions and the cancellations in the weeks and days before April 17 was that only eight sorties were flown (on D-2) prior to the Brigade's landing instead of the more than forty originally planned.[8]

The State Department earlier had become worried over the troubles at the United Nations. As the defector scheme failed, Secretary of State Dean Rusk felt the second strike could not come from (or at least could not appear to have come from) Nicaragua, since U.S. involvement no longer could be plausibly denied. After consulting with an agreeable McGeorge Bundy of the National Security Council, Rusk called Kennedy and persuaded him to issue the cancellation order. No further air strikes would be carried out until the exiles had secured the beachhead and the flights could be made at least to appear to have originated in Cuba.

At 7:00 P.M. Rusk received Bissell and Gen. Charles Cabell, who was taking the place of the absent Dulles, to explain the decision. The two stunned CIA men protested and tried to impress upon Rusk the necessity of the strikes as planned.[9] The secretary offered to call the president and did so. Passing along the CIA's arguments to Kennedy in front of the two men, he recommended cancellation, arguing, according to Bissell, "that developments at the United Nations made another air strike politically disastrous for the president." Rusk then told the two men that the president agreed with him.[10]

With the U.S. hand now exposed, Kennedy feared, besides being branded an aggressor, a Soviet or Chinese response—anywhere from Laos to Vietnam to Berlin. Strongly worded statements condemning the U.S.-backed bombings already had been broadcast. Just how seriously President Kennedy should have taken such threats is a matter of debate. Some believe the gamble in Cuba was not worth the global risks; others feel the president overreacted. In *The Crisis Years: Kennedy and Khrushchev, 1960–1963*, eminent presidential historian Michael Beschloss told of Kennedy's meeting with former president Eisenhower after the invasion:

> During a private meeting with Eisenhower at Camp David, the President had to bite his tongue while his predecessor dressed him down like an errant schoolboy: "Why on earth" hadn't he provided the exiles with air cover? Kennedy said he had feared the Soviets "would be very apt to cause trouble in Berlin."
>
> The veteran of Iran, Guatemala, Berlin, and the early Cuban planning gave Kennedy one of the chilling stares that the public never saw: "That is exactly the *opposite* of what would really happen. The Soviets follow their own plans, and if they see us show any weakness, then is when they press us the hardest. . . . The failure of the Bay of Pigs will embolden the Soviets to do something that they would not otherwise do."[11]

At any rate the CIA in Washington and Nicaragua reacted to the cancelled strikes with dismay and bewilderment. The outraged team at the agency's control center in Washington hounded General Cabell to go back and to be more forceful with Rusk. Marine Corps colonel Jack Hawkins, the operation's chief military planner, called the cancellation "criminally negligent."[12] Gen. Lyman Lemnitzer, chairman of the Joint Chiefs of Staff, said it was "absolutely reprehensible, almost criminal" when informed later that morning of the cancellation order.[13]

Cabell called upon Rusk once more—this time at his apartment at 4:00 A.M., April 17th. He asked for jet cover from the U.S.S. *Essex*, just over the horizon, during the unloading of the Brigade ships, which had already begun. This request was also denied.[14]

Meanwhile, José Miró Cardona and the Cuban Revolutionary Council had been spirited out of New York and returned to Miami, where they were escorted to a barracks at Opa-Locka airport at around 2:00 A.M. on Monday morning, April 17. There, they found a radio and heard the news of the invasion. They listened furiously to communiqués issued in their name by a CIA-hired public relations firm. Their anger grew when they learned they could not leave the barracks and that the doors were barred by U.S. soldiers. They demanded news and to be immediately transported to the beaches. By that time, the men of Brigade 2506 had reached the soil of their beloved homeland.

April 16 and 17

On the afternoon of April 16, Pepe San Román and Manuel Artime led a moving ceremony aboard the LCI *Blagar*. After praying for safety and listening to a patriotic speech by Artime, they saluted the Cuban flag and prepared for the liberation of Cuba.[15] That night, the U.S.S. *San Marcos*, an LSD (landing ship dock), rendezvoused with the Brigade flotilla and turned over the landing craft to Brigade pilots. Within minutes, the *San Marcos* disappeared into the night and the little armada headed toward the Bay of Pigs.[16] Meanwhile, the men had changed into their camouflage uniforms with the Brigade 2506 emblem sewn into the sleeve.

The first landings took place shortly after midnight, April 17, on a beach near the town of Girón. Five frogmen accompanied by Grayston Lynch descended the *Blagar* and made their way to shore to set up the landing lights for the rest of the men scheduled to land at Blue Beach. They altered their landing spot by two hundred yards because of unexpected human activity at a local bodega. Just offshore, one of the landing lights accidentally turned on in their boat and, despite efforts to smother it, was sufficient to alert a local militia outpost. Two militiamen, believing the light had come from a fishing boat stuck in the coral rock, drove their jeep to the beach and flashed their lights on the frogmen, who then were about forty yards from the shore in knee-deep water. Led by Lynch, the frogmen opened fire and riddled the jeep with hundreds of rounds, killing one militiaman. The Bay of Pigs invasion had begun.[17]

The frogmen charted a path for the landing craft through the coral reefs (reefs they had not expected to find). Soon thereafter, the Fourth Battalion came ashore, followed by Pepe San Román and his command staff. A squad from the Fourth Battalion quickly captured the airfield, which to their relief was intact and ready for operations.[18]

Back aboard the *Blagar*, however, Lynch received the disturbing news: Castro still had operational aircraft, and the Brigade should expect to be attacked at dawn. He was instructed to unload all supplies and men and to move the ships out to sea.[19] Hence, the Green Beach landings were scrapped and the Third Battalion was put ashore at Blue Beach, from where they would be shuttled up to their positions on the coastal road to Cienfuegos, east of Girón.[20] Through the hours before first light, the men raced against time and frantically unloaded supplies, tanks, and troops. The coral rock offshore did not help matters, nor did the drifting cargo ships.[21] As anticipated, a number of citizens began assisting the liberators.[22] Just as daylight emerged, a Castro B-26 appeared in the distance.

Meanwhile the *Houston*, which carried the Second and Fifth Battalions, had made its way to Red Beach accompanied by the *Barbara J*. As at Girón, Brigade frogmen were the first to land. After easily repelling small-arms fire, they lit the way for the men aboard the *Houston*.[23] The soldiers at Red Beach landed on small boats lowered into the water by very loud winches. The men of the Second Battalion discovered early that some of the outboard motors were inoperable.[24] This difficulty they surmounted by developing a towing system and using a catamaran that belonged to Rip Robertson. Some engines were started with batteries from the *Barbara J*.[25] Despite losing precious time, the entire Second Battalion made it ashore under their commander, Hugo Sueiro. Erneido Oliva, the Brigade's second-in-command, landed with them. They were to take the beach, then link up with the paratroopers and block the road to Jagüey Grande and Central Australia.

The Fifth Battalion, meanwhile, was waiting to land and join the Second Battalion. Although there are conflicting accounts as to the reason, the Fifth Battalion did not disembark and was still aboard the *Houston* when a Castro B-26 appeared at first light and fired at the ship. As the *Houston*, accompanied by the *Barbara J*, made its escape down the bay, it was attacked again from the air by two T-33s and a Sea Fury.[26] This time, in spite of poor shooting, they managed to hit the *Houston* with one rocket.[27] Water began to pour through a giant hole in the bottom hold. Luis Morse, the *Houston*'s captain, skillfully beached the ship near the bay's western rim, about three to four hundred yards from shore. As the men of the Fifth Battalion struggled to land, they were strafed by Castro planes; some of them drowned in the attempt. Once ashore, battalion commander Montero Duque established radio contact with Oliva, who ordered the Fifth Battalion to Playa Larga, now a few miles down the coast. After encountering some light resistance, the battalion commander stopped his march.[28] Stranded on the beach, they remained cut off from the rest of the Brigade. Except for a brief skirmish later, the Fifth Battalion's war was over.

Events at Blue Beach were likewise adversely affected by Castro's minis-cule air force. Despite strong fire from the *Blagar*'s .50 calibers and the down-ing of one Sea Fury, the planes caused havoc for the liberators.[29] The Heavy Weapons Battalion, as well as the Third and Sixth Battalions, landed under fire.[30]

At first light, the First Battalion paratroopers were dropped into the battle zone. One company was supposed to land at the road extending north from Red Beach and link up with the men coming from Playa Larga. Thanks to the presence of Castro aircraft, it was thrown off course and its men and supplies were dropped off-target. Despite brave fighting, sometimes alone, they were unable to regroup. The other company, under battalion commander Alejan-dro del Valle, landed safely at San Blas. The advance units landing at nearby Yaguaramas and Covadonga also were dropped successfully. At San Blas, citi-zens helped the men by serving as nurses and by supplying them with food and water. Five joined the fighters. In all, over fifty people joined the Brigade that day, including members of Castro's militia.[31]

Off the coast of Pinar del Río, Cuba's westernmost province, the CIA radio scheme served to catch Castro off guard temporarily. He sent a large force of men to the area and went himself to Havana after having arrived near the Bay of Pigs.[32]

The Brigade suffered a major blow later that morning: Castro planes, unre-lenting in their attacks, hit the cargo ship *Río Escondido* with a rocket off the shores of Blue Beach. Because the ship carried fuel and ammunition, it ex-ploded in a giant mushroom-shaped fireball. According to Grayston Lynch, who was aboard the accompanying *Blagar*, the mushroom was over a mile in diameter and several thousand feet high.[33] The *Río Escondido* also carried critical communications and medical equipment as well as food supplies.[34]

With only two cargo ships still afloat—the *Caribe* and the *Atlántico*—and half the supplies lost, the decision was made to take the ships out to sea, since the critical materials that remained stood little chance of getting ashore in the daylight under incessant aerial attacks. Expecting, although never receiving, naval cover at the twelve-mile limit, the two LCIs (the *Blagar* and the *Barbara J*), three LCUs (landing craft utility), and the two cargo ships pulled out. The plan at that point was to load the equipment from the cargo ships into the LCUs past the twelve-mile limit and, with the *Blagar*, return that night and unload them at the beach. Unfortunately, the men aboard ship spent the rest of the day on the high seas fighting off Castro planes. The cargo ships, on their own initiative, eventually pulled away from the LCIs and LCUs in a mad dash from the battle zone.[35]

On Red Beach, meanwhile, the Second Battalion discovered a microwave station that only minutes earlier had been beaming messages. The CIA has been criticized for not knowing of the station's existence. However, Castro could not have remained ignorant of the invasion for very long even without it: There were telephones within driving distance of the beach and militiamen with jeeps and cars to get to them.

Castro decided to make his major breakthrough at Playa Larga, the furthest point inland. Although the rebel army and police battalions were used, much of the battle was fought by the Castro's militia—a volunteer army that defended the regime from counterrevolutionaries on all fronts. Castro's main objective was to prevent a provisional government from landing.[36] It seems the dictator sensed the psychological impact and international political repercussions that a democratic government established on Cuban soil would bring about. The first encounter on the Playa Larga front came around midday when the Brigade's Second Battalion spotted a group of Castro militiamen approaching. The men of the Brigade, well concealed, waited until they were within range and opened fire with a white-phosphorus grenade and with their weapons. Scoring direct hits, the Brigade forced the surviving militia to flee.[37] Castro's troops did not challenge the men for another two and a half hours. Meanwhile, the Brigade captured over forty prisoners.[38]

The Second Battalion—now with support from a squad of the Fourth Battalion and two tanks sent by San Román from Girón—dug in along the road north of Playa Larga. At around 2:30 P.M., they spotted a Castro column moving down the road. When it was several hundred yards in front of the Brigade's advance units, the Brigade opened fire with their rifles, machine guns, recoilless rifles, and tanks. Just then, two Brigade B-26s appeared overhead. Although denied permission to hit Castro's planes on the ground that morning, they were allowed to fly support missions over the beaches (and in some cases were shot down by those same Castro planes). The planes, coming from Nicaragua with only a little flying time over Cuba because of fuel restrictions, strafed the Castro troops with their .50 caliber guns and hit them with bombs and rockets. In the end, only a handful in the group of advancing Castro troops survived. The ease with which such stopping power was employed leads one to imagine the impact the B-26s could have had if they had the air superiority they expected and a base at nearby Girón.[39] At any rate, after about twenty-five minutes, a Castro T-33 appeared and downed one of the Brigade B-26s on the spot. The other was disabled and crashed into the water on the trip back to Nicaragua.[40] No remains were ever found.[41]

Shortly after the battle, two ambulances and a Red Cross truck approached the Red Beach road, ostensibly to pick up wounded. The men of the Brigade held their fire. A few minutes later, forward scouts reported that the ambulances and truck were unloading men and mortars and that troop-carrying trucks were pulling up behind them. The men were ordered to open fire. It was another rout.[42]

On the Girón/San Blas front, paratrooper advance units had secured the roads outside of Yaguaramas and Covadonga. Each was held by a group of nineteen men who operated a .57-mm cannon, a .30 caliber machine gun, and a bazooka. The nineteen men also included a rifle squad and forward observers. On the Yaguaramas front, the paratroopers came under a direct attack. When reinforcements arrived, they counterattacked and sent Castro's troops retreating.[43]

By sundown on April 17, the Brigade's ground units had achieved their objectives despite the troubles they had encountered. They were on the ground in Cuba along the roads that ran through the Zapata swamp and had repelled the first waves of enemy attacks. Grayston Lynch relates: "The first of Castro's men spotted the invasion force when it was less than forty yards away, and they died ten seconds later. It took three and a half hours to notify Castro. . . . exactly seven hours after these patrols spotted the invasion force, the brigade had seized a beachhead forty-two miles long and twenty miles deep, at the cost of less than a dozen men killed or wounded."[44] Nevertheless, the survival of Castro's few planes, because of the cancelled air strikes, doomed the Brigade. Their supply ships were either sunk or forced out to sea. The B-26s—which by then were supposed to be operating out of Girón against Castro troop movements—could not land and were left to fly support missions all the way from Nicaragua, three and a half hours away. This gave them very little time over Cuba. Moreover, instead of controlling the air, the Brigade planes flew into skies dominated by faster enemy fighters, against which they were completely vulnerable. In all, one Brigade plane crash landed on D-Day and a transport plane landed on the last day to drop off some supplies and to pick up a few wounded. The Brigade was thus left defending a beachhead with a day's supply of ammunition, no naval support (the *Blagar* and *Barbara J* were supposed to provide cover from offshore), and virtually no air cover. Nonetheless, they maintained their faith in the United States.

Along the San Blas front on the night of April 17, the advance units defending the roads to Covadonga and Yaguaramas began retreating. With insufficient ammunition and no air support, they were forced to fall back incrementally while resisting numerically superior forces.

The night of April 17 also saw the most intense battle of the Bay of Pigs: the Battle of the Rotunda, at the traffic circle north of Playa Larga. By this time, the Second Battalion had received further reinforcements from the Fourth Battalion, additional mortars, and another tank. By nightfall, the troops and tanks were set up along the rotunda and had a wide range of fire. Shortly after 7:30 P.M., the attack began. The Brigade first came under a barrage of shells from Russian 122-mm howitzers. The men were ordered not to move and to stay silent. In four hours, Castro's forces fired over 2,000 shells. The men held their ground as the shells came ever closer; a few experienced shock. Nevertheless, because of their long and narrow positions, the howitzers had trouble finding the Brigade and soon the shells were going overhead.[45] Less than ten troops were killed and about thirty were wounded in the howitzer attack.[46]

Shortly after midnight, the first Castro columns appeared. Stalin tanks, each followed by infantry, made their way down the road toward the rotunda. The ideal positions into which Oliva and Sueiro had placed the Brigade were such that the first two Castro tanks were completely knocked out by the Brigade's tanks and guns. One was permanently disabled after a Brigade tank, out of ammunition, rammed into it repeatedly and split the Castro tank's gun barrel.[47]

Next down the road, now blocked by the tanks, came several infantry assaults. A feverish battle was fought throughout most of the night. The Brigade held off wave after wave of tank and infantry attacks. In the darkness and the intensity of the battle, the exhausted and desperate men of Brigade 2506 men fought on despite having had no rest and little food or water for over twenty-four hours. Oliva learned later that morning that the small Brigade force of less than 370 men and three tanks had faced a Castro army of over 2,000 troops and about twenty tanks. It is estimated that 500 Castro soldiers were killed and over 1,000 were wounded that night. On the Brigade side, 40 to 50 were wounded and 10 to 20 were killed.[48] Castro had also lost half his tanks.[49]

Throughout the night of the seventeenth, Pepe San Román desperately radioed the *Blagar*, which had sailed out of radio range. At one point, he even sailed six miles out to sea to try to establish radio contact.[50] Lynch, for his part, had been faced with attacks from Castro planes throughout the day, the disappearance of the cargo ships despite orders to return to Point Zulu (fifty miles from the coast), and a short-lived mutiny by the rescued merchant seamen from the *Río Escondido*. He nevertheless wanted to make it to the beaches that night to drop off what little ammunition was aboard the *Blagar* and *Barbara J*. He later was ordered to wait for the cargo ships, unload them into the LCUs, and go in on Tuesday night.[51]

On Monday night, the Brigade air force was given permission to try to attack Castro's planes, as had been planned for Monday morning. It was too late. As they arrived at San Antonio de los Baños, where the main airfield was located and from where the Cuban air force had flown all its sorties, the town was blacked out and covered by a thick haze. The fliers turned back after failed attempts to draw fire and locate the target.

April 18

On Tuesday morning, contact with the *Blagar* was reestablished, and San Román received word that four unmarked U.S. Navy jets would arrive over the beachhead shortly. The thrilled Brigade, as instructed, set up panels marking the front lines. However, the navy jets flew back out to sea soon after arriving. Apparently, they had been authorized to fly only a reconnaissance mission. Later, American planes flew another mission, and it is possible they hit a few targets, although U.S. strikes have never been officially confirmed.[52] What is certain, however, is that many U.S. pilots watching the Brigade torn to pieces because of Castro's small, outdated aircraft were moved to tears of anger.[53] Knowing they easily could have knocked out the Cuban planes, they felt the United States was letting down its allies in a despicable manner.

Early on Tuesday it was decided that, despite the previous night's effort, the Brigade's position at Playa Larga no longer could be held, as they were critically low on ammunition and could not expect to be resupplied soon. In addition, a major force was being amassed at the other end of the road. Thus, they released the prisoners they had taken, loaded on to trucks, and headed down the road to Girón to link up with San Román.[54]

By late Tuesday prospects seemed dim indeed for the Brigade. Air drops of supplies over Girón were blown into the swamp and the sea. Despite heroic efforts by the frogmen and local civilian volunteers, most of the supplies were lost. The Third Battalion, meanwhile, had been sent from the beach's right flank to San Blas, where they were to see their first action. The Fourth, back from Playa Larga, took the place of the Third. The Sixth Battalion was sent to defend the road from Playa Larga.[55]

In Nicaragua, the Cuban pilots at Puerto Cabezas were angry, frustrated, and exhausted by late Tuesday. Flying around the clock from Central America and shot at by planes they had not been allowed to destroy the morning before, many could not continue flying. By this time the Cuban pilots were supposed to have been taking off and landing from the Girón airstrip, not making the long sorties from Nicaragua into skies dominated by enemy aircraft. Thus, two CIA contract pilots flew along with a group of Cuban pilots on Tuesday and scored major hits on columns of Castro trucks and tanks. In all, they destroyed seven tanks and inflicted numerous casualties.[56] Having to make the long trek back to Nicaragua, they only stayed a short time over Cuba. Again, the damage caused in less than half an hour leads one to speculate what total air superiority and a Girón air base would have meant.

Later that afternoon, the paratroop units defending the roads to Yaguaramas and Covadonga, desperately short of ammunition and facing an ever-larger Castro force, fell back to San Blas and joined the paratroopers stationed there. Del Valle later positioned the entire group just south of the small town. At the other end of the perimeter, on the road from Playa Larga, Oliva took charge of the Sixth Battalion and prepared for an attack. Throughout Tuesday night, skirmishes occurred.[57] The next day was the Brigade's last at the Bay of Pigs.

The Brigade's remaining supplies, meanwhile, lingered in the Caribbean throughout Tuesday night. Lynch and his crew unloaded the *Atlántico*, now back in the fold after having fled over one hundred miles, into the LCUs. (The *Caribe* still had not arrived.) As they departed for the shore, they calculated their arrival at Girón at 4:30 Wednesday morning. Knowing they would be caught in the daylight by Castro planes during the unloading, Lynch requested air cover from Washington. He warned, to make an impression, that the ships would be lost without it. Apparently his superiors were impressed—so much so that they ordered him to stop and to return to Point Zulu.[58]

Throughout the day on Tuesday, President Kennedy had followed events as best he could. He resisted Adm. Arleigh Burke's push for greater U.S. participation. Peter Wyden observed, "It clearly pained the admiral [Burke] to see the president bypass all channels of command—and all tradition."[59] There were also rumblings from the USSR., as Khrushchev threatened to assist the Castro government against what everyone knew was an American-backed invasion. The president made it clear to the Soviet premier that the United States would defend the hemisphere against any "external aggression."[60]

Tuesday night, after a formal white-tie affair, the president met with General Lemnitzer, Admiral Burke, Vice President Johnson, Secretaries Rusk and McNamara, and Richard Bissell. As Burke laid out options for U.S. assistance to the Brigade, the president, responding angrily, told the admiral he wanted no U.S. involvement. Burke, reportedly distressed, answered in kind: "Hell, Mr. President, but we *are* involved."[61] It was at that meeting the president and reportedly the chairman of the Joint Chiefs learned from Bissell that there was no guerrilla option. Kennedy thus compromised once again: He agreed to allow American fighters to provide a one-hour umbrella for Brigade B-26s between 6:30 and 7:30 A.M. the next day.[62]

April 19

Three B-26s left for Cuba during the predawn hours on Wednesday—two of them manned by American crews and the other by Cuban flier Gonzalo Herrera. For some reason the B-26s arrived an hour before the American jets. Some believe it was because the time difference was not taken into account when the orders were issued. Whatever the cause, the two planes flown by the Americans were shot down and their crews were killed. The other, flown by Herrera, strafed Castro artillery and troop positions near San Blas and then returned to make a direct hit with two bombs.[63]

At San Blas, meanwhile, Del Valle took advantage of the confusion caused by Herrera's attack and ordered a quixotic counterattack by the troops under his command. The men—almost out of ammunition, starving, and fatigued—went forward. Castro's troops, surprised, broke and ran. The Brigade men were forced to retreat a short time later when many ran out of ammunition.[64]

On the road from Playa Larga, Oliva positioned his men for a final showdown on Wednesday morning, placing the Sixth Battalion, seven bazookas, and three tanks along a curve in the road. The Second Battalion was then called out of reserve and joined the Sixth at the front. In the first engagement, Oliva's men knocked out three Castro tanks and an armored car with the bazookas. Hit also by white-phosphorous shells and Brigade rifles, the Castro troops retreated a little after noon.[65] Shortly after 2:00 P.M., infantry assaults and hand-to-hand combat ensued. A company from the Second Battalion was ordered to counterattack through thick vegetation, where the fighting took on nightmarish qualities. The company briefly stopped the advance after an exhaustive effort.[66] Nearly out of ammunition, the men defending the road were ordered to fall back two hundred yards into trenches.[67]

At midday Lynch received a message from Washington authorizing a navy-assisted rescue mission. He radioed San Román on the beach and told him of the planned extrication. San Román valiantly refused to be evacuated. Lynch then, with no hope for air cover, set off for Girón with the LCUs, the *Blagar*, and the *Barbara J*. He called San Román and told him to hang on.[68] San Román meanwhile had been forced from his command post and was crouched in the sand twenty feet from the water. In the calm and respectful manner for which he was known, he detailed his collapse over the radio. Finally, shortly after 2:00 P.M., San Román reported that enemy tanks were breaking into Girón and that he was destroying his radio. It was over. He sent orders to the commanders at both fronts to divide into companies and to go into the woods until reinforcements came. He and his staff then took to the swamps.[69]

In Miami that morning, Adolf Berle and Arthur Schlesinger met with the Cuban Revolutionary Council. They traveled back to Washington together, where they met with Kennedy. The young president, obviously distraught, was shocked to learn the Cubans had been under virtual house arrest. He obviously sympathized with the men and, knowing that three of them had sons in the Brigade, shared how he had lost a brother and brother-in-law in World War II. He explained his reasons for not intervening and then assured them of his commitment to a free Cuba.[70]

As the vanquished Brigade soldiers made their way into the swamps and woods around the Bay of Pigs, they became pursued outlaws in the land they had come to liberate. Whatever their condition Wednesday afternoon, they had fought beyond anyone's expectations. With a day's worth of ammunition and nowhere to retreat, and facing 20,000 enemy troops who possessed tanks, artillery, airplanes, and a faithful ally, Brigade 2506 performed magnificently. Never surrendering, the Brigade retreated and dispersed only after they had run out of ammunition. In the end, they inflicted over 1,600 enemy deaths and

2,000 wounded. The Brigade itself lost around 114 men, including those who had drowned. Just over 60 were severely wounded.[71]

A couple of days after the collapse, Lynch, Robertson, and the frogmen aboard the *Barbara J* and *Blagar* were transferred to a U.S. Navy vessel, where they were briefed on a rescue operation. They were to go on land and bring out any Brigade members they could find. By that time, U.S. ships and planes were all over the Bay of Pigs area. Lynch recalls, "Now that the battle was over, we had more ships and planes in Cochinos Bay than we could use. If only we had been given just one of these jets a few days earlier, there would have been no need for a rescue mission."[72] Despite heroic efforts by the CIA men and the Cuban frogmen, only a few were rescued. The U.S. jets overhead, which were helping to find and flush out survivors, at this stage were still restricted in their actions: Washington had denied permission for them even to fire over the heads of the Castro forces pursuing Brigade members who were seeking rescue. A U.S. Navy captain quoted a pilot: "We had to watch the Cubans capture the survivors we flushed out! Like playing Judas—delivering the poor CEF (Cuban Expeditionary Force) to the Cubans."[73]

The navy and CIA personnel involved with the operation were seething. Feeling they were ordered by the White House to act in such a way as to betray their allies and bring about a national humiliation, they were infuriated with President Kennedy. In Guatemala, U.S. personnel were in great despair. "Their fury at the politicians in Washington was limitless," wrote author Peter Wyden, who later quoted the CIA station chief as saying, "If someone had gotten close to Kennedy, he'd have killed him. Oh, they hated him!"[74] The navy captain quoted above describes the mood aboard a U.S. ship during the rescue mission: "The emotional climate on board built from sorrow and humiliation to anger and frustration toward those who had let this operation be governed by indecision, incompetence, and cowardice in high places."[75]

On Thursday, the president addressed 1,000 members and guests at the American Society of Newspaper Editors in Washington. Again he expressed his intention not to abandon Cuba and spoke highly of the men of Brigade 2506. He likewise warned of the strength of Communism and the threat it posed, in a sort of call-to-arms. Kennedy later spoke his famous line concerning the invasion: "There is an old saying that victory has one hundred fathers and defeat is an orphan."[76]

This chapter traces the experiences of numerous Brigade veterans from their departure from Central America through the final collapse of the invasion. Again to provide the widest representation possible, I have included interviews with two B-26 pilots, a member of the Nino Díaz group, members of the battalions that landed at Girón and Playa Larga, a paratrooper who landed at Yaguaramas, a member of the Fifth Battalion, a Brigade infiltrator, a letter written by Rogelio González Corzo ("Francisco") moments before his death, and the recollections of a resident of a nearby town. One member of the Second Battalion, Luis Morse, was the son of the *Houston's* captain. In his testimony, he discusses his experience both as a soldier and a son going into battle with his father.

D-2

Gustavo Ponzoa, B-26 Pilot

Born in Pinar del Río in 1924, Gustavo Ponzoa was raised in Havana and graduated from the Baldor School, an independent private school. His stepfather was a medical doctor who owned a well-known Havana clinic. Gustavo spent three years studying architecture at the university to satisfy his parents but ultimately, against their wishes, dedicated himself to his true passion: flying airplanes. He studied at Spartan Aviation in Tulsa, Oklahoma, and eventually received full-time work as a pilot for Cubana Airlines. During the struggle against Batista, he was a member of Castro's 26th of July Movement for a time. Disillusioned with the revolution's turn toward Communism, he left Cuba in July 1960 with other Cubana pilots when they learned something was being planned against Castro. He went to Guatemala to begin his training in late August. In the years following the invasion, he continued combating Fidel Castro and flew numerous overseas missions for the CIA.

B-26 pilot Gustavo Ponzoa poses with his Bay of Pigs flight records in his Miami home, 1999. Photograph by author.

On April 5, we were told we would be moving to Puerto Cabezas. We knew the invasion was on, and we were all very gung-ho. On the fourteenth, an unmarked constellation arrived, and they began to unload all sorts of munitions, arms, bombs, and boxes filled with maps and other documents. We were taken to an isolated operations room, where we sat around a couple of long tables and listened to the first briefings. Gonzalo Herrera and I were assigned to bomb Santiago de Cuba on the first raids. Our mission was code-named Gorilla. I was Gorilla One, he was Gorilla Two.

At 2:15 A.M., April 15, we took off. We assumed our altitude and flew in radio silence. When we got near Montego Bay, Jamaica, I noticed that I was ten minutes ahead of schedule. Without telling Gonzalo, who was flying at a comfortable formation about one hundred meters from me, I made a wide 360-degree turn to kill the ten minutes. When we left the Montego Bay area, we were at about 8,000 feet, but then we slowly descended to 500 feet. We knew they could have had radar, and when the first rays of the sun came out we went down to 200 feet and then to 50 feet and then to 10 feet above the water.

We soon saw the outline of the hills around Santiago de Cuba. Our original mission was to go in near Guantánamo and to approach Santiago de Cuba from the east with the sun low and behind us. But when we were twenty or thirty miles from the coast, we saw one of their naval ships and I thought it signaled us. I thought I couldn't waste even a minute now, because it was possibly communicating with the airport. So I signaled Gonzalo, and instead of going in all the way through Guantánamo we went directly at the airport.

As a Cubana pilot, I had flown to that airport perhaps thousands of times. There was a daily 6:00 A.M. flight, and the airplane for the flight was parked just above the hydrant I hit with my first five-hundred-pound bomb. I saw a red, intense fireball and a wing flying two or three hundred feet in the air. In all, I had two five-hundred-pound bombs and ten fragmentation bombs. The second five-hundred-pound bomb was earmarked for a place fifty meters from the fuel tanks, but it did not explode when I released it. We continued fighting and dropping our bombs nevertheless. At one point the airport was so covered with smoke, you could barely see. We spent twenty minutes over the airport. We knocked out everything.

When we finished, I was euphoric. I said, "We've done away with that airport!" By the time we left the combat zone, I dropped the "Gorilla" and just addressed Gonzalo directly. He informed me that he had been hit a few times. I followed him back to Nicaragua. We were the first to land, and everyone began shouting *vivas* and all that. We were then taken to a debriefing where they showed us pictures taken by a U-2. About half an hour later, the others began to arrive. That was when we learned that one plane had been knocked down, another had to land at Grand Cayman, and a third had landed in Key West.

We had gotten back at 9:30 A.M. We were supposed to leave again at around 1:30 P.M. At about 11:00 A.M. General Reid came over with a big paper and said, "Gus, we have to hold the mission forty-eight hours." I said, "Goddamn it, General, the whole fucking invasion is going to hell right here." How in the hell were we going to give those people forty-eight hours? Eight planes had gone out that morning, and seventeen could have gone. If seventeen would have bombed three times a day for three days straight, they would have done away with all the airports in Havana and knocked out all their planes on the ground. Then we would have had a great chance to win, because once we could land and get loaded up at Girón and carry out missions from there, not even a truck or a tank would have come over to that side of Matanzas.

José Flores, Special Group

A native of Matanzas Province, José Flores lived most of his life in Havana. He owned a construction business and was an active member of the Auténtico Party. An opponent of the Batista dictatorship, he helped supply Castro's rebels in the Sierra Maestra. Delighted about Batista's ouster, he soon became disillusioned with Castro when known Communists began assuming important posts in the government. He fought against Castro as part of the Auténtico Organization and finally came to Miami in March 1961. After shipping arms to the opposition in Cuba, he joined the Brigade at the Frente offices. After the invasion, he settled in Hartford, Connecticut, where he continued in construction and re-mained active in anti-Castro efforts. He currently resides in Miami, Florida.

We signed up for the invasion at the Frente office on Twenty-seventh Avenue in Miami. When we were leaving for the airport aboard a truck, someone showed up and told us that former president Carlos Prío, an Auténtico leader, had called for a group of us. We were told that we would join a group in Louisiana under the command of Nino Díaz and that we were to go as volun-teers to be the first to land in Cuba, on April 15, to draw Castro's troops away from the main invasion force. We spent the afternoon in Carlos Prío's house

The Special Group's José Flores standing in front of his paintings depicting a Cuban scene, Miami, 1999. Photograph by author.

and were soon taken to Opa-Locka. My whole family, including my children, were in Cuba and had no idea I was part of all this.

We arrived in Louisiana around the twenty-sixth of March. I trained for less than three weeks, and some trained there for only three days. We trained on bazookas, recoilless rifles, rifles, and mortars. It was a very simple training. One day, we were given a special breakfast, and we felt there was something strange in the air. When we finally departed on April 13 for Key West, we were all happy and sang patriotic songs. At Key West we boarded our ship, the *Santa Ana,* and sailed toward Cuba. Everyone was thrilled and anxious to land already and liberate Cuba. There was great camaraderie among us.

We learned about the air raids the morning we were preparing to land. While trying to find the beach, we could hear the airplanes. Nine of us went out from the *Santa Ana* on small boats to try and look for the landing spot, but we lost the propellers because of the coral rock and turned back. Aboard the *Santa Ana,* we prepared for a landing the next day. The next night a small group of us returned on our small boats and got to the beach, at the mouth of a dried-up river; thousands of Castro's soldiers were there waiting for us. When we got to within about a block of the beach, we radioed to shore to see if we could reach our reception team. We said our code, "Bacardí," and they were supposed to say "Hatuey." Instead, we heard responses like "Rum" or "Oriente" or "Coca-Cola" or "Cuba Libre," but never "Hatuey." When we got back, we reported what we had seen and heard.

The next day, we sailed away. We later heard of the invasion at the Bay of Pigs and about how poorly things were going. So from the southern shores there off the Guantánamo Naval Base, we headed for the Bay of Pigs. Everyone was saying we had to go. On the way, we came across one of the Brigade ships. We were in olive green uniforms, and they were in camouflage. Fidel's people also wore olive green, and the people on the Brigade vessel nearly fired before they recognized us. We were told the invasion was a lost cause. So we turned back toward Oriente and then to the north of Cuba. They had us moving around from one place to another for the next eleven days. Two U.S. destroyers finally came, and we were transferred from our ship to the destroyer and taken to the base at Vieques Island.

The Invasion: Blue Beach, Girón

Grayston Lynch, CIA

CIA agent Grayston Lynch at his Tampa home, 1999. Along with Rip Robertson, Lynch was the CIA's top person at the invasion site. Photo by author.

A native of Victoria, Texas, Grayston Lynch was the son of an oil worker. Lying about his age, Lynch joined the army in 1938, right after he graduated from high school at the age of fifteen. His duty came to an end in October 1941, but he reenlisted on December 7. During World War II, he landed at Normandy and was seriously injured during the Battle of the Bulge. He also fought in the Korean war and afterwards joined the army's Special Forces. In 1960, he was recruited by the CIA and, following a tour in Laos, found himself as part of the Cuba operation. The first person to land during the Bay of Pigs invasion, Lynch served as the unofficial CIA commander throughout the battle. In the years following the invasion, he was a central figure in the U.S. actions against Castro; during this time he worked with numerous exiles. He is currently retired and recently completed his first book, Decision for Disaster: Betrayal at the Bay of Pigs.

We had a catamaran boat and towed the rubber raft alongside it and then got into the raft when we were a couple of hundred yards from the coast. I was planning to stay in the catamaran, but when we got close enough to look the area over, we saw these guys standing outside this bodega, "People's Bar" or something like that, right at the point we were going to land. They had floodlights on the outside of the building that lit up the whole area. We were supposed to land right at the bodega and then go out to a short stone jetty to the right of it where they were constructing a building; the fingerlike jetty was all lit up because of the lights from the bodega. It looked like a ruin because only parts of the wall were up. A road ran behind the area along the coast, and behind that it was all vegetation, and it was dark. Any beach defenses would have been there.

My orders were to determine if we were walking into a trap. If there was one, we would order people not to land and to move to an alternate site. I thought, "I have to be sure, so I may have to land and go in there and look myself." So I got into the rubber raft with the frogmen. We had marking lights for the beach with us, and we had them in the "off" position; I had even taped them. Then we had water splashing all around there, and somehow we got a short and one of the lights came on. We were about fifty yards from the coast, and this Goddamned jeep came down this road because he saw the flash of light. We found out later on that they thought it was a fishing boat and that they were going to warn them about the coral. He stopped in front of us, turned, and put his headlights on us. That's when we started blasting.

We landed, and I went across the road. We checked behind the jeep, and nothing was there. We went back and placed landing lights on the beach and went out to the building and put a light on top of that.

The first landings came in, but because there was so much going on I forgot to warn them about the coral and to come in slowly. These people had been trained down in Vieques on the landing craft; so when they hit the beach, they did so at full speed to ride up on it and just rammed into the coral. They dropped their ramps, and everybody ran out onto the beach. Every man on that first wave was carrying extra supplies, and they dumped them in a pile by the bodega. They took off and went straight up that road into Girón. There was a little bit of automatic-weapons firing at the edge of the village, but that was it, and they took the town. Pepe San Román landed and loaded up troops from the Fourth Battalion into two old cars, and they captured the airport.

Then, I got a radio message that said I had to go back to the *Blagar* because I had an urgent message. I got back to the ship—the landing was still going on—and the message said, and this is verbatim, "Castro still has operational aircraft. Expect you to be hit at first light. Unload all troops and supplies and take all the ships to sea." Yeah, and while you're at it, make the world in one day! The landing of all supplies and troops, by our own schedule, wasn't going to be complete until the next afternoon. We had been on schedule up to that point.

After I got the message, I told Pepe San Román that I thought it was best to land the Third Battalion at Girón and to shuttle them up to their positions instead of taking them to Green Beach on the deck of the *Blagar* if we were going to get hit by aircraft. The Fourth Battalion, meanwhile, immediately took the airport. The Sixth Battalion moved in and started unloading supplies into the new resort houses.

The Sixth had been the last to land off the *Río Escondido*. I had sent two of the big LCUs to take the whole battalion ashore. When the LCUs were going back to the *Río Escondido* to unload the fifty-five-gallon drums of aviation fuel, the damn Sea Fury came down and put a rocket in it. We got the crew onto the *Blagar*. The captain, meanwhile, had put the *Río Escondido* into reverse before he left the ship, so it was going out to the middle of the bay. Then there came a small explosion, and then came this massive one, like an atomic bomb, and this mushroom cloud that this thing formed came half way to my ship. When the stem lifted, you could see two propellers slowly turning as the ship went into the water.

Jorge Herrera, Heavy Weapons Battalion

Born in 1938 in the city of Bayamo, Oriente Province, Jorge Herrera graduated from La Luz School, a private academy, and subsequently attended the University of Havana to study medicine. When the university closed, he left Cuba to attend the Wharton School of Business at the University of Pennsylvania. When Herrera returned to Cuba in 1959 for a vacation, concern for his family in the rapidly developing political situation motivated him to stay. Meanwhile, he finished his bachelor's degree at Villanueva and left for Miami in November

Jorge Herrera, Heavy Weapons Battalion, at his Coral Gables home, 1999. Photograph by author.

1960, whereupon he enlisted in the Brigade. He departed for Guatemala on December 12 and was trained on 4.2mm mortars as part of the Heavy Weapons Battalion. After his release form prison, Herrera continued his studies. He is currently a stockbroker for Merrill Lynch.

Everyone was ready and had a great desire to go to Cuba. If they would have canceled the invasion, I think 70 percent would have refused the order. I went to Cuba aboard the *Atlántico*. The trip was characterized by terrible heat as well as hunger, since they only gave us little sausages to eat; yet we all went with great hope. With the presence of a U.S. destroyer, which we could see most of the way, we believed this was something organized and that we were really going to get the support we needed. The day before we landed, we received our briefings.

We were several miles out when we saw the tracers from the firefight in which the frogmen were involved with the enemy. After several hours, at about 5:00 A.M., the landing craft came to the side of the ship. They placed ropes alongside, and we descended into them. The man piloting our landing craft made a mistake of some sort and went out into the open sea. We began going in circles because we couldn't see land, but luckily we saw a light on one of the ships and went to it; it guided us toward shore. Since it was daylight by then, a Castro B-26 strafed us on our way in. That was really scary, to see the plane shooting at you while you're incapable of doing anything about it. We disembarked about three blocks' distance from the shore near Girón, and we had to walk on the coral in chest-deep water with all our equipment.

We stayed at Girón that day. That night, in the hours before dawn, my group left for Playa Larga with Harry Ruiz Williams to support the people there, and we had a terrible accident along the way. We were loaded with ammunition and mortars, and I don't know how it happened but the driver put the truck right into a crater and we flipped over. Nobody died, because God is great. Just imagine all of that equipment—the mortars alone weighed six hundred pounds. Ruiz Williams and I thought we should get the boxes of ammunition out of the truck and cover them with rocks off the side of the road, because if the planes shot at the truck, we could still have what we needed to keep fighting. We spent the rest of the night in the woods near the side of the road.

The next morning, we captured a couple of *milicianos* who told us that numerous Castro officers had surrendered. Then, at about 1:00 P.M. we found out, standing close to the dirt road, that our forces were in retreat. We stopped one of them and asked what was happening. We made them load the mortars and the boxes of ammunition we had hidden the night before. We then went to Girón.

When we returned to Girón, we took up positions about five or six hundred meters south of the airfield. We set up our two mortars there and waited. A plane came by and dropped a couple of giant bombs. They looked bigger to us than they actually were, and they lifted us all off the ground. The next day, Wednesday, we had around eighty grenades left. When the enemy troops began coming in, we received their position. Manuel Granado did an outstanding job as my forward observer. I would make the calculations and then fire. We were hitting them very effectively. An .81mm unit was also firing at them, and we held up their advance to Girón for hours: They had no idea we had no more ammo, and they were scared to advance.

We knew nothing until about 3:30 P.M., when Gabriel Gomez del Rio, the other forward observer from the battalion, came and told us that we were in retreat and that we had no air support, no help at all. So, we blew up a couple of grenades in the tubes of our mortars and went toward Girón. Erneido Oliva was there—he was a real military man, we were just kids. He told us that we had to go into the woods. We separated into small groups and tried to stay together until we were caught.

Tulio Díaz Suárez, Sixth Battalion

Tulio Díaz Suárez was born in Havana in 1935. His father was a lawyer, and his mother was a public school teacher. A graduate of El Instituto del Vedado, he entered the University of Havana law school, where he took part in student protests against the Batista government. He became disillusioned with Castro in early 1959 and by the following year had been expelled from the university for trying to rally students against the regime. He came to Miami in April 1960 and subsequently departed with other students on a tour of Latin America, on which they spoke out against the Cuban government. He departed for Guatemala several weeks before the invasion. After his release from prison, he settled in Miami and went into business.

I was trained to load a .57mm recoilless rifle. I went to Nicaragua from Guatemala a little bit before everyone else; a small group of us was taken to help load the ships. The trip to Cuba was very tense. There were 130 fifty-five-gallon drums at the front of the ship, and with 150 people on deck, a cigarette could have caused a disaster. We were also short on food and water.

We could see the small lights on the shore while we were waiting to disembark. When we heard the first shots from the frogmen, I thought, "Now this is getting good." When one is young, such things are very inspiring. About 156 of us boarded one of the landing craft in the morning with all our armaments. When we were close to shore, a Castro Sea Fury came in and released its two rockets. I saw when they hit the *Río Escondido:* The explosion looked like a giant mushroom, like an atomic bomb, but on a lower scale.

When the landing craft dropped its ramps, people began going toward shore; the water was over their heads. When I disembarked, I went underwater with all the rockets, an M-3, a pistol, and three boxes of bullets. I was finally able to jump atop the coral and swim toward shore. When I arrived, everyone was already there. I was exhausted and with the nervous tension of the moment and all of that on my back.

By that time, a lot of people were in the mangrove. They began to scream, "Sea Fury, Sea Fury!" In front of me, from the east, I saw a Sea Fury coming towards us. The landing craft departed, and I was caught between the beach and the woods. I found the darkest spot on the grass, and I lay down and opened fire on the plane when it came over me. It was a difficult moment, but I felt good because he didn't hit me. I acted like a man, and that filled me with spirit.

They came to pick up my battalion on a truck. Because the truck they sent had filled up, the .57mm shooter and I stayed behind and joined the Third Battalion when they went to San Blas. On the third day (at San Blas), we saw some American planes, and I thought, "These people are at least coming through here." But it seems they were just there to take pictures, nothing else.

We knew it was over when we began to retreat back to the beach. The expressions on people's faces changed. Fifteen minutes after we got there, the howitzers began to hit us. I heard Pepe San Román telling off the Americans. At first, he was very serious and very dry. Later he told them we were going to die, that they had abandoned us, that with a little help we could have done what we came to do, and that this was not something that should be done to men who had been loyal to them. There were many people standing there, and we didn't know what to do. We finally went into the woods.

Ricardo "Ricky" Sánchez, Paratrooper

Ricardo Sánchez was born in 1941 in Havana. His father was a medical doctor and his mother a nurse. A graduate of Ruston Academy, he began working as a translator at the education ministry after his graduation in 1959. Sánchez was turned off by the Castro regime because of the obvious Communist and anti-American direction it had taken. Ironically, his first cousin Augusto Martínez Sánchez was one of Castro's chief subordinates. Ricardo left Cuba in November 1960 and joined the Brigade in Miami in January 1961. After his release from prison, he received a degree from St. Joseph's College in Philadelphia and en-

Paratrooper Ricardo Sánchez, at head of line on left, shortly after his capture at the Bay of Pigs. Photograph by permission of Bay of Pigs Veterans Association.

tered banking. He is currently an executive for Union Planters Bank in Miami, Florida.

Ricardo Sánchez at his Miami office, 1999. Photograph by author.

Our battalion commander, Alejandro Del Valle, was standing at the door when we came over the beach. He was very excited, like a little kid. He was saying, "This looks like Normandy! Look at that!" You could see the activity and all the ships down there. We jumped at 7:30 in the morning and landed near Yaguaramas, on target.

There was nothing where we landed, just a little group of houses. We set someone up near a hut to look out behind us for anything that came up the road from San Blas. Before us lay the road to Yaguaramas with cane fields on either side of it. I set up on my .57 recoilless rifle beyond a curve on the road facing Yaguaramas, and there was also a .30 caliber machine gun, an .81 mm mortar, and bazookas. The infantry people were spread on both sides of the road.

About a week to ten days before we left, all of our heavy weapons were taken from us to be packaged to get them ready for the drops. I don't know how it happened, but the .57 I received was not *my* .57. What happened was that we got new equipment on the drop, and I attribute it to someone saying, "Hey, let's help these kids, let's give them new equipment." What they didn't know was that by giving us new equipment they gave us equipment that was not ready to be handled and that was not zeroed in. I also never received the telescopic sight. Besides that, the .57 came only with antipersonnel rounds and no antitank ones, even though it had that capacity. The idea was that we had a bazooka, and we would have something that was antitank (the bazooka) and something antipersonnel (the .57).

When we had set up, we all bunched up under a tree. We were chatting, and all of a sudden, all hell broke loose. They started shooting at us from the cane field from about one hundred yards away. We went back to our weapons and set up. We saw about four truckloads of *milicianos* [militia] coming in and getting off a truck. I was instructed to shoot at them with my .57—and I was pretty good on that thing. I shot and hit somewhere way out, and I thought, "What the hell is this? These things aren't in sight!" I had to start playing around with it to get my bearings. In the meantime, all these guys were getting off trucks and setting up. Our radio got shot up at that time, and we lost touch with San Blas.

Then the *milicianos* started sneaking up behind us, around the hut where we had left our scout on lookout. The scout had also seen the *milicianos*, but instead of coming to warn us, he went to a tank he saw coming up the road from San Blas; he realized it was one of ours. Since we had no communication with San Blas, we didn't know a tank was coming to pull us out. Anyway, the scout went and informed the people in the tank that we were surrounded. So the tank comes in and blasts around the hut where we still thought our scout was on lookout. We immediately thought it was a stray Castro tank coming in from the beach, and the bazooka guy was told to shoot at him. When he did, I heard this sickening "click, click, click." The bazooka wasn't working. So I was told to shoot at the tank with the .57. I only had antipersonnel rounds, and I thought "All I'm going to do is to throw gasoline into a fire—this guy is going to get pissed off at us and start shooting." But I shot, and luckily enough I had no bearings and missed.

The tank backed off; about twenty minutes later, it came in again and stood right in front of us and began to shoot. There was nowhere to go. The guy with the bazooka went into some trees, as did my assistant. When I was going to get up and run, our scout came over running, saying "Hey, it's us!" According to him, they had been shooting low but over our heads to get the guys in the cane field.

The enemy pulled back when the tank came, and we moved forward into a dried-out irrigation canal by the cane field. I saw my first dead body there. We stayed there until about 7:00 or 8:00 at night, when Néstor Pino—who later became a colonel in the U.S. Army—came and said we had to get out since the tank had to go back. Once the *milicianos* realized the tank was gone, they would come in force and slaughter us. We went back about four miles that first night and set up again. Our goal was to reach San Blas, but because we had no communication with them, we thought we couldn't just allow the enemy to go straight in there. So, as they came down the road, we'd hit them and move back again.

The next morning we were encircled once again, and a truck came in with a .30 caliber and got us to San Blas. We arrived there the second day at about 1:00 in the afternoon and picked up Radio Swan on a shortwave radio. They were announcing: "The invasion troops are moving into Matanzas and taking over such and such a town." We started looking around saying, "What the hell is happening here? Did they leave us behind? The whole thing went somewhere else, and we're here in the boondocks waiting to be creamed!" [he laughs].

Del Valle was convinced we would be supported with a heavy aerial bombardment, and he sent two people to set up panels for our air force. By that time, the Third Battalion had joined us. At about 3:00 or 3:30, we began being hit by artillery fire in San Blas, and Del Valle decided to fall back around two hundred yards from the town. The artillery fire lasted all night, but it was all in front of us and never hit us.

Very early the next morning, our planes came in and hit the enemy. Then I heard all this rumbling behind me, and I saw two tanks and the whole Third Battalion and some people from the Fourth ready to advance. Del Valle was riding on top of a tank saying, "Let's go troops!" Néstor Pino just looked at him as if to say, "What the hell are you doing?" Del Valle was charging like Custer, and we were happy as heck. Del Valle was a super gung-ho person, the image of a swashbuckler, a John Wayne type. My impression of him was that he felt he could walk through a wall. He was the ultimate man of action. He was a fiery leader. Anyhow, about an hour later, they were back because they had run out of ammunition. There was also a long column of tanks coming, and they had nothing with which to face them.

We retreated after that. We were told there was going to be an ammunition drop, and we set up. The wrong ammunition was dropped, and that's sort of when we gave up. Meanwhile, one of their commanders, Félix Duque, came through our area in a car, and we stopped him and took him prisoner. Del Valle took off with him in a convertible to Girón. It was the highest-ranking prisoner taken by the Brigade during the invasion. Meanwhile, the road ahead was full of tanks. Later, the scout I mentioned earlier, who wasn't a bazooka man, borrowed a bazooka and hit the first tank. It blocked the road, and the whole column was stopped. As they started hitting the tank to move it off the road, we all started getting the hell out of there. We had nothing to shoot at them with.

Walking to Girón at about 5:00 in the afternoon, we bumped into a group of civilians with white flags. We asked them how far it was to Girón. They said we were five or six kilometers away but that there was nothing there. We said, "What do you mean there's nothing there? What about all our people?" "Oh, no," they said, "they're all gone." So when we got to Girón, we decided to try and make it to Cienfuegos and to the mountains. They told us Oliva had gone that way.

We spent all night on a truck with some wounded on a path off the coastal road to Cienfuegos. At about 6:00 the next morning, one of us went to the road to see if he could see anybody. Some time passed, and all of a sudden we started hearing gunfire. So Julio and I got off the truck with our handguns. When we came out of the bushes, every *miliciano* and every Castro soldier you can imagine was there, all over the highway. We were captured. Castro was less than a block away, with a whole bunch of newspaper people. He came and stood right in front of us and asked, "Where are the rest of your people?" We told him, "We are alone, with a truck full of wounded." He asked, "How many of you were in this thing?" We told him, "Just a few, around a thousand." He asked, "What about the Americans?" He wasn't hearing what he wanted to hear; he didn't want the press people to hear it.

They took us to the beach and then to Central Australia, where they placed me in a garage with my hands tied behind my back. My cousin Augusto walked in, and all of a sudden he was standing in front of me. He said, "What the hell are you doing here?" I told him, "All I want—let's not get into an argument—is for you to go and tell my parents that I'm alive." My father had been responsible for Augusto going to the university, as his father died when he was very young. My mother had gotten him his first job. He shoved me and said, "You don't deserve the parents you have." He really loved my parents. From there, he sent somebody over to put them in prison. I think he realized I could damage him politically, so he needed to do something not to be associated with us.

The Invasion: Red Beach, Playa Larga

Pepe Hernández, Second Battalion

I landed at Playa Larga aboard one of the first three boats that went ashore. While we were landing, one of our ships was firing a .50 caliber machine gun toward the shore to give us cover; but they were firing too low, and the bullets were coming too close. I think there was someone in another one of the landing boats who was shot and killed. The pilot of my boat, trying to avoid the shots, kept going to the right, away from the landing lights. We ended up on the rocks, and I had to jump into the water. When I did so, I went completely under with all my equipment, which weighed around forty pounds—I only weighed around 135 pounds back then. I got out with all my equipment, but I was all scratched up from the coral rock.

Our group was made up of about forty men whose mission it was to move up the road and make contact with the paratroopers when they landed near Central Australia later that morning. We had to walk a great distance to get there, but supposedly there was going to be no resistance along the way. When we came ashore, there were some *milicianos* there, and the first words I heard when I landed in Cuba came from one of them, who said, "Long live Fidel Castro!" We did away with that small resistance and went up the road. When we got to the rotunda, a flat-bed truck came up carrying *milicianos* and civilians, including women and children. We didn't even know at first that there were civilians aboard. We told them to halt, but they stopped and the *milicianos* started shooting at us. A guy next to me with a BAR hit the gas tank on the truck, and it blew up and caught fire. It was a very sad scene, because I saw some women and at least one young girl—some were covered with flames. But we didn't have a choice; we had to respond to the fire. In fact, one of our men had been shot through a lung there.

Later that day, I was at my forward observer post about seven kilometers from Playa Larga, with around forty of our men who were off to the side on a semicircular clearing about five hundred meters in diameter. From there, I saw Castro troops far away coming in from Central Australia. I later went to the other end of the clearing, on the road, with my binoculars. I saw an armored car in the distance in front of a bunch of white buses. I counted nineteen of them. When they were six or eight hundred meters away from us, they stopped and got off the buses. They lined up and began to march and sing. The armored car was with them. We opened fire when they were within five hundred meters. We had an M-41 tank, a .50 caliber, and a .57mm recoilless rifle.

In the middle of all that, two of our B-26 bombers showed up. We had an airplane spotter with us, and he put an L-shaped panel on the road made of pieces of shining metal to guide the planes toward the enemy. When they made their first pass, they dipped their wing; Castro's people—because the planes were painted like Castro's air force—thought it was theirs and began to shout *"viva!"* When the B-26s passed the second time, they shot their rockets. The planes came in so close that I remember being on the ground and looking back and seeing them only about fifty feet above the road. I saw them release the rockets, and they looked like they buckled when they did so. The whole thing lasted for about a half an hour or forty-five minutes. Those airplanes were later lost.

Later we saw ambulances coming, and we stopped shooting. But we saw that people were getting out of the ambulance with guns and that they were shooting from it. In other words, they were using the ambulance to try and continue advancing. So after we saw that we continued firing.

Rafael Montalvo, Second Battalion

Rafael Montalvo, Second Battalion, at his Coral Gables home, 1999. Photograph by author.

Born in 1943, Rafael Montalvo was from one of Cuba's oldest families. His uncle and namesake was the youngest general in Cuba's war of independence, and his great-grandfather was imprisoned by Spain and sent to Africa during the same conflict. Rafael's father, a pediatrician, was the head of Havana's Children's Hospital. At the age of fifteen, Rafael was sent to an English boarding school after a scuffle with Batista's military police. He returned from England after the revolution to a Cuba that he found increasingly repressive and abusive. He went on to Georgia Tech, where a sizable colony of Cuban students constantly discussed the situation in Cuba. Upon his eighteenth birthday in February 1961, after a soul-searching three-day retreat in Conyers, Georgia, he joined the Brigade against his parents' wishes.

On the docks in Nicaragua there was a mass of people moving back and forth. The aluminum boats we used to land were practicing up and down the beach; other people were practicing going up and down nets; Somoza's P-51s were flying overhead. It was totally euphoric. We thought we were involved with something big, that this was going to work, and that it was a serious effort. We couldn't wait.

The trip over was highly emotional. It was very uncomfortable for some, but at eighteen you're not uncomfortable with anything. I remember the other people complaining, but we were fine. Those two or three days went by very fast; it was a time for meditation, a time when you come to grips with yourself. The closer you get to the moment, the more you become absolutely sure you are going to die. It's the only way you're going to deal with it, so that you could act.

The last day we began picking up radio stations, and Castro, of course, was playing the national anthem and other patriotic music. It was getting us all completely fired up. We were so enthusiastic, we were so emotional about it. It was incredible. When we saw the shoreline, it was a great moment.

We went into the bay, and the winches from the ship were making a tremendous noise. Then we went down the nets and into the landing boats with one hundred pounds of equipment; I had never been down a net in my life. There was a light on the beach that we could see as we got closer. From next to the light they started firing at us. The tracers went over us by quite a bit, but it looked to us like they were firing right at us. I was on the first boat that landed.

We landed to the right of the beach on a rocky shore. I had two belts of BAR, and I could not lift my leg. I finally had to pull myself up to the shore. By the time I got there, I had lost my squad and there was shooting in every direction. The second boat landed, and I was told to follow its leader. So the two of us went hut by hut on the beach where some militiamen had gone into. By this time, my adrenaline was way up: You're ready to blast things up; you're not afraid anymore. We asked them to throw their weapons out, and to our surprise, they started to throw them out the windows. From there I joined my squad.

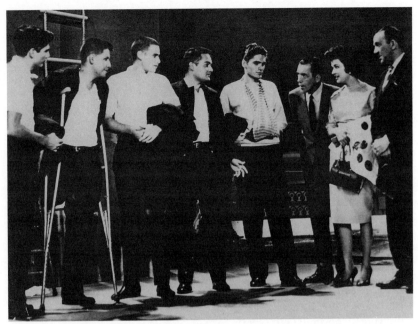

Injured prisoners with Ed Sullivan, 1962 (*left to right*): Felipe Silva, Juan Figueras (interviewed for the book), José Smith, Carlos Allen (whose wife was interviewed for the book), and Luis Morse (also interviewed). Photograph by permission of Bay of Pigs Veterans Association.

That night we went to the front, at the rotunda. It was a hell of a night. Before we went there, we spent about four hours under heavy artillery fire. It was scary as shit. The shells were hitting in the water, as they were pointing too high. At the rotunda it was horrible. The tanks, the white-phosphorus grenades blowing up on the tanks, people moving in the shadows, shooting; you don't see shit, you just shoot and shoot and shoot, and every time you hear a noise, you shoot. It went on for most of the night. Our tanks were hitting their tanks; the two tanks were hitting each other like this (body to body). At some point, I peed in my pants because I wouldn't get up and turn around to unzip my fly. I was as flat as I could be, the firing was continuous and incredible. The enemy was really close in front of us. We had no trenches, nothing. The only illumination was from the grenades; you saw people when something exploded.

At 4:00 or 5:00 in the morning, it got awfully quiet. All you could hear was their wounded screaming. One guy was screaming, "Lieutenant, lieutenant, don't leave me. You son of a bitch, lieutenant, come get me." He spent the whole night like that, until he got weaker. At some point I fell asleep. I woke up just before first light, and there was a fog, and it was eerie. We went across the road, and there was no one there—only the dead and people run over by tanks.

Later we went back towards the beach. It was just daylight, and it was very quiet. You could see there were a lot of dead militiamen. A little while later, Sueiro came over and ordered the retreat. We couldn't believe it, because we had beaten the shit out of those people. When we got back up on the road—I don't know who started it—we all started singing the national anthem. Everyone got on trucks and went to Girón.

When we got back to Girón, we rested and dug trenches and so on. While we were there, they shot my friend Eddy de las Casas. We had been talking when we heard a plane coming. I dove into a trench I had dug and heard bullets all over the place as the plane strafed. When I got out, I went to look for Eddy in the house he had gone into. I found him lying on the floor, and the walls were all covered with blood.

The last day, we were called early in the morning to go to the front on the road to Playa Larga; the Sixth Battalion was there already. My company, G Company, was told to pass them and to advance as far as we could. We went into the vegetation between the road and the sea, which was an area maybe one hundred yards wide. We were thirty-five men, and we went about a mile and a half or two miles to where there was a bend in the road. In the vegetation, we were twenty or thirty feet from the enemy. We didn't leave anyone alive; we couldn't, because we were so few people. It was the first time I actually saw the people I was shooting. We kept going forward; one group would advance, and the other would fire. At some points we all just ran forward, shooting. Once you got into the emotion, you'd just keep going. One of our tanks went up the road and hit one of their tanks, and our mortars put up a barrage in front of us that confused them. When we came back, I thought I was going to die. I was totally dehydrated, and my legs could hardly move. Yet we still had to fight our way back. It was a very long mile and a half. Fourteen of us got wounded and were carried back by another fourteen, leaving seven of us up front without a radio.

When we got back, the bosses had already left. There was a boat leaving the beach with people in it, and I almost fired at it—we were fighting, we were not supposed to leave. I got two canteens full of water and a .45. I checked in on the wounded, and there was nothing left to do there. Five or six of us went to a town near Girón looking for some sugar, but they didn't have any. The people there were scared. As we were leaving, one of Castro's planes strafed the townspeople. When it was all over, one of the peasants came out holding his son. And that's the thing that really gets me every time I remember: His son had a hole right through him, and the guy was crying. I felt like, "Why the hell are we here?" I felt terrible at that point. We went into the woods. By that time, Castro's people were everywhere.

Luis Morse, Second Battalion

Former Florida state representative Luis Morse, Second Battalion and son of the captain of the *Houston*, in his Tallahassee office, 1999. Photograph by author.

Born in Havana in 1940, Luis Morse was a graduate from El Colegio Columbus, a small private school. His father was a public high school principal and worked as a sea captain during the summers. His mother was a store owner. At the university, he was an active Batista opponent, but turned against Castro when the leader geared the revolution toward Communism. He left Cuba in July 1960. After a recruiting trip for the camps, he went to Guatemala in October 1960 and was made part of the Second Battalion. Little did he know his father had been asked to captain one of the ships. Luis was released from prison in April 1962 with the other injured prisoners and worked for his companions' release. A graduate of the University of Florida, Morse served in the Florida House of Representatives for fourteen years. He is currently the deputy secretary of the Florida State Department of Elder Affairs.

It was an emotional moment when we traveled to Nicaragua and saw the ships on the docks. When I went into my ship, the *Houston*, I suddenly saw my father there as the commander giving orders to people. I thought, "Hey, what are you doing here?" It was a total and complete surprise when I saw him.

The trip over was good. Apart from having to participate in briefings, I spent my time up in the command office with my father. It was a very nice time; instead of being by myself and thinking about where we were going, I was simply enjoying the company of my father. It was a happy moment. I was proud that I was there with him going into combat.

When we saw the tracers from Girón, it was pure adrenaline. We were ready. We were happy and excited and just wanted to go in. We landed at Playa Larga in small aluminum boats. We took the positions on the beach that had been indicated to us, and set up our mortars on the beach side of the town.

I remember firing our mortars a lot. I spent all of my time going back and forth trying to be active. Then I saw the planes hit the *Houston*, and I thought my father was dead. After that, I actually didn't give a shit about anything else. I didn't even care if they killed me. I would say that I was acting very recklessly.

After the invasion, I was wounded, captured, and eventually taken to the hospital at the Columbia military base. That was where I finally found out my father was alive. He had been chosen by the naval guys in the prison to be their representative in the negotiations for the release, and Castro's people had allowed him to go to the hospital to see me before he went. It was an emotional reunion. Later in prison at *Castillo del Príncipe*, [Principe Castle] I asked to be transferred to the cellblock where my father was. It was an interesting experience. We talked a lot and got closer.

Jorge Marquet, Fifth Battalion

A T-33 hit the *Houston* while the Fifth Battalion was still aboard. This caused the ship to begin sinking. The *Houston's* captain, Captain Morse, knew the area and, instead of taking the ship to the shore, decided to look for a sand bar. He did so and beached the ship.

The first person to get off the *Houston* was an officer who, without any authorization, jumped ship. We never heard from him again. When the order came to abandon ship, I was with my cousin, who didn't know how to swim, and it was quite a distance to the shore. I found a life jacket for him, but it went straight down when I put it in the water to test it. Then I found a large piece of wood, like the size of a door, and I helped him get ashore on it.

When I came ashore, my squad leader told me, "There are still people on the ship, many who haven't been able to disembark because they don't know how to swim. There are also injured. I want you to take a rowboat from here with someone else and go to the ship." I said "okay" and I went with Frank de Varona to the *Houston*. When we got there, we took the injured and some others to shore. We made several trips, and I eventually asked to be relieved, as I was extremely tired.

On shore we built some trenches. Whatever supplies we could get out of the ship, we covered with camouflage. Later we tried to link up with Erneido Oliva's forces at Playa Larga, where we had been supposed to land. Montero Duque, the head of our battalion, designated two people to go as forward observers and see what our chances were of joining the Second Battalion and Oliva. An hour or so later, they came back and said there was no way to get through and reach them—and that's the reason we never joined them. That's what I could tell as a soldier; I was not an officer, and I don't know exactly what the situation was.

The Fifth Battalion stayed there on the shore. We dug trenches, to be able to repel an attack if it came. After about three days, Castro's forces came. He sent a reconnaissance unit, and we ambushed them. We told them they were surrounded, and they said, "¡Patria o Muerte! ¡Venceremos!" [Fatherland or death! We shall win! (both were popular revolutionary slogans)]. The people in the trenches shot at them. I was one of the ones in the trenches. Later on everyone left and did the best they could. With my cousin and a group of around ten or twelve, we went into the swamp.

Juan Figueras, Fourth Battalion

A 1955 graduate of Belén, Juan Figueras became an active opponent of the Batista regime as a university student. His father, a Camagüey medical doctor, had served in Cuba's house of representatives until Batista's coup d'état in 1952. In 1957, because of his activities, Figueras had to leave Cuba in exile. He returned to Cuba in 1959, but seeing the

Juan Figueras, Fourth Battalion, at his Coral Gables office, 1999. Photograph by author.

Castro regime's Communist leanings (and thus believing the revolution had been betrayed), he left Cuba again in November 1960 and departed for the camps the next January along with his brother. He returned to the United States with the injured Bay of Pigs prisoners in April 1962 and assisted the Cuban Families Committee in the public relations campaign for the release of his fellow Brigade members. He later graduated from the University of Florida and currently resides in Miami.

We were the first battalion to land at Girón. When we got there, there was no resistance or anything. At about 4:00 or 5:00 in the afternoon my company was ordered to Playa Larga. On the way there, we were attacked by several airplanes, and we had to dive to the sides of the road. We finally got to Playa Larga at about 8:00 or 9:00 that night. The Battle of the Rotunda was going on, but we couldn't tell what was and what wasn't a rotunda, because one could see nothing. I was with a .57, and they told us to stay close to the headquarters — which was right on the water! It was then they began shelling us with howitzers, and I was hit by one of them.

Some of our paramedics and my brother attended me with tourniquets and morphine. For the rest of that night, I came in and out of consciousness. The next thing I knew, it was the morning and they were boarding us on trucks to evacuate Playa Larga. Back at Girón, the doctors were attending to us, and I lost consciousness again until that night. When I awoke, I was told that we were in Cayo Ramona, a tiny village in the swamp, where there was a hospital. A small group from the Brigade, with Brigade doctors and injured soldiers, took it over to operate on us. Dr. Juan Sordo operated on me there.

The next day, the third, I woke up in a truck. I asked my brother where I was. I was told that we were next to the Girón airstrip awaiting an airplane that was to take away the injured members of the Brigade. The airplane came, but we stayed in Girón because they said they had no time to wait as the sun was about to come out. I lost consciousness again and woke up that afternoon at about 4:00, when Girón came under a howitzer attack. They then loaded up some of the injured into a truck and began driving towards Cienfuegos. Later on we were forced to drive it off the side of the road. Some of our paratroopers showed up with other injured Brigade members and stayed with us. The next morning, the militia came and arrested us.

I was taken on a truck driven by a *miliciano*, who told me, "When there are people present, I have to speak to you harshly, but I don't really mean it, I just have to act that way." They took me to a nearby town for a couple of hours, and they told me I was in bad shape, so they took me to Cienfuegos. They amputated my leg there the same day.

Juan Sordo, M.D., Medical Staff

Born in 1916 in Pinar del Río, Juan Sordo received his medical degree from the University of Havana in 1941. He worked as a police doctor for fourteen years and then in private practice. When he left Cuba in exile, he visited the Brigade camps for a few days. After his short tour, he was inspired and decided to stay. Sordo landed at Girón but was transferred to Playa Larga shortly thereafter. He was later imprisoned and released with the rest of the Brigade. When interviewed for the present work, at eighty-three years of age, he continued to practice medicine full-time.

Juan Sordo, M.D., at his Hialeah practice. Photograph by author.

We received our final briefing in Nicaragua. They showed us the pictures of the place we were supposed to disembark, and I saw something that was obvious: There were coral reefs along the shore under a foot or two of water. I told the instructor, "Look, Sir, there are coral reefs there blocking access to the beach. To go there, we either have to go through the mouth of the Bay of Pigs or to the east of the reefs, because nothing could navigate there." He said, "No, no. Those are clouds." I said to him, "Sir, I know what it is." I knew the area, and I told him what it was and that the water there was only a foot or two deep. He said, "Look, don't worry, Sir. You are going to be taken in like this [he cups his hands]." I said, "Yes, just 'like this' above coral reefs." Of course, there were coral reefs, and we had to jump into eight feet of water next to the reefs. People were cut and hurt.

I spent the first night in Girón, and then Oliva, in Playa Larga, sent for me. I was in Playa Larga all night under an intense bombardment from the howitzers. I took a small house to use as a hospital, but it was hit by a howitzer and I had to get the people out of there and go to the shoreline. We had about fourteen injured people there.

The next day I took some men, including Juan Figueras, to Cayo Ramona after one of the paratroopers told me about the hospital there. It was a rudimentary facility with a few beds and a small operating room, designed for basic medicine and childbirth. I took a squad with me. There were two doctors there; one decided to cooperate and the other didn't. I told one of our men, "Sit this man (the uncooperative doctor) down. If he moves, put a bullet through his head." The man remained frozen. The other one offered to help; his father was the hospital's administrator. They gave me lunch. That day, I operated on around seven men and went back to Girón.

On the nineteenth, I stayed with the injured soldiers until about 7:00 P.M., when we saw the lights of Castro's arriving troops. I went into the woods, leaving the injured in the care of some *milicianos* we had captured, including one who said, "Doctor, don't worry; I will attend to your injured." So, I went into the woods. The next morning, I was captured and I was taken back to Girón. When Fidel learned they had captured a doctor, he sent for me. He looked at me and said, "They tell me you are a doctor. What is your name?" I told him, "Juan Sordo." He put his hand on my shoulder and said, "How is it you came here to kill your brothers?" I told him, "I didn't come here to kill anybody. I am a surgeon. I came here to help the injured." He told me, "But how could you have gotten involved with the Americans?" talking to me in a tone as if he was a lifelong friend of mine. So I told him, "Don't you remember what you said when you attacked the barracks in Santiago? You said that any Cuban not pleased with his government had a right to rebel. I took advantage of the same right you did." He then said he was going to execute me. I said, "Well, what am I going to do? You won, and I lost. Do with me what you will." Then a commander, I learned later his name was Duque, came and punched me. Fidel told him not to hit the prisoner.

Luis León, Resident of El Perico

The son of a Chinese immigrant father and a mother of Canary Island ancestry, Luis León was a young barber from El Perico, a town about fifty kilometers from Playa Larga. He witnessed the return of Castro troops from the front.

The Castro people's main activity in my town was centered in the police station they had taken over. There was a tremendous amount of movement, and a lot of *milicianos* with diarrhea. Some later told me that they acted as if they were sick to their stomachs so that they wouldn't have to go to the front. Those who came back from the beach commented that the invaders had armaments that made it impossible to fight against them. They were totally impressed.

Toward the end of the invasion, a person from El Perico named Lazaro—a butcher who had become a *miliciano*—called the town together. I remember as if it just happened. I went over with everyone else and watched as he opened a van and threw out two cadavers wearing camouflage. He threw them on the floor; one of them cracked his head upon impact, and the stream of blood went out into the street. Lazaro told the townspeople, "The Americans have attacked us, but there is nobody who could defeat us!"

The Invasion: Air War

Esteban Bovo, B-26 Pilot

On Monday morning I went to the beaches. By then, the *Río Escondido* had been sunk already and the *Houston* was already beached. We got the order to release our auxiliary tank, and when we did so it got caught on a rocket. Gus Ponzoa got under us and told us the situation and instructed us not to shoot the rocket. We completed our mission and returned to base. As we approached, we told them to put foam out on the runway. They laughed and said, "What foam?" They had used it the week prior for an American plane that had experienced trouble. We told them we would make a pass so they could tell us how it looked. They told us the tank was hanging from a rocket and to jump out in parachutes. We decided we would land the plane. Everybody got the hell out of the way [he laughs]. We stopped the plane in about one to two hundred feet and ran out.

On Tuesday morning, I went back to Cuba and hit a convoy from Jagüey Grande. We came in low, and they launched everything—I think including their shoes—at us. There was also a great amount of anti-aircraft there. When we got back to base, we told them about the convoy, but they didn't believe us. Later a group of six planes went out and finished what we had started. Later that day, I went with two other to San Antonio de los Baños. We had engine trouble and had to go back to Nicaragua. One plane made it, but the town was blacked out.

After Tuesday, the problems began. We had flown nearly eighteen hours in two days. Some of the beds were empty already. They asked for another mission, and we said we would do it. Then the Americans said they would fly for us because they saw we were exhausted. That was the flight in which the American pilots died.

Gustavo Ponzoa, B-26 Pilot

On April 19—I have it written down as the nineteenth although everybody tells me it was the eighteenth—we went out in six planes, two piloted by Americans and four by Cubans. We got to Girón at 3:45 P.M. Along the road between Central Australia and the Bay of Pigs, we saw the dust from a convoy. It looked sort of like white dust rising from a desert. I began flying at about one hundred feet to release appropriately the napalm I carried. There was a column of thirty to fifty vehicles—trucks, buses—jammed with people. There were also two large tanks and a small one. We caught them all in a straight line. I was told later that in that attack there were over 4,000 of them who were either killed, burned, missing, or injured.

The Invasion: Infiltration Teams/Underground

José Basulto

José Basulto poses before Brothers to the Rescue airplane, Miami, Florida, 2000. By permission of José Basulto.

Born in 1940 in Santiago de Cuba, José Basulto was raised in Havana and graduated from Baldor Academy. His father was a vice president for a sugar corporation, and his stepmother worked at the University of Havana. After a brief time at Boston College in 1959, Basulto decided to return to Cuba, where he had close contact with the Agrupación Católica. He joined the MRR and after a couple of months returned to the United States and was part of the original group sent to Useppa Island. Basulto went to Santiago de Cuba in early 1961 and, while posing as a physics student, beamed intelligence information back to Miami. Following the invasion, he spent some time in the U.S. Army and later graduated from the University of Miami with a degree in architectural engineering. He remained active in anti-Castro activities and founded Brothers to the Rescue, a Cuban exile group that gained international attention when its unarmed airplanes were shot down by Castro's air force in 1996.

In Santiago de Cuba, I sent information back on how the underground was organizing and the capabilities that we had. I was asked for information on the defenses at the entrance of the bay at Santiago, because they were planning an attack on the Texaco refinery there. I was also asked to provide information on fuel at the airports and on the number and types of airplanes they had.

I reported to "Francisco," Rogelio González Corzo, as soon as I had arrived in Cuba. Since the Americans wanted to keep the Cuban infiltrators away from one another, the radio operators responded to a central operations base in Miami. That way, they would keep us divided and they could control of us individually. We were not happy with the idea, so we developed a code among ourselves so that if we ever had to communicate with each other, we could do so directly without using the Americans. Already by that time, we were beginning to have our suspicions that things could wind up upside-down.

On April 15, I was doing my job in Manzanillo, looking for some intelligence for preparing a maritime reception of ten tons of weapons, when the bombings took place at Santiago airport. I was outside the town, so I heard of the bombings on my way back in. Afterwards, I received messages saying "stay away from the airport."

A couple of days later, maximum priority messages started coming in. On the day of the invasion, I received a message saying that it was time for all the patriots to fight for a free Cuba. It said to proceed to destroy bridges, disrupt communications, and to tell the patriots to do this and that. I got pissed off with that message. I sent a message back saying, "It's impossible for us to rise. Most patriots are in jail thanks to your damned invasion." I was a kid, and I knew that thing couldn't succeed.

I took the men working closest with me to a beach called Siboney, east of Santiago de Cuba. We spent the day there swimming, and I said, "Well, guys, anything we could have done, we did. This is something that caught us off guard. We weren't prepared, we weren't asked, so we're not responsible for whatever happens from now on." For us to try to use the six pounds of explosives and the three or four machine guns that we had in all of Santiago de Cuba would have been suicidal and stupid. So I thought we would keep a low profile and see what came next.

I stayed in Santiago after the invasion and kept sending my communications. I left on May 22 as it had become more difficult to obtain the support of our own people in Cuba. The assistance we received before all but disappeared after the invasion. The feeling was that the Americans had abandoned us and that our premise had been wrong. They realized they were hanging from a sky hook that had no support from the top and that the United States was not going to provide us with what they had promised.

We made the decision to evacuate. There was the very real danger that many people in the Brigade knew our names and where some of us could have been. So it was time for us to leave and to try to come back again later. We pretended we were going for a picnic next to the U.S. Naval base at Guantánamo, and jumped the fence. We had to go through a minefield, and it was kind of scary because we did this in broad daylight. A group of Marines picked us up and took us for debriefing. Later that day, around sixteen others who were working with us also jumped the fence. That night we were all put into a plane and landed in Miami during the early hours of the morning. We were put into a bus and taken to the Columbus Hotel. And that was it; it was like, "Hey you guys, good-bye."

Rogelio González Corzo, "Francisco"

Born in Havana in 1932, Rogelio González Corzo was a Belén graduate and a member of the Agrupación Católica. A devout Catholic concerned with the problem of poverty in Cuba, he joined the Ministry of Agriculture in 1959 but was soon disillusioned by Castro. He joined the MRR and became its national coordinator and the head of the

Rogelio González Corzo, code-named Francisco, the devoutly Catholic head of the MRR in Cuba, was executed at the end of the invasion. Photo by permission of Dulce Carrera Jústiz.

underground in Cuba. He was arrested on March 18, 1961, and executed by firing squad on April 20, just after the invasion. Below are excerpts of a letter he wrote while awaiting his execution.[77]

Dear Parents and Siblings:

I know what the moment you receive the news of my death will mean to you, far from where I am. I want to tell you that this was always what I had asked God for. I think it would have caused you great moral and perhaps physical suffering if you would have been here, and if you would have had to live through these thirty-two days between my arrest and my death.

You need not even for a moment feel ashamed of my imprisonment and execution; on the contrary, I hope you are proud of your son and that you know how to assume the proper attitude at this moment that God and the Fatherland have asked for the sacrifice of your son. I want you to know that it is the only attitude there could be in situations like the one that the Fatherland is going through during these moments.

I am writing to you at 1:00 A.M. on April 20. I am in a cell they call the chapel, and my death is only a matter of minutes away. I want you to know that my last thoughts on earth were about you and my siblings.

During these moments in which death knocks at the door, please know, parents and siblings, that I am at peace, the same as all my companions who shall open for me the gates of heaven and eternal happiness. My death also takes me to the side of my grandparents, where, God willing, I shall wait for all of you.

Remember, do not lament, this is for the best. Remember that I await you in heaven. Have strength as I do during this time. I leave only with my worries about your spiritual lives. Please, do not abandon it; may my problem not in any moment affect your Catholicism, but instead, may it strengthen it.

Waiting for you in heaven, your son, who shall never forget you, and who waits for you with his grandparents,

Rogelio.

The nights in the swamps were unbelievably freezing. I don't recall ever having been in such a cold place in Cuba.

Mario A. Martínez-Malo, Second Battalion

4
RETREAT AND CAPTURE

After the collapse on Wednesday, the men of the Brigade did their best to escape the area. They were certain that, if captured, they would be executed. A handful were lucky enough to be rescued by Lynch and his crew, and at least one made it to a foreign embassy in Havana. One group escaped aboard a sailboat and was rescued in the Gulf of Mexico just under two hundred miles from the mouth of the Mississippi River near New Orleans. By the time they were picked up, the dispirited men had been at sea without food or water for fifteen days and had lost twelve of their original twenty-two passengers.[1]

The majority of the Brigade took to the swamps and woods and tried to reach Cienfuegos, Havana, or some other location such as the Escambray Mountains. Pursued by Castro's militia, who set up almost impenetrable encirclements around the perimeter, the men hid during their attempted escapes. Unable to find potable water, many suffered from extreme dehydration, and some went as far as to drink their own urine. They ate crabs, lizards, snakes, and whatever animals they could capture—all without cooking, lest their fires alert a Castro patrol. In addition to ground forces, they were pursued by low-flying helicopters that constantly hovered overhead and strafed the areas where they were hiding. Many suffered deep cuts from the thick vegetation. The government ordered many of the local people, mostly peasants and *carboneros* (charcoal makers), out of the area while the Brigade was pursued.

In the end, around 1,180 of the nearly 1,300 men were captured by the Castro forces.[2] Although some *milicianos* acted maliciously, a few were discreetly kind and compassionate toward the invasion force even as they took them prisoners. Some considerate captors got word to prisoners' relatives that they were alive and even held some of the captives' jewelry in safekeeping. The men greatly appreciated such acts, pointing to them as evidence that support and sympathy for the Brigade's cause existed even among those who were supposed to be Castro's most ardent supporters.[3] The Brigade soldiers were herded back to Girón, where they were paraded before the Cuban and international press. At the beach, the captured men of the 2506 were insulted and assured that they would all be executed. Afro-Cubans were reportedly the most mistreated, as they were a public embarrassment to Castro, who claimed racial equality as one of his greatest achievements. Two black men reportedly were tied to a tree for three hours while Castro's men insulted them, calling them "niggers."[4]

This chapter follows the experience of Brigade 2506 in the immediate aftermath of the invasion. The majority of testimonies are from the ground forces, including a priest, as they tried to escape the Castro encirclements. The ordeal in the swamps was, in many cases, worse than the horror of battle. The insecurity of not knowing their fate, the fear of execution, and the intolerable thirst, combined with bitter feelings of betrayal created a nightmarish experience for the men. Also in this chapter, a member of a surgical team recalls the fate of the *Lake Charles*. The story of a Brigade infiltrator's last hours before seeking asylum at an embassy and an aviation ground crew member's memories of the invasion's end are also included.

Humberto Cortina, Second Battalion

Born to a wealthy and powerful political family in 1941, Humberto Cortina was a graduate of St. Thomas Military Academy. A cousin of Néstor Carbonell, Cortina was an opponent of Batista as a student. Like most Cubans, he was hopeful that the revolution would restore the 1941 constitution. Disillusioned by the numerous executions and the redirection of the revolution to Communism, Cortina left Cuba in August 1960 and joined the camps in October. He eventually became part of the Second Battalion and saw action in Playa Larga and Girón. After his release from prison with the injured prisoners in April 1962, he

Former Florida state representative Humberto Cortina, Second Battalion, poses before a Brigade flag in his Coconut Grove home, 1999. Photograph by author.

worked for the release of fellow Brigade members. In later years, Cortina served in Florida's house of representatives. He currently resides in Coconut Grove, Florida.

On the last day, I came back to the beach with Sueiro and Oliva. At that time, the decision was made that we needed to get to the mountains, and everyone sort of hugged one another. A group of around twenty of us went into the swamps. We divided into groups, first of ten and then five. I was with Luis Morse, Tito Freyre, Eddy Lambert, and Giro.

We started into the swamps going northwest, trying to make it to Havana. We were right in the middle of the swamp, where there were only little patches of trees. While advancing toward the trees, we were seen a couple of times by helicopters looking for people like us. We were able to hit an empty *bohío* [a peasant hut] later and change into civilian clothes. At one point, we encountered and fought Castro militia. Giro got hit in the leg, so we had to leave him. I had already spoken to everyone and said that since we were trying to make it to Havana, whoever got shot was going to be left behind. If it was possible to carry the person I would do so myself, but if he was hit badly he would need to stay.

Later, on dry land, we were walking off the sides of a road close to the Central Covadonga sugar mill town. Eddy Lambert and I were walking in front, and Tito Freyre and Luis Morse were behind. At our first encounter, I told the individuals that I was the son of "old man Molina," a name I just invented. The two peasants didn't believe us, but we just kept walking. They stopped a jeep full of militia and talked to them, and those guys started to shoot at us. We shot back a couple of times and escaped.

We ended up at Central Covadonga. At about 7:00 or 8:00 that night, we made the decision to go into the town and look for a church to see if we could disguise ourselves as priests or if we could hide with them. At this time, Tito Freyre and I were at the front and Eddy Lambert and Luis Morse were well behind. As we walked in, we could see the church. Then, a group of around ten *milicianos* turned into the road, and I said "good evening." They said the same and walked by us. As we continued walking, four militia from another group stopped us. They asked us who we were, and again I said I was old man Molina's son. They said, "Hold it, put up your hands. What are you guys doing here?" We told them we were literacy volunteers. They moved Tito Freyre to my left. The militia guy started to search me; I had a .45 in the back. Suddenly, firing broke out; it was Morse and Lambert fighting behind us. When that happened, I hit the guy searching me with my elbow. There was another guy ten or fifteen yards in front of me turned around toward the shooting. I pulled out my .45 and shot at the guy. They then shot me twice in the legs, and I continued trying to shoot towards the flash of the shot. I think I hit the guy in front of me. So I was lying on the ground and a militiaman came over and put a bayonet on my neck and said, "We're not killing you guys." I couldn't feel my legs.

Tito Freyre was taken away, and Eddy Lambert escaped but was eventually caught up in a tree. They took me to Covadonga, where there were many wounded militia. I was lying on a stretcher where they were cleaning my wounds, and a couple of guys came over and tried to choke me, one telling me I had killed his uncle. Ten or fifteen minutes later they brought in Luis Morse, who had already been hit. Luis and I were then taken to the small hospital at Cayo Ramona. While there, as soon as I mentioned my name, people came over and told me I was a *bitongo* [spoiled rich kid], the son of a wealthy landowner, and they just picked on me. A commander came and I had a few words with him.

One *miliciano* brought me a can of guava juice. He was a young guy I had known because he was the one who sold the books at the dog track my family used to own. He was a *miliciano* now, but he brought me the juice and said he would try to contact my family. I will always remember that. Those things you always remember.

Luis Morse, Second Battalion

Oliva gave us the order to move inland, and we split up into groups. I was with Humberto Cortina, Tito Freyre, Giro, and Eddy Lambert. The first day was very uncomfortable because of the helicopters. Whenever we heard them, we would try to hit the ground and hope they didn't see us. They were strafing, but luckily they just didn't hit. The helicopters were so close that I could see the faces of the guys in them.

The second day, we found an abandoned peasant's hut; we took some civilian clothing, some yuccas, some potatoes, and some chickens, which we ate raw because we had no matches. It doesn't taste any good that way—I don't recommend it.

On the third day, we started to cross the encirclement posts. The next day we were very hungry, and at one of the last posts we decided that instead of simply crossing we would take one of them in order to take their food. So we sneaked up on those guys, put a gun to their heads, and took their food. It was sweetened condensed milk and guava paste. At another post, they fired and hit Giro. The four of us continued.

We finally reached the outskirts of Central Covadonga and had a disagreement among us. Humberto was recommending that we go into the town and enter the church. I thought we should skirt the town and get farther away from the combat zone before we approached anybody. So we decided to separate. Tito went with Humberto, and they started walking in. Lambert and I finally said, "What the hell, we've been through hell already together." So we started following. Suddenly I noticed we had five militiamen walking about ten feet behind us. I turned around with a cigarette and asked them for a light. They said, "Keep on walking; you're under arrest." Lambert and I had our pistols, and we had talked about what we would do. So I turned to one side and he turned to the other, and we started shooting at them. When it was all over, they were all on the floor, shot. One was killed, and the others were simply wounded. I was shot through the shoulder. Lambert suddenly looked around, and he was the only one standing. He just walked away.

I was told that I would be shot immediately because of the dead guy. Later they sewed up my bloody wound, and they had the TV cameras there filming—they wanted to see a *gusano* [a worm—what Castro supporters called opponents, especially those who had left the country] cry. A very nice nurse gave me a tongue depressor. She said, "Bite on it so they won't see you cry." We were later taken with a whole bunch of our wounded to the hospital in Matanzas, where they gave us minimal care. I have always been suspicious that in some cases they actually did some surgery that was really not necessary, including some amputations. All they did for me at first was to sew the exit hole of my shoulder wound. About a week afterwards, they had to reopen the exit wound because it was totally infected. They had not given me any kind of antibiotics or kept the wound clean. I have no use of my left arm now. According to doctors I saw later in New York, if they had taken the trouble simply to sew both ends of the nerve together within the first couple of months, I would have had full use of my arm.

Pedro Encinosa, Headquarters Staff

Born in Santiago de las Vegas in Havana Province in 1932, Pedro Encinosa was the son of a local farmer and city councilman. Encinosa graduated from a technical-industrial school named after Gen. José Braulio Alemán. He later became a technical teacher and a councilman himself. At one point, he was Erneido Oliva's teacher. Encinosa left for exile in Miami in mid-1960 and arrived at the camps in December. He was made part of the headquarters staff and assisted with various duties during the invasion. After his release from prison in December 1962, he went into business but always remained active in the anti-Castro cause—an effort that has taken him as far as Central America and Africa. He currently hosts a Saturday night show on a Cuban radio station in Miami.

A young man from my town and I eventually ended up alone, trying to find a way out of the encirclements. We were shot at with machine guns from helicopters every day. We spent twenty-one days trying to escape in the swamp, trying to go north in search of a town or a farm. We couldn't find any civilian clothing in the empty *bohíos* because our people had already sacked them.

We turned ourselves in at the *bohío* of a charcoal maker, who lived there with his wife and three sons. They had already returned because twenty days

Pedro and Josefina Encinosa at their Miami home in 1999, sitting before a mural of Pedro's farm in Cuba. Photograph by author.

after the invasion the government thought the area had been cleared and the people had been allowed to go back. They gave us food, water, and even coffee. The family convinced us to turn ourselves in. They explained to us that it was useless to try and continue to escape while they, for example, could turn us in with the guarantee that we would be protected. In fact, it was the government's order: Any "mercenaries" found in the woods would be turned in with the guarantee that no harm would come to them.

We had some possessions with us. The family told us, "If you go there tomorrow with all those things, they are going to take them away. If we have it, they won't take them away, because we are with the government. I don't have any of the things you have; if you give us the M-3, the pistol, and all those things, it would be a good thing and something we shall appreciate." What were we going to do? We said, "Here, have them." But about our personal things—like our watches, rings, and chains—they told us, "If you give those things to us, we promise to take them to your home. Where do you live?" I told him, "Santiago de las Vegas." He said, "Give me the address and I promise I'll take it." Of course we gave it all to him. Could you believe that about five or six months later—when we had our first visits in prison—my family asked me about such and such a young man. I asked them, "How do you know him?" They said, "He went to the house and took us all you had given him to turn over to us." It was a gesture I always appreciated. It also showed that there was a sentiment in those woods that wasn't so committed to Fidel Castro or the Communists or anything like that.

Fernando Martínez Reyna, Heavy Weapons Battalion

Fernando Martínez Reyna, Heavy Weapons Battalion, at his Miami office, 1999. Photograph by author.

Fernando Martínez Reyna was born in 1940 in Havana, where his family owned businesses. A La Salle graduate, Martínez Reyna attended the University of Villanueva. Although never involved in politics, he was nevertheless hopeful about Cuba's future after the overthrow of Batista. When it became apparent that the revolution was leading Cuba toward Communism, however, he joined the MRR and sold bonds for the organization. He was arrested during the protest against the Mikoyan visit, left Cuba in December 1960, and departed for the camps in February 1961. Martínez Reyna was released with the injured prisoners in April 1962 and actively campaigned for the release of the men still in prison. In the years following the invasion, he entered banking and is currently an executive with Hamilton Bank in Miami.

On the nineteenth of April, six of us went into the swamp. We planned on waiting until May 1—May Day, when there were always rallies—to try to make it to Matanzas. But we wanted to go into some *bohíos* first and try to change clothes. So the six of us went into the swamp with that in mind.

We didn't have a compass, so many times we began walking without knowing where we were going. Meanwhile, Fidel Castro's helicopters were strafing the area, and we had already run out of water. On the afternoon of the twenty-first, we were sitting eating some raw crabs—which were delicious because we were starving—when we saw two *milicianos*. Although we had a machine gun and pistols, we went to the ground and tried to go unnoticed, as we knew that if we had a confrontation with them the rest would come. They went by us and kept going. We sat up again, with our guns next to us, to eat the crabs.

I guess they had seen us, because suddenly the *milicianos* started shooting at us from behind some rocks. As a result, three of us were injured—I was hit in the leg and in the arm. We killed one of the *milicianos*, and the other one fled. The bullet in my leg completely fractured the femur, and I now have one leg shorter than the other. Manuel Rionda asked me to open his shirt, and I saw the white T-shirt he had on underneath was soaked in blood. We told those who weren't injured to keep going. I stayed there with Manuel Rionda and Mandy Cañizarez. A little while later, they both died. Some *milicianos* came later and took me away on a stretcher. Twice they put me down and wanted to leave me there.

They took me to the beach, where I received first aid in a small house with the other prisoners. The next day I was taken on the bed of a truck with other injured prisoners to the military hospital in Matanzas. The drivers would speed up every time we went over railroad crossings. People would bounce, and with their broken bones it was very painful.

Julio Sánchez de Cárdenas, Paratrooper

Julio Sánchez de Cárdenas, paratrooper, in Miami, 1999. Photograph by author.

Born in Havana in 1937, Julio Sánchez de Cárdenas was a graduate of La Salle and was a university student when Fidel Castro came to power. His father worked for Bank of Boston. Not politically involved before the revolution, he joined the AAA (Amigos de Aureliano Arango) after the new government began to repress university protests. He left Cuba in June 1960 and departed in February 1961 for the training camps, where he became a paratrooper. After his release from prison, he received his bachelor's degree in history from the University of Florida and his Ph.D. in anthropology from Tulane University. He is currently on the faculty of Universi-

dad Interamericana in Puerto Rico and is a noted expert on Caribbean religions.

We got to Girón on the third night. There were several injured there—some very badly. It was a grotesque spectacle. We thought about what we should do: One said he wanted to get into a tank with a .30 caliber machine gun and go forward killing people until he was killed, that type of crazy thing. What seemed the most intelligent option was to divide into small groups and to go into the swamps. I went into the swamp with seven or eight people.

We were in a wet part of the swamp and had to drink the swamp water. I ended up having an allergic reaction that caused pimples to break out on one side of my face—one hell of a strange thing. My face nearly fell off from the number of pimples. Destroyed and demoralized, we went into some holes there to sleep. At my suggestion, we started praying the rosary, and even the one among us who was a Protestant prayed it with a hell of a lot of fervor. I don't know how it happened, but while we were praying he saw there were some drops of water falling. It was then we noticed that those holes we were in worked as a kind of filter that made the water drip along the wall. We were able to open a hole and gather some water in our canteens. We thought that since we saw it while praying the rosary, it seemed like a miracle. I believe in miracles. I believe God intervenes in people's lives.

The next day, we decided to divide up into smaller groups. There were militia posts all over the roads, at short distances from one another, trying to prevent those of us in the swamp from crossing the roads and escaping. Where we stopped to sleep that night, there were machine guns only about two hundred paces away, which would strafe the area every so often. When we fell asleep, I began to snore. When the militia heard it, they began shooting in our direction. I could feel and see the tracers coming over me. I was on the ground, face down, and I tried to make a hole with my chin to bury my head, saying, "Our Father who art in heaven, hallowed be thy name. . . ." That is the closest I have ever been to death. It was the worst experience of my life.

The next day, we separated into smaller groups. I went with two other men to look for a way to cross to the other side of the road and escape the encirclement. We planned to go the next evening, but at about 4:00 that afternoon some *milicianos* heard us and came into the swamp a little. They saw us and told us to halt from some nearby woods. One of my companions, who had a theory that bullets were thrown off track by leaves, ran. I froze and raised my hands. The *milicianos* disarmed me and took me prisoner. I noticed they were just as afraid of what I was going to do to them as I was about what they were going to do to me.

I was put on a jeep, and they were friendly to me even though they took my boots, my watch, and whatever property I had. We were taken to the beach, where other prisoners were kept. While I was there, I began to discuss Marxist theory with some of the guards. One of them told me, "You know quite a bit; how is it that with your conscience you came here with these worms?" We ate there, and later we were put on some buses. But before that, we were passed in front of some soldiers and townspeople who spat at us and hit us. There was a young black man in front of me who, because he was black, received many of the blows. They said to him, "Negro, how could you have joined these people now that blacks could do the same as whites in Cuba?" The poor guy held his head down, and he was really hit hard. He hadn't really even come with us: He was a sailor aboard one of the ships that had been sunk.

Sergio Carrillo, Paratrooper

Besides being the head of an .81mm mortar squad and a sacristan, I was also a medic. Late on the third day, while we were going back toward Girón, a jeep came filled with people. After some bickering, we loaded the wounded on the jeep and continued toward the beach. The Sea Furies continued to attack, shooting at us every time they passed. We had nothing to shoot back at them with, and many were throwing away their guns because they were out of ammunition.

When we got to the beach we found a boy of about six to eight years who had been hit by a bullet from an anti-aircraft gun. It had opened up his whole stomach. The parents were, as you could imagine, simply beside themselves. I had nothing left to give the boy; but, in any case, he was not going to survive in his condition. We stayed and comforted his parents and prayed the rosary with them. A little while later, the little boy died. There is a story that I went outside and shot at the Sea Fury with a machine gun, out of rage. What really happened was that when I went into the boy's house, I had put my gun aside. The father was the one who took the machine gun and went out and shot at the Sea Fury. We were finally caught on the beach the next day.

Tomás Macho, S.J., Chaplain

Tomás Macho, S.J., Brigade chaplain. Miami, Florida, 2000. By permission of Tomás Macho.

Tomás Macho, S.J., was born in Santander, Spain, in 1916. The Jesuits sent him to Cuba in 1949 to serve as the chaplain to a Catholic workers' group, and a year later he became a teacher at Belén school. He left Cuba in the mid-1950s for the United States to study at the Jesuit-run Georgetown University. He later attended the Jesuits' Fordham University, where he studied for his Ph.D. Shortly thereafter, he found himself in Miami for what he thought would be a temporary stay en route to a teaching position in El Salvador. In Miami, while meeting up with several Cuban friends who were by then in exile, he joined the Brigade. He was aboard the Houston *when it was beached at the Bay of Pigs. He is currently retired and lives in Hialeah, Florida, where he assists at the parish of Santa Cecilia.*

Silence came—silence because formerly you could hear the bombings and the planes. Then in the morning—you know how the Cubans are—some said they were going to Havana. The commander had already given the order, "Boys, this is over. You are free to do whatever you want." It moved me that so many people said, "Father, come with us." I said I would stay with Llaca and Villaverde and a few more individuals I knew, and that I would go whenever they went.

Not long before that, I was saying mass. While I was saying mass, one of our men came over screaming, "*Milicianos! Milicianos* are coming!" There were two reactions there. The first was to reach for the guns and go fight. The other was to reach for the food and leave. I hit the ground and heard the gunfire. They tell me the *milicianos* screamed "*Patria o Muerte!*" and our men screamed "Surrender!" In the end, one of their men died, one was left unscathed, and others were injured. The ocean's water passed over the dead one, and a group of us went to pick him up. I gave him last rites. One of them almost began to cry and lamented "that Cubans should have to kill Cubans."

A large group of us started to walk—with great optimism because we had a radio and we heard the secret codes from the Americans. That night, we stopped and saw a ship on the horizon signaling the coast. We dropped to the ground, as we did not know if it was friendly or an enemy ship. The next day, the group was only half of what it was before. We slept out there for another night and later camped near a place where we had found water. The battalion commander and his second-in-command told us, "We are leaving you and going on our own. All of you go your own way, because if they catch us we'll be executed." They ended up catching them before they caught us.

We continued walking in no specific direction, and we could hear the fire from the helicopters above. I told Villaverde, "This seems ridiculous. Where are we going? Why don't we turn ourselves in at a *bohío*, and tell them, 'Here we are,' and if they are bad they will execute us; but, at least we would have reached some end. Do you realize we are just going to keep walking this way?" We decided to go back to the place where we had found the water. We found a different place with water and decided to make camp and organize ourselves from there. I went away to pray, and at around 10:00 in the morning, a helicopter came and landed. They ordered: "Mercenaries! Surrender!" I told them from far away, "Look, of course we'll surrender. We don't even have guns. There is no problem at all." As far as I knew, no one had guns in our little group of five or six. When I came out, one of them said, "Here is the famous Father Macho!" I asked, "Where do you know me from? Are you are from the Catholic workers' group, from Belén?" He said nothing.

We were taken to a place—I didn't know the name—where there was a school. We sat on the sidewalk. All I remember is the impression of the people of that town: They showed no hate or satisfaction, and there were no insults. It was such indifference. I asked, "Is there anything to eat?" Someone said, "Here is a can of Russian food." I said, "Who cares if it is Russian? We are hungry." A *miliciano* then came to me and said, "Give me your boots." I thought that if that boy could go around with such miserable boots as his, I could go around the same way. I told him, "Okay. I will give them to you, but you give me yours." So, we traded boots.

José "Pepe" Regalado, Infiltrator

One day, after dinner at the Reboredos' home in the days following the invasion, I went to the doctor's study to listen to the Voice of America. Then, there was a knock at the door. It was the G.2, who had come because they had received news that there were counterrevolutionaries in that home. I said an Act of Contrition and went into the living room, thinking I was a dead man. They came in with machine guns and searched the whole apartment. I sat down with my back to the balcony where the mimeograph operator was—there were some curtains that made it look like a window from the inside.

Two *milicianos* stayed with me in the living room. Meanwhile, the members of the Brigade were being interviewed on television. I started criticizing the Brigade members along with the *milicianos*, saying, "These are traitors, they all have to be executed. We have to execute all the priests." They were there for over an hour. They didn't look inside the sofa bed (where there were explosives), and they did not look out onto the balcony. Since they found nothing, they stayed in the living room and visited. We invited them to coffee. They then begged our pardon and left. The Lord God was with me; my guardian angel protected me.

Later that night, I could barely get up from my chair. For the first time, I felt my legs weaken. At that moment, I knew I was good for nothing because I had become gripped by fear. I left the Reboredo home for my apartment above, desperate to talk to a family member. I needed family. I grabbed the phone and called my godmother, who was in Havana. When she answered, I hung up. I had to take medicine to go to sleep that night. Every time I heard a car door from the street, I thought they were there to get me. I knew I was no longer good for underground work. That's when we went to the Italian embassy.

Alberto Sánchez de Bustamante, Surgical Team

Born in 1937, Alberto Sánchez de Bustamante came from a family in which five generations had included medical doctors. A graduate of La Salle, he was a medical student at the time of the revolution. He came to Miami in October 1960 and joined a group of medical personnel that was supposed to staff a hospital ship during the invasion. They were informed only when they arrived in Guatemala in late March 1961 that the plans for the hospital ship had been

Left: Alberto Sánchez de Bustamante, surgical team aboard the *Lake Charles,* in Miami with fiancée, Margarita, a few days before his departure for Guatemala. Photo by permission of Alberto Sánchez de Bustamante.
Above: Alberto Sánchez de Bustamante, M.D., at his Orlando practice, 1999. Photograph by author.

cancelled. Thus, they were trained with weaponry and put aboard the Lake Charles *with the Operation Forty group, with whom they were supposed to land to carry out their medical mission. After the invasion, Bustamante attended medical school and is currently a gynecologist in Orlando, Florida. He is also deeply involved in Cuban cultural projects with a group called Cuban National Heritage.*

We were supposed to land on the third day; but the night before, we began hearing the messages from the beach about Russian tanks. In other words, we knew it was lost. Yet we wanted to disembark. The spirit of fraternity that emerges in an ideological crusade like that of Brigade 2506 was such that one felt part of a body in which one considered himself a traitor if he did not participate. We felt that if we turned back and were not willing to go in there and die with the rest of the force, we would be betraying those people. We wanted to die fighting.

We received an order the next morning to disembark. From our ship, we heard all the messages from the American pilots asking for authorization to shoot at the Russian tanks. They never received it. We also received all the messages from the different groups asking for reinforcements—because the Brigade was left with no ammunition. While we were lowering the aluminum landing boats, we were ordered to stop and to proceed to Puerto Rico. Soon afterward, we were ordered to go back to Puerto Cabezas.

In the combat zone at that point, we saw various submarines. We never knew what they were doing, but our opinion was that they were Russian and U.S. submarines filming how the Cubans beat the hell out of each other. For them it was a game; for us it was our freedom and our lives that were at stake. For them it was a joke—the little Cubans killing one another.

The *Lake Charles* went back to Puerto Cabezas after going in circles for several days. We feared Somoza, who had come out when we departed saying, "Bring me Fidel's whiskers!" We thought that now that son of a bitch was capable of getting rid of us to wash his hands and to make it look like he had nothing to do with this mess. When we arrived at Puerto Cabezas, they decided to take away our guns. We saw no Americans there, just Somoza's people. They put the guns in the hold of the ship. That made us feel insecure, because even if we thought there was only a small chance of survival, at least with the guns we could have defended ourselves. They later came and told us the group would be divided in two: Those with family in Miami would go there by airplane; those without family would go in the ship. I had no family in Miami. Several of us got together and decided we had to do something, because we thought those sons of bitches were going to kill us. We thought of getting out of the town and going up into the nearby mountains and to the Mexican border to save ourselves.

We had a great deal of firepower on the ship, and, although the Nicaraguans outnumbered us, we felt we could defeat them. We found an opening to the hold of the ship where one of my companions, who was short and thin, could get in and open the door from the inside. So one night at 4:00 in the morning, we started to take out the guns and armed ourselves to the teeth. At 6:00, we sent a messenger to Somoza's people telling them that either they get us out of there in twenty-four hours or they would have to kill us, because we were going to get out of there. Many hours passed, and we thought Somoza's armored trucks would be arriving any minute. At about 3:00 in the afternoon, two or three U.S. Air Force cars arrived. The American officials told us not to worry, that they were going to get us out that night and that we would be taken to our homes in Miami.

We arrived at Homestead Air Force Base aboard the same blacked-out planes that had taken us earlier. There were about fourteen or fifteen CIA and FBI cars there. Three or four of us got into each car, and they dropped us off at our homes all over Miami.

Jorge Giró, Air Force Ground Crew

When the invasion failed, we stayed at the camp for a few weeks. A rumor was going around that we were all going to be killed by the CIA and the American mercenaries that were working with us, so that there would be no witnesses. We were terribly scared and spent about a week to ten days locked up in the camp, prohibited from leaving. Finally, Tony Varona, Antonio Maceo, and others showed up to visit the camp. It seems the American authorities had allowed them to visit us. They promised us that they were going to get us out of there. The next day some planes arrived, and we were taken in them to Opa-Locka Airport in Miami. I remember I was given a shirt, pants, thirty-eight dollars, and a good-bye.

The only thing we did not have was the freedom to leave—but we had a great freedom inside of ourselves. We did not feel imprisoned or ashamed.

Father Sergio Carrillo, paratrooper

5 PRISON AND LIBERATION

The men of the Brigade were held at Girón between their capture and being transferred to Havana, except for the severely injured, who were treated temporarily in hospitals in the cities of Cienfuegos and Matanzas before being sent to a military hospital in the capital. Over the course of a few days, the captured men were taken to Havana aboard military trucks, buses, and *rastras* [trailer trucks]. Some of the vehicles stopped occasionally in towns so local revolutionary mobs could taunt the men. Onto one forty-foot, tightly sealed, unventilated *rastra*, Osmani Cienfuegos—a leader of the Castro force at Central Australia—herded 149 men. Cienfuegos, the brother of the 26th of July's Camilo Cienfuegos (who had died mysteriously in a 1960 plane crash) was repeatedly warned that the truck was dangerously full, to which he replied, "Let them die! It will save us from shooting them."[1] The men inside the *rastra* could barely breathe during their eight-hour ordeal. By the time the doors were opened in Havana, nine had died of asphyxiation. One more died a short time later.[2] The rest were taken with the others into the Palacio de los Deportes, Havana's Sports Palace, an arena used for events such as boxing and basketball.

For twenty days, the captured men of Brigade 2506 were forced to sit by battalion in hard chairs as they waited to be interrogated at the Sports Palace.

At one point, they were asked to stand and state their name and place of origin before television cameras—a moment when many families learned that their loved ones were alive. The broadcast informed some families for the first time that their relatives had been in the invasion force. Conditions in the Sports Palace were horrendous. The men were not permitted to bathe, change, or shave; with the mud and grime of battle still covering them, they had to remain seated for up to twenty-one hours at a time. For about three hours each day they were allowed to lie on dirty mattresses in the center court under bright lights. At one point, *jalapa*—a type of powerful laxative—was mixed into their food to make them violently sick. Firehoses had to be brought in to flush out the feces that had accumulated on the floor.[3] The stunned and tired men—not completely knowing who among their comrades was dead or alive—did experience some joy when a friend or acquaintance was escorted in to join the rest of the group.[4] The Brigade's leaders, meanwhile, were kept separate from their troops and went through their own ordeals. One of them, Manuel Artime, was brutally interrogated and tortured.[5] According to the documentary film *Brigade 2506*, several peasants from the Bay of Pigs region who had helped the invaders were also held at the Sports Palace. Their fate was never known.

On occasion, Fidel Castro himself would show up to see the men at the Sports Palace and would even debate them informally. In probably the best-remembered incident of the Sports Palace experience, Castro stopped before the Afro-Cuban Tomás Cruz and said something to the effect of "You, Negro, what are you doing here? Didn't you know blacks could now go to the beaches with whites?" Cruz boldly and quickly responded that he had no complex about his race and that he had not come to go swimming at the beach but to liberate his homeland. Castro's men also carefully selected a group of Brigade soldiers for a television appearance before a panel that included Communist leader Carlos Rafael Rodríguez. One small group—exhausted, demoralized, embittered by feelings of betrayal, and fearing execution—agreed to answer questions in a manner that suited the revolutionary propaganda machine. One prisoner, Felipe Rivero, feigned fear and weakness and was selected to be part of that group. Instead of answering the questions in the manner the panel had expected, however, Rivero lured the members into a debate, in which he caught them off guard and made several points that embarrassed them.[6] In addition to that first group, sons of wealthy families were highlighted, as were the sons of Miami's political leadership. The greatest coup, however, was when Castro found former Batista war criminals among the Brigade. Although only a miniscule group, the regime presented them as further examples of the invasion force. Henceforth, these groups were used to bolster his argument—however false—that the "liberators" were merely *Batistianos* and members of the upper classes. To add to the humiliation, those appearing on television were interviewed under a large sign that read: "FATHERLAND OR DEATH. WE WON."[7]

After two weeks at the Sports Palace, the roughly twelve hundred Brigade prisoners were given the yellow T-shirts they would wear throughout their captivity. The color was chosen to emphasize publicly the idea that the men, to whom Castro referred as "yellow worms," were cowards ("worms" was the term applied to opponents of the revolution, especially those who had left Cuba). The men were also given soap and finally allowed to bathe.

Following the ordeal at the Sports Palace, the Brigade was transferred to a nearly completed naval hospital in the capital. Although they were kept in cramped conditions, their overall treatment improved. The men were also allowed family visits. Prompting this change was a ransom offer Castro had laid out a few days earlier: $28 million worth of Caterpillar-type tractors. The dictator allowed a commission of ten Brigade prisoners (elected by the men) to go back to the United States and present the terms to the U.S. government. President Kennedy, unable to negotiate because of the break in relations, organized a bipartisan group of private citizens called the Tractors for Freedom Committee to deal with the negotiating team. It included Milton Eisenhower, Eleanor Roosevelt, labor leader Walter Reuther, and former Eisenhower official Joseph Dodge.

The Tractors for Freedom Committee was beset with problems from the start. Some members of Congress complained that the United States would become a laughing stock for allowing Castro to make demands. For many, any deal amounted to blackmail. Others felt it was against the nation's security interests, as Castro could possibly use the tractors for military purposes. The legality of a private citizens' group concluding such an agreement with the Cuban government was also questioned. Milton Eisenhower, moreover, became frustrated by the president's reluctance to state publicly that the Tractors for Freedom Committee was a strictly private group with the task of raising funds and that the decision to negotiate with the Havana regime was governmental. Nevertheless, they finally made Castro an offer in early June: five hundred regular tractors, not the type Castro had requested. Castro rejected the committee's offer, and shortly thereafter the Tractors for Freedom Committee was dissolved.[8]

On June 17, when it was clear there would be no deal, the Brigade prisoners were taken from the naval hospital to the *Castillo del Principe* [Prince's Castle], an eighteenth-century Spanish fortification that served as a prison. The prisoners were forced into the castle's depths by guards who insulted them and poked them with bayonets. Many were herded into large, crowded, dungeonlike cells, where every one hundred men had an uncovered hole that served as a toilet.[9] While at the *Castillo,* many of the injured prisoners joined the rest of the Brigade.

As the Brigade once again began to suffer under wretched conditions, the Cuban exile community in the United States mobilized. Under the guidance of exile lawyer Ernesto Freyre and the Harvard-educated Alvaro Sánchez, both of whom had sons among the Brigade prisoners, a new group called the Cuban Families Committee began to work in mid-July. They eventually set up their headquarters on Madison Avenue in New York City. Working alongside other relatives and members of the Brigade who had managed to get to the United States after the invasion, the group endeavored to gain the release of the prisoners.[10]

In August, meanwhile, the entire Brigade was transferred to the roof of the castle, where they were placed into *galeras,* or cellblocks. The leaders, now rejoined with the men, helped unite the Brigade and once again instilled military discipline. A regular pattern soon emerged which included laying out plans in case of an anti-Castro uprising in the outside world. In addition, classes were conducted, and cleaning details were appointed. Religious worship reemerged and included many men kneeling together each night to pray the rosary.[11] Protestant ceremonies were likewise held. Only during their long prison experience did many of the men truly get to know one another, as they earlier had been divided and trained as separate battalions and some had been at the camps for only a short time.[12] Throughout the fall of 1961, morale and hope for release were high.

Hopes were dashed, however, when their release was not realized by Christmastime. The men nevertheless tried to keep their spirits up through study, teaching, and making items such as rosaries with articles they found in the prison. Consecrated hosts were smuggled in and were used during masses.[13] A band made up of crude instruments the men had made was put together in one of the cellblocks. In time, a group of women organized by the

Families Committee's representatives in Havana volunteered to help by bringing in whatever goods they were allowed to bring for the prisoners. Nicknamed *madrinas* [godmothers], they were also sources of information for the prisoners. Despite all their efforts, the men suffered greatly in prison.

While the Families Committee worked around the clock to obtain the men's release, Castro launched a great propaganda effort in late March 1962: the trial of Brigade 2506. Conducted in the prison's courtyard, the case was heard by a five-man commission under labor minister Augusto Martínez Sánchez. A defense attorney was appointed for the Brigade soldiers, but they believed he acted more like a prosecutor than the prosecutor. Expecting at least a few of the Brigade members to denounce the United States openly, as had occurred the Sports Palace almost a year earlier, the regime's representatives were shocked and angry when the same men (with only two exceptions) refused to do so at the trial.[14] At one point, an inquiry was made whether anyone chose to make a statement; at first, there was no reply, but one prisoner finally raised his hand. Excitedly, a member of the commission asked what he had to say, to which the Brigade member responded, "Request permission to pee." This reply prompted raucous laughter from the rest of the men.[15] During the trial, in another memorable incident, a fight broke out between some Brigade members and guards. When it seemed things would get out of control, the Brigade's second-in-command, Ernesto Oliva, took the microphone and shouted "¡Brigada, Atención!" At that point, everyone froze—including the guards—and things quickly calmed down.[16]

In the end, the men were sentenced to thirty years in prison. Castro, however, still held out the offer of a ransom. This time each man had a price on his head: $100,000, $50,000, or $25,000. The Brigade leaders (Artime, Oliva, and San Román) each had a price of $500,000, bringing the total amount of the ransom to $62 million. In the meantime, Castro released sixty of the most seriously injured prisoners after receiving a pledge of nearly $3 million from the Families Committee.[17] The group of injured veterans soon joined the committee in New York and thrust themselves into the public relations effort to release their comrades in Cuba. Once in the United States, many met with American officials and private groups and tried, through the press, to raise public awareness of the men in prison. Some appeared on television programs such as the *Ed Sullivan Show* and the *Today Show*.[18] One veteran, Luis Morse, even agreed to be a contestant on *To Tell the Truth* in an effort to raise awareness.[19]

The condition and treatment of those who remained in Cuba took a serious decline after the trial. Making matters worse was that the over two hundred men with a $100,000 ransom, as well as the Brigade leaders, were taken to Cuba's most dreaded political prison on *Isla de Pinos* [the Isle of Pines]. Conditions for all of Castro's political prisoners on the island were indescribably brutal and harsh. The men were kept there for the next eight months, away from the rest of the political prisoners, and were subjected to all sorts of deprivations and abuses.[20]

The Families Committee, meanwhile, was advised by attorney general Robert Kennedy (who had taken a special interest in the prisoners' cause) to organize an aggressive fund-raising campaign and to secure the help of a professional agency. After a great deal of work, the committee was unable to raise even $1 million. Robert Kennedy believed the committee should bring aboard a tough negotiator who could deal directly with Castro. He recommended the eminent attorney James B. Donovan, who promptly agreed to represent the committee free of charge.[21]

Donovan met with Fidel Castro in late August and persuaded the leader to accept, in lieu of cash, $62 million worth of medicine and food. In the ensuing weeks, hard negotiations over prices, acceptable goods, and shipments were held.[22] Meanwhile, Robert Kennedy mobilized the Justice Department to cover all legal issues concerning the transfer and played a key role in persuading drug and baby food manufacturers to contribute to the ransom in exchange for tax benefits. The Red Cross was brought in to coordinate the shipments to Havana.[23]

In the days before Christmas 1962, the men of Brigade 2506 were informed of their impending release. Many thought it was a cruel trick. On December 23, they were taken to the San Antonio de los Baños airfield and issued new clothes. They were also given fresh beds and good food. When the *African Pilot*, the first ship carrying ransom goods from the United States, docked in Havana, the first of several flights carrying the Brigade to Miami departed. At one point, the flights were stopped when Castro demanded the $3 million that had been pledged earlier for the wounded prisoners. Thanks to the last-minute generosity of Cardinal Cushing of Boston and Gen. Lucius Clay, the money was released the next day, and the remainder of the Brigade was flown to Miami. One thousand relatives of Brigade members in Cuba were allowed to travel to the United States aboard the returning *African Pilot*.[24] In the end, a small number of Brigade members did not return with the group, as a handful were executed or given long prison terms.

Upon their return to South Florida, the men arrived at Homestead Air Force Base. They were later taken aboard buses to Dinner Key Auditorium in Miami, where they were reunited with their loved ones. The men were ecstatic to see their families. Many had been separated nearly two years; for some it had been even longer. They had lost so much weight in prison that, in some cases, their families did not immediately recognize them. The men whose families left Cuba aboard the *African Pilot* were reunited with them at Miami's Tropical Park, where the relatives had been taken. When the Brigade leaders arrived in Homestead, they were met at the airport by saluting Brigade members and numerous patriotic well-wishers. Minutes after their arrival, Robert Kennedy called Pepe San Román from Washington and welcomed him back. When they arrived at Dinner Key Auditorium, they were cheered wildly and carried on the shoulders of their men.[25] For the Brigade, the battle was over; but for many, the war against Castro had just begun.

On December 29, President Kennedy visited the Miami Orange Bowl for a ceremony in which he inspected the Brigade and publicly addressed several thousand Cuban exiles. Having met with the Brigade leadership a couple of days earlier at his Palm Beach home, he now faced the Brigade and the Cuban exile community as a whole. At the ceremony, upon being given the Brigade banner, the president boldly stated, "I can assure you that this flag will be returned to this Brigade in a free Havana." When he spoke those words, the crowd erupted wildly in applause and cheers. Although many exiles and Brigade veterans were resentful of Kennedy for having abandoned them (and, in fact, many boycotted the ceremony for that reason), the men and the crowd were caught up in the moment. The young president still offered the greatest—and only—hope for a free Cuba. Though perceived as having mishandled the invasion, his commitment to the cause was seen by some as genuine. That so many men took the president's words literally made the sense of betrayal they felt in later years even greater. After the president praised the heroism and significance of the Brigade, First Lady Jacqueline Kennedy addressed the crowd in Spanish and promised someday to tell her young son of the Brigade's courage and bravery.

This chapter details the experience of the men of Brigade 2506 from their transport to Havana from Girón to the Orange Bowl ceremony in December

1962. After a few lengthy testimonies in which individual Brigade members cover most of the period, I have added a section dedicated to shorter vignettes. In this chapter, I have attempted to include the largest possible number of interviewees.

Jorge Silveira, Third Battalion

A militia patrol captured us, and we were taken to a small hut and thrown on the floor. While we were there, they gave us some Russian canned meat; we didn't wait for it to be cooked, because we were afraid they would change their minds and take it away from us. Later we were taken on a truck to Girón and placed in some houses there. On the same day, we were taken to Havana.

I went aboard the *rastra* in which those nine men died of asphyxiation. Until then, the *milicianos* had not mistreated us physically, although they had attacked us verbally, calling us mercenaries, worms, *Batistianos*, sons of bitches, faggots, saying "you killed my brother," etc. They took a group of us to the *rastra* where Osmani Cienfuegos was in charge. They told him that all of us didn't fit in the truck and that people would die. His response was that it didn't matter, that we were going to be executed anyhow—that "either they'll die here or they'll die there." They put us in the truck, locked it up, and went towards Havana.

The experience aboard the truck was very Dantesque. We would hit against each other when the truck moved, and people grew very desperate from the lack of oxygen. The screams were horrible. I remember some of my companions were praying out loud; they were prayers of desperation. One man asphyxiated right next to me, although I don't know who it was because it was so dark. Someone had opened a tiny hole with a piece of metal. If it were not for that hole, many more would have died.

During the trip, which lasted eight or nine hours, they stopped at different places and we screamed. I have no doubt they knew what was happening back there. It was all premeditated. Osmani Cienfuegos gave the order directly, and I personally hold him responsible—as well as his superiors for never punishing him.

When they opened the doors in Havana, the sensation of being able to breathe was great. The *milicianos* looked horrified when they saw us. It must have indeed looked terrible to them. When we departed we had all been standing, but we all ended up lying on the floor and on top of one another. They asked about the water all over the floor: It was sweat and urine. I was completely nude when I got to Havana, as I had lost my clothing aboard the truck; some I took off because of the heat, and the rest I lost from having it ripped off me during the ride. One of my companions carried me off the truck. I couldn't walk, because for part of the trip I had two or three men lying across my legs.

They dropped us at the entrance of the Sports Palace, a stadium used for boxing. Those of us who were injured were thrown in front of the doors, and the rest were taken to the stadium seats. Doctors came to see the injured, and some were taken to a hospital. The doctor who saw me—he wasn't Cuban—mentioned that perhaps I had gangrene in my legs. One of the Brigade doctors who was with us looked at me and told me that I had nothing and that I should get out of there lest they amputate one of my legs. Later I heard the doctor who had seen me earlier tell the guy with him that if I wasn't better by tomorrow that they'd have to amputate my leg. That night some companions massaged my legs, and I was walking the next day—with difficulty, but I was walking. It was simply a lack of circulation.

The Sports Palace was almost the first time the whole Brigade was together as a unit. Until that moment, our training had been by battalions. I would say that our morale was extremely high. Castro's people tried to create division among us. First they sat us by battalion, and when they did so, the solidarity was immense. They then tried to divide us into the proletariat, the ex-military, children from rich families, members of country clubs, etc. Fidel Castro came while we were there with international press people, but he had to send them away because he didn't get the reaction he expected from us. Throughout the entire prison experience, Castro's chief objective was to get us to say that the Americans had sent us and abandoned us. Any one of us at that time could have gone over to them. They even asked the paratroopers to train a paratrooper battalion for them in exchange for their freedom. Although we had been abandoned, we had enough dignity not to admit it to Fidel Castro and his regime. The Brigade remained united.

After more than twenty days, we were finally allowed to shower. I remember that when I got out of the shower, I ran over my skin with my fingernail. I realized I still had a layer of crud over my body. After that we were taken to the naval hospital.

The naval hospital was the Hilton of our prison experience. It was where we were best off and where we were best treated, because it was more or less when Kennedy assumed responsibility for the invasion and the possibility of exchanging us for tractors came about. That was when the first delegation of the Brigade was sent to the United States to try and get the tractors. While at the naval hospital, we created many ways to get information. For instance, we had a *miliciano* in our room we called Pinocchio, who was against the system and who gave us information in addition to bringing us some medicine and food.

From there they transferred us to the *Castillo del Principe.* When we were moved, they took all the things our families had sent us. We arrived there at night, and they put us in the *estrella* [star], an open central courtyard, and separated us by alphabetical order. Because my name starts with one of the last letters in the alphabet, they put us in what were probably the worst cells—the ones called the *leoneras* [the lions' dens]—which were low in the prison with no windows and terribly humid. That's when I realized I was really imprisoned. On the way down, we were forced to run past guards who hit us with bayonets. The next morning, they gave us *café con leche* [coffee with milk] and bread made by prisoners—which was great for us at the moment. They also allowed us to bathe. The next day, they came and asked if there was anyone who wanted to go to a different cell. A group of friends and I volunteered. We ended up in one of the best cellblocks there were: It was on the roof, and it had an outdoor courtyard.

Conditions overall were very poor at the *Castillo.* We had so little food that when we would lie down, we sometimes could not get up, because we would become dizzy. There were times when they gave us only eight or ten boiled pieces of macaroni three times a day. We were physically debilitated. To give you an idea of the conditions, when I went to the invasion (and I had rowed and swam in Cuba) I weighed 165 pounds. When I got out of prison, I weighed 118 pounds. Remember, too, that we had done very little physical activity in prison. During my time there, I also contracted hepatitis.

Things took a turn for the worse when the negotiations in the United States broke down. That's when the rumors began about a trial and possible selective executions. During one of the family visits, we arranged that an aunt of mine in Cuba and the mothers of two other men would dress in black and stand on a street corner we could see from the prison if they heard that the rumors about the trial were true. On the agreed upon day, they were there not only dressed in black, but they also had black umbrellas, black shoes, and black socks.

One must bear in mind that the Brigade represented a cross section of Cuban society: There were country people, poor people, rich people, professionals, and illiterates. Those in the Brigade who were lawyers got together and decided—so that no one would get themselves into a position in which they could not defend themselves—that we would simply say that we came to fight Communism and that we had nothing more to say.

My aunt was one of the *madrinas*, a group composed of mothers and other family members of the prisoners who helped us. Usually, the cellblock *madrina* had a son or a nephew in that cellblock. They brought us some food, medicine, and served as intermediaries between the prison and the families.

In December 1962, they told us we would be released in a few days. Some believed it; others did not. Our families were then allowed to bring in food baskets, and our treatment improved. The day before we left, we finally turned in the yellow T-shirts they had first given us in prison, and they gave us new clothes. I left with a group on the last flight of the first day. We were received at Homestead Air Force Base by U.S. Army officers, and most of them were apologetic for what had been done to us. I got the impression that they felt ashamed. They gave us new clothes and took us to Dinner Key Auditorium. I had asked for my usual pants size there at the air force base, but I had lost so much weight that I could have wrapped them around twice!

When we got to Dinner Key Auditorium, I remember we were taken to a stage. We walked down some steps from the stage, like in a graduation, to where our family members were. There were many hugs, great happiness, and weeping when one saw his family. When we found out the next day that one of the flights was being held up, we went to Dinner Key to tell the Americans that if the plane wasn't allowed to leave, they would have to send us all back to Cuba.

The Orange Bowl ceremony was a moment of hope. We thought the president was going to support a new invasion. We were willing to go back to the camps at that moment. I believe that was where the Kennedy family's total betrayal occurred, especially when we were told they would return the flag to us in Cuba. I believe when one is the executive, one must be responsible for the acts of everyone under his authority. I am convinced that Kennedy betrayed us.

Mario A. Martínez-Malo, Second Battalion

It was so cold in the swamp. I don't recall ever having been in such a cold place in Cuba. One night, I was so thirsty I drank my own urine. It was a mistake. On the third day I saw some bees flying, and I thought maybe I could follow them to a hive. When I found it, there was militia there. They said, "Put your hands up!" I said, "Wait!" The bees were all over me [he laughs]!

We were taken to the beach in a column. There were press people there. It was the first time I saw people from Communist countries, as most of the news people were from Communist countries. Then they put us on trucks to the Sports Palace.

The Sports Palace was quite an experience. They sat us in chairs for twenty to twenty-two hours at a time. At night, they had us sleep in the ring with all those lights on us and it felt like we were on a barbecue grill. We also got diarrhea from the *jalapa* they gave us—all of a sudden the twelve hundred of us jumped up and began defecating. It was so horrible that they had to bring in fire trucks to clean the place with the hoses.

At the Sports Palace, people assimilated what was going on. We were also waiting and counting people who were missing. While we were figuring out what happened to them, all of a sudden another group of people would show up and we cheered and screamed that so and so was alive. We were also interrogated at the Sports Palace. They asked us the reasons we had joined the Brigade and who our families were. They also presented us to the general public on television, and one by one we had to stand up and give our names. I bent my head down a little and gave a different name—I gave my mother's family name—because I didn't know if they would hurt my family.

My parents didn't know I was in the invasion; the only one who knew was my sister in Miami. She didn't hear my name (among the prisoners), and everyone in Miami assumed after a few days that I was dead. A friend of mine had come into the Sports Palace, and I had asked him to visit my parents to tell them I was part of the Bay of Pigs invasion. He went there and told my family; my mother said he was a liar and didn't want to believe it. Later, they saw me on TV.

At the naval hospital we were in a clean place, but we were really cramped. Twenty of us were in a small room, but the sanitary conditions were much better. It was also the time when there was talk about the exchange. We had the first visits there, but it was the only time I saw my family, because I told my father to get the hell out of Cuba and to go to Miami.

After that we were sent to the *Castillo del Principe*. Our first impression was terrible, because they took us into the dungeon. It was a drippy place, and the humidity was unbelievable as we were below ground. The sanitary conditions also left much to be desired. We were divided into groups of about four hundred, and we stayed in the dungeon for a couple of months before they sent us to cellblocks on the roof.

After our trial, we each received thirty years in prison. But they also put a ransom on each one of us, and I was in the $100,000 group. The men in that group were taken one day from the *Castillo del Principe* to San Antonio de los Baños airfield and put on a small plane. Some people thought we were flying to Miami. I said, "How in the hell are we going to fly to Miami if there are six guys in here carrying guns?" At the time, we didn't have the slightest idea where we were going. All of a sudden the plane made a turn, and we started thinking "Where are we going?" I said I thought we were flying south. Oh, my God, the Isle of Pines.

When we got to the airfield, they were waiting for us. I knew the days ahead were not going to be easy because the militia guys guarding us there had a different mentality. They put us on trucks and took us away. All of a sudden, we heard a big noise as we went in front of the buildings where the other political prisoners were held. We were received like heroes.

They put us in a place where they told us Fidel had been when he was imprisoned by Batista. He had been there with two or three other people; we were 209 people. I had just enough room to sleep on the floor with my legs bent. It was an underground, L-shaped cell with a small window about ten feet high. We had no pillows, and we were naked except for our shorts. We had no soap, one toilet, and three showers. Life in there was tough. The food was unbelievable, and we were very crowded. We considered a glass to keep water in a treasure. When we joined *La Pacifica* (a hunger strike at the prison), they walked into our place and took everything away from us, beat some of the people, and made life miserable for us.

We tried to stay alert and busy. We organized classes, seminars, whatever, to keep our minds busy. We also used to collect different recipes for cooking; at one point we had over six hundred. We also planned trips. I became very close to Father Macho, who had been my professor at Belén. He would also sometimes celebrate mass for us.

About fifteen or twenty of the men became really sick. They were vomiting because they had gotten some sort of dysentery, and we had to put them beside the shower and the toilet. They realized many of us were sick when the negotiations for our release were almost concluded. They knew how to multiply: If fifteen or twenty guys would die, they would lose money. So, they brought in IVs and medical doctors. The day before we left, they brought us food. After having been so long without good food, the smell and the taste made people sick. It was terrible because everyone was vomiting at the same time in a closed place. It reminded me of the time we all got the diarrhea at the Sports Palace from the *jalapa*.

It was beautiful when we landed in an American place. I recall that at Homestead Air Force Base they gave us ice cream. We were taken to Dinner Key Auditorium, where there were hundreds of people. I realized that I was so skinny that my family wouldn't recognize me. Besides, my head had also been shaved. I went over to my father and stood in front of him. He moved his head around me, like looking for me, and I said, "Hey, it's me!" He said, "Mario! Wait here! I'm going to get everybody!" When I got home, it was 3:00 or 4:00 in the morning. There was a cousin of mine who was twelve years old, and he wore size twenty-eight pants. I put on a pair, and I started laughing in the mirror because I could count my ribs. I weighed ninety-five pounds.

I went to the Orange Bowl ceremony, more out of curiosity and to see the people than because of Kennedy. I knew it would be the last opportunity that I would be with my commanders from the Bay of Pigs.

Eduardo Zayas-Bazán, Frogman

I was wounded on the morning of the third day near the bodega where we had first landed. When Castro's troops finally arrived that afternoon, we were in the clubhouse where our people were keeping all of the wounded. Out of the five frogmen who were left at the Bay of Pigs, two of us were wounded, Felipe Silva and I. Yet the rest stayed with us. They could have tried to escape, but they said they would not leave us and that we would stay together. I will always be grateful to them for that.

It was a most difficult moment; we were totally demoralized. They separated me from the other wounded prisoners for some reason and put me on a truck to one of the sugar mills, where they gave my wound a little first aid. They then put me in a 1956 Buick with another wounded prisoner who had shrapnel all over his back. There were two militiamen taking us; the driver was wearing a priest's Sunday felt hat he had taken from a priest, and the other one had a machine gun pointing toward us. They turned the radio on to Radio

Swan. The station was saying how Ché Guevara had committed suicide, that we were arriving in Havana victoriously, and all types of propaganda that was totally misleading. I remember the guys were making conversation with us. One of them asked me, "Are you married?" I said, "Yes." He asked, "Do you have any children?" I said, "Yes, I have a five-month-old son." He said, "What a pity, because you're never going to see him again." It was a horrible feeling. My world had crumbled.

Before the invasion, we didn't question anything the Americans did, because we had total faith in them. Not only did I think I was not going to die, but it didn't even cross my mind that the invasion was not going to be successful. The Americans were there with me; remember, Gray Lynch had landed with us. When we had traveled together from Puerto Cabezas to Playa Girón, there were six American ships on the radar. At that time, Americans had never lost a war. We felt like with the CIA and the FBI we were dealing with supermen who knew all the answers. We totally believed in our cause and in the Americans who were helping us return Cuba to democracy.

They took the other prisoner and me to Yaguaramas and then to a police station in Matanzas Province. They placed us in a cell, and they took turns harassing us. They told us, "Take off your boots. You don't need them, because we're going to execute you." They had us there for several hours; I suppose they were waiting for orders. They put us back in the car and took us to the G.2 headquarters on Fifth Avenue in Havana, where they left us in the car for about an hour or two. After that, they took us to *Ciudad Militar* at Camp Columbia during the early hours of the morning. We slept there the night of the nineteenth with fifty or sixty other Brigade prisoners. We spent the next day there, and the evening of twentieth they put us into two buses and took us back to Playa Girón. We were back at Playa Girón the morning of the twenty-first, where by then there were two or three hundred more prisoners. I believe someone made a decision that rather than executing us, they would take us in front of television cameras. That day they took us to Havana for the second time. They took us to the Transportation Ministry and gave us a good meal, and a number were put in front of television cameras. I was not selected, because my pants were torn and I was bloody. I was then taken to the military hospital at Columbia, where they put a cast on my leg. I spent ten days there before I was taken to the Sports Palace.

During the day the prisoners in the Sports Palace were forced to sit in the bleachers. Those who were wounded were on the floors in some of the side rooms. During my interrogation they wanted to know about our training, and of course we tried to give as little information as possible. From the Sports Palace we were sent to the naval hospital. Again I was united with the frogmen. My father and sisters visited me while we were held there.

A couple of months later, we were taken to the *Castillo del Príncipe*. That was the worst of all the stays. There were a lot of common prisoners there, and the guards were borderline animals who used bayonets to harass us. My wife wrote me three times a week, and I received pictures of my son. Those photographs meant everything to me. They gave me hope; you had to have hope, otherwise you became desperate. Family visits were rare, depending on how the negotiations with the Americans were proceeding.

The trial occurred because they fundamentally did not know what to do with us. They truly thought that when the trial took place there would be many of us who would bad-mouth the United States. They were counting on that, and it didn't happen. So they didn't know what to do; they didn't know how to end the trial. As a matter of fact, they postponed the trial for a couple of days in the middle of it. The trial was a kind of a spectacle, with a tribunal of them and the rest of us sitting in this big patio surrounded by guards. Castro finally came up with this idea—or someone gave it to him—to give us a sentence of thirty years or a ransom on our heads.

When I got out (with the injured prisoners), several of us were taken to New York and three of us were on the *Today Show*. We also went to see the governor of New York, the governor of New Jersey, and Cardinal Cushing. Those of us who spoke English were doing public relations for the prisoners, and in May I had a knee operation in New York Hospital.

Sergio Carrillo, Paratrooper

My family learned I was in the invasion when I appeared on television at the Sports Palace. I had a cousin who was poor and lived in a tenement who had a television. She was the type who would shout, "¡*Paredón!*" [to the execution wall] and all that. When she saw me, she said she changed her views totally. Nobody had known where I was. In fact, my father and my brother were in the militia at the time, and they had shot at us without knowing I was there. Of course I didn't know they were there, either.

The racial problems began in the *Castillo del Príncipe*. I had various conflicts with the guards there because they asked me how it was that I, being black, had come in the invasion. One time during an inspection after a visit, I was in the middle of the line. There was a mulatto guard who had it in for me, and he sent me to the back of the line. When everyone left, I was ordered to stay. Then, right there in front of the women and everyone else, he made me undress completely. There was racism in general but not by everyone. Castro had tried to give the impression that blacks and whites had no problem under his regime, and they couldn't accept that a black person could have come with the invasion. It was as if to say "Now that all of you are free, and have everything," according to them, "how could you, being black, come to invade us?" That was their problem—it was bad propaganda.

Tomás Cruz was a military man. He was also an evangelical pastor who preached a great deal in prison. He helped many people spiritually and morally. While we were in the Sports Palace—I was about four or five seats away— Fidel Castro passed by but stopped when he saw a few blacks. Fidel asked Tomás Cruz, "What are you doing here? Didn't you know blacks could now swim at the beaches with whites?" Cruz said he had not come to go to the beach but to overthrow him. It was a famous incident. It was such a quick response, and Fidel could not have imagined it. He couldn't answer back, because he was in shock.

Within the Brigade, there were never any racial problems. The great thing about the Brigade was that there was everything—from the poorest to the wealthiest, middle class, upper class. Yet there was never any discrimination. A sense of friendship developed that still exists. There was great harmony and love among us because we went through so many difficulties together. I believe that what most unites people is difficulties.

The great thing about the trial was Erneido Oliva's valiance. I was near him. I don't know what happened, but a problem broke out between a Brigade member and a guard. The Brigade member took the guard's gun, and a fight broke out that could have resulted in numerous deaths. Because they couldn't stop it, they called for Oliva. By that time, there was a large group fighting. So Oliva went to a microphone and all he said was, loudly, "¡Brigada, Atención!" Everyone stopped, and a paralysis set in. At that instant, everyone came to attention and the situation was saved.

Hector García, one of the greatest classical guitarists in the world, was in my cellblock at the *Castillo del Principe*. Somehow he got a guitar, and at night he would give concerts. He formed a choir, and we celebrated a Christmas mass in Latin that dumbfounded the guards. Our relatives had smuggled hosts to us in cotton. We used a cup as a chalice and had some wine that had also been smuggled in. Besides that, we all prayed the rosary each night and gave religious instruction. The Protestants also held their ceremonies, and there was much respect between us. In prison, many people who were illiterate were taught to read, and history and English classes were also given; it was like a small university. The only thing we did not have was the freedom to leave, but we had a great freedom inside of ourselves. We did not feel imprisoned or ashamed.

Sports Palace

José Basulto, Infiltration Team

Seeing my own friends marching in front of the TV there giving testimonies and being manipulated by the Castro government was one of the most difficult experiences in my life.

Rafael Montalvo, Second Battalion

I don't know how to convey the state we were in—the total defeat. What happened? Shit happened! We felt very bad. Yet we were very cocky, and we were very proud; we knew the reasons for which we fought were valid. We never questioned them or our purpose.

Andrés Manso, Sixth Battalion

My family found out I was in the invasion when they put the television cameras on us at the Sports Palace. They passed out. We were all also interrogated. One by one we had to stand before a *miliciano* who would take all our information—our age, where we were from, our battalion. They also asked us our motive for coming to Cuba. It was very normal, very decent.

Julio Sánchez de Cárdenas, Paratrooper

When we were on television, we each had to say our name. My mother learned that I was in the invasion while she was watching television. She was alone and widowed, and I was her only son. It was a very hurtful experience. On television, Castro began asking us several questions in order to argue with us. Some people even asked him questions. One of the questions was about the Communist Party. He said he wasn't tied to the Communist Party. So I raised my hand and asked him that if he in fact had no ties to the Communists, what it was about the Communist Party that he found so offensive. When a question didn't benefit him, he would cut the person off and begin talking about something else.

Jorge Herrera, Heavy Weapons Battalion

Once detained en masse in the Sports Palace on the first night, those sons of bitches put something in the food that gave you an incredible diarrhea. People were defecating even in the hallways. Firemen had to come to clean the place up with the firehoses. You could see how far the malice and cruelty of that system reached.

Injured Prisoner

Fernando Martínez Reyna, Heavy Weapons Battalion

I was in the military hospital. One day, the guards came to see me and told me to get dressed. I had no idea what it was for. They put me into a car; there was one guard next to me with a machine gun, another guard, and a driver. When we pulled into my house, I saw the flower arrangements and figured someone had died. One of the guards told me, "Your father has died, and we have let you come to the funeral. You shall be here for half an hour. You are allowed to speak to no one except your mother. If you speak to someone else, we will take them prisoner." So I saw my mother. The guards were next to me the whole time, armed. When we left, I thanked one of them. Of course they were despots and said "thank the revolution."

Naval Hospital

Juan Clark, Paratrooper

Castro had a special interest in the paratroopers. It was, I believe, the first time that paratroopers had jumped in combat in the Americas. Castro came to the fifth floor of the naval hospital (where I was) in a very jovial way, saying, "Boys, how have you been treated by the revolution?" He spent an hour with us. I asked him why he hadn't held elections. He said, "I'll let you go talk to these people"—he referred to the ones constructing an apartment block—"and see how many would like elections." I said, "How many of those who would like to have elections do you think could come to work the next day without having any problems?" That he did not like. He didn't show it, but those who were with him did.

Negotiations for Release

Néstor Carbonell, Operation Forty, Frente Advisor

It was a very delicate situation. I was working with Miró and Varona in Washington, D.C. They had their sons in prison and were clearly interested in avoiding executions. (There was the fear that the sons of the leaders might be executed along with the heads of the Brigade.) But at the same time, they had the primary responsibility of waging battle against Castro and not getting bogged down in negotiations and certainly making no concessions to the tyranny. It was a very delicate situation. They did not oppose the Families Committee, but they certainly weren't involved in their negotiations.

I was in Washington at the time when we received reports that there were going to be executions. Varona went to the White House with two or three other members of the council and met with National Security Advisor McGeorge Bundy. Varona said, "We hear that Castro is going to execute some of the prisoners, and that has to be prevented. We don't care what has to be done diplomatically or otherwise." Apparently Bundy became testy or defensive and certainly evasive. Varona confronted him, saying, "You've got to stop that; otherwise, the blood of these innocent people is going to *splash* against the White House and stain this building and those who are here today!" Miró became very pensive and wrote a letter to his son, sent through diplomatic channels, basically saying, "I have offered my services as a criminal lawyer to defend the Brigade. Unfortunately this may not be feasible. May you accept your fate with dignity. It is a privilege to suffer and die for our homeland. God bless you all." So those were the reactions of these two leaders. They complemented each other: Varona, confrontational; Miró, equally firm but less emotional.

Hugo Sueiro, Second Battalion Commander, Prisoner Representative

We went to see Miró Cardona and told him what was going on. We then went to Washington, D.C., and then came to Miami to talk to the family members at the Columbus Hotel. We had some hard experiences there. I had two men named Gilberto Hernández in my battalion. The father of one of them asked,

"How is my son?" I asked, "What is your son's name?" He said his name. I had to tell him his son was dead. He said, "No. I saw his name on the list." It was so hard.

Humberto Cortina, Second Battalion

I was released with the injured prisoners. At that time, I was elected by the companions in my group to be able to speak and to try to raise the $62 million. I participated in everything, since I spoke English very well. One day in New York, Harry Ruiz Williams, who headed our group, called me and said we had to go down because we were being picked up. So Harry and I went down, and it was Bobby Kennedy. He said, "Let's go have dinner at Quavares." So, we went to the restaurant, and we sat at a table outside. Bobby called Harry "Enrico," and I spoke very little. Bobby said, "I have somebody here who is going to come over and have a drink with us." It was Frank Sinatra. Of all the Kennedys, Bobby was the one I liked the most. I was nineteen, and it was very impressive.

We stayed at the Schuyler Hotel. We always continued to dress in our yellow T-shirts. I spoke many times in the paper. I said that if we did not find the necessary funds to bring all our prisoners back, we would return to Cuba and stay with them.

Castillo del Príncipe

Mario Abril, Second Battalion

I was put into cellblock number one. The windows faced the city and you could see Havana. During that period I became acquainted with Hector García, the guitarist, who was also a member of the Brigade. One day I had seen him writing a musical score, and so I said, "Hey, look, I am a musician myself." So, we talked and became friends and organized a choral group. I remember on December 24 we had a midnight mass, and the choir sang. They couldn't read music and had to be taught by rote; I was made the teacher. That Christmas I saw a guard outside throwing little rocks all by himself with his rifle on his shoulder. I said, "Hey, have a little hot chocolate. Let me have your canteen." So he gave me his canteen cup, and I fished a cup of chocolate and gave it to him through the bars on the door. We talked for a while, and I asked him if he had kids; yes, he had kids. No acknowledgement was made of the circumstances, a tacit acceptance of the roles that we had to play. So, I said, "Merry Christmas to you," and he said, "And to you too," and I went back to the mass.

The Trial

Antonio González de León, Second Battalion

The trial was emotional. By that time one had a different feeling than when we had just lost, when we were totally demoralized. A year had passed, and we had a combative spirit. One saw human quality there, the sense that although one is routed one is not defeated.

Rafael Montalvo, Second Battalion

One of us, after being captured, had admitted to working for the CIA, the FBI, the U.S. government, the Boy Scouts; whatever they suggested, he agreed to. He scared very easily, and he was afraid of confrontations. When the trial came, they would take him outside every night and return him after they had put the fear of God into him.

The first day of the trial, they asked us to testify. They went to the first guy in the first row, and he said, "I have nothing to say; I refuse to defend myself." The second one said the same. They kept asking, and they were puzzled because they thought people wanted to testify. In the back, Luis González Lalondry raised his hand. The judge said, "You—what is it that you have to say?" Luis said, "I request permission to pee." The place went wild. The guards freaked out, and we had a riot. The judges ran and locked themselves up. They took us back to our cells, and we spent all night singing, "Tu ves yo no lloro," [You see, I don't cry].

The next day they called the guy I mentioned who was very fearful. He was way in the back. He walked all the way—at first very slowly with his head down. Then as he kept walking, he started picking up his head and picked up the pace and picked up his posture. When he got up there, this man who always spoke in such a low tone you couldn't hear him spoke this time with a firm voice, loud and clear. They ordered him, "Now, you are going to testify." He said, "No, sir. I am not." It was a great act of courage. The place went wild. They sent him back. Unfortunately, a couple of guys did speak against the United States.

It got really rough there after the trial, with the food, the guards, everything. The one exception was during the missile crisis: Then the guards would come and tell us, "Hey, I'm your friend, you know" [he laughs].

Jorge Marquet, Fifth Battalion

A companion of mine called Juan Torres Mena had a problem during the trial. The guard insulted his mother, and Juan hit the guard. He was hit with a bayonet. Chaos broke out, people went after the guards, and there was swinging and punching. Erneido Oliva screamed, "¡Brigada, Atención!" Everyone stopped. Oliva spoke to the troops, saying, "Gentlemen we did not come here for this: We came to die, to liberate Cuba. We must give an example of dignity."

While we were imprisoned, we had a great sense of unity. A great fraternity emerged. Many of us got to know one another in prison, because while we were split up into different battalions, you knew only those in your battalion or company. But in prison they stuck us in the cellblocks and we met different people.

Isla de Pinos

Tulio Díaz Suárez, Sixth Battalion

I had a ransom of $100,000 and was sent to the Isle of Pines. Life was monotonous, and they did not let us out into the yard except for two times. There came a time when they would give us spoiled food, and some people got dysentery. Our water was also in very short supply. The worst part of being in that place was the screams of the people in the punishment cells. In cold weather, the guards would throw buckets of water and feces on the prisoners every hour or so; in turn, the prisoners moaned and swore at the guards who were punishing them.

Tomás Macho, S.J., Chaplain

When we were transferred to the prison on Isla de Pinos, five of us—the three leaders San Román, Oliva, and Artime, a man called Arozarena, and myself— were selected to be in solitary cells. A guard passed by who started to laugh and make fun of me. He said, "Do you want me to bring you a young girl? What would you do with her, Father?" Another came and stood before the iron door and said, "Do you believe in God?" I said, "Yes, I believe in God." He said, "Deny Him." I kept my mouth shut, as I didn't want to provoke him. I kept looking at the guard. He said, "Quickly," and he put his rifle between the bars and cocked it. I said nothing, and he left, laughing and saying, "May Saint Peter come down with his keys and get you out!"

Reunion

Jorge Marquet, Fifth Battalion

We arrived at Homestead Air Force Base and they gave us new clothes. It was very official. There were some people around who cheered, but there was no sort of demonstration. We met with some doctors; if they thought you had something contagious, they sent you to the hospital. I had a cyst on my side from a lack of vitamins. Coincidentally, the doctor I saw had treated me in Cuba when I was young. I told him, "I really want to see my family." He told me, "Look, come see me in my practice later and forget about it. I'll just say you have nothing."

From there we went to Dinner Key Auditorium, where our families were waiting. I was on the last plane that was held up because Fidel Castro wanted the money for the injured prisoners. The environment at Dinner Key was wonderful. My parents, my wife, the baby who had been born while I was away, everyone was there. The baby called my father "Father." She had never seen me in her life. Everybody was extremely happy.

Pedro Encinosa, Headquarters Staff

There was a ship called the *African Pilot*. It went to Cuba loaded with merchandise for our release. The agreement was that when the ship returned, it would bring back some of our family members. Sadly, neither my mother nor my father chose to go. But my wife and son did.

After landing in Fort Lauderdale, they were taken to the famous reunion at Tropical Park. They were brought by bus to the park, and we were there waiting for them. One could see the families as they came out. When I saw my wife and son . . . well, you can imagine.

The Orange Bowl

Juan Sordo, M.D.

I was at the head of the medical corps. Kennedy passed by and stopped and shook my hand. I shook his hand and all that, but under my breath I muttered "son of a bitch."

Fernando Martínez Reyna, Heavy Weapons Battalion

I did not go to the Orange Bowl ceremony. I repudiated that act. Along with a group of fifty to a hundred, I refused to go. I thought it was demagoguery for Kennedy to give the flag back to the Cubans after he had betrayed us.

Grayston Lynch, CIA

It was the first time it ever snowed in the Orange Bowl: Kennedy gave them a snow job. I wasn't even allowed to be in town. Rip Robertson and I were barred from even going near any of the Brigade, because we would contaminate them: We were going to tell them the truth. These people had been in prison all that time; when they came back, they didn't know what had happened. So when the Brigade came back from prison, we were down in Key West for a whole week. Kennedy grabbed all the leaders and took them up to Palm Beach, and Bobby snow-jobbed them again.

Andrés Manso, Sixth Battalion

Undoubtedly, I felt good that day, but I wasn't enthusiastic. Any way you look at it, it was politics. He said he would return the flag to us in a liberated Cuba. In the end, I was not surprised. It wasn't such a great joy to know I was with the president who had betrayed us. Any way you cut it, it was he who betrayed us.

Alberto Sánchez de Bustamante, Surgical Team

We were very excited about it. We thought that Kennedy, because of his guilt about what he had done, would do something. You have to put yourself in Kennedy's place. There was the guilt of what he had done to us, plus the humiliation from the international standpoint: the most powerful country in the world losing to a butcher like Castro. I am convinced that he and his brother were carrying that with them. The ceremony was very emotional. He went there and said, "I'll return this flag in a free Cuba" and all that. By then, the missile crisis had ended when he betrayed us a second time.

What made me give my blessing to his activities were
my own feelings of duty: God asked it of me; the
church was indicating it was the correct path.

Myrna Pardo Millán

6 THOSE LEFT BEHIND

The desperate emotions the men of Brigade 2506 felt throughout their experience were matched only by those of their families. Some of the "men" were
mere teenage boys. One could only imagine the worry the parent of such a
youngster could have experienced. Some men were in their fifties, and the
oldest was sixty-one. Most, however, were in their twenties and thirties. Nearly
all the men had left loved ones behind in Miami or Cuba or both.

The parents, wives, children, and siblings had some notion of where the
men were being trained during 1960 and early 1961. Certainly, informed
people had told them of the training camps in Central America. Nevertheless,
because of the secrecy surrounding the entire mission, one could not trust any
information completely. Brigade families differed in some important ways
from standard war families, as many were recent exiles in a strange land and
others lived under the rule of the government their men sought to overthrow.
Those in exile struggled with new surroundings and suffered material depriva-
tion in addition to loneliness and worry.

The role of religion was paramount for many families. The Catholic par-
ishes of Gesu and Corpus Christi in Miami were among the most frequented
places of community prayer for those in exile. Like their religious faith, the
families' faith in the United States was also unshakable. They believed that, in

the end, they would win and live freely again in their homeland. Their primary concern was that their loved ones would come out of the conflict alive.

When news of the invasion came to those in Miami, the families were joined by many in the Cuban community at a Gesu prayer service. Such acts, including a demonstration at Bayfront Park demanding U.S. intervention, also occurred when the invasion clearly had failed. In all cases, the families spent a great deal of time listening to the radio, awaiting news. Those families who remained in Cuba suffered and hoped in greater isolation and feared for their own lives as well as for those of their men.

The worst time for most families was the period that followed the invasion. It was then that the families of the men who had perished were given the bad news. For the rest, it was the beginning of a long and lonely ordeal. Certain that their loved ones would be executed, many became desperate, only to be reassured by talk of a release. Like the men, they were put on an emotional roller coaster for twenty months. The experience was all the more grueling for many wives who found themselves in the United States with families to care for single-handedly. The close relatives still in Cuba, meanwhile, had to endure the taunts and insults of revolutionaries.

The exhilaration felt when the Brigade returned from Cuba was probably greater for the families than it was even for the men. It was the end of one road and the beginning of another: Life as Cuban exile families had begun.

This chapter details the experience of eight women. Three became young widows because of the invasion: Two had husbands among the nine who perished in the *rastra*, and the other lost her husband when his B-26 bomber plunged into the ocean after action over Playa Larga. One woman, whose husband was released with the injured prisoners, worked closely with the Cuban Families Committee; another, who was in Cuba during the entire episode, left the island aboard the *African Pilot*. Also included in this chapter are the fiancée of underground leader Rogelio González Corzo ("Francisco"), and two brief testimonies from the mother of a surviving veteran and the cousin of a Brigade member who was missing in action.

Myrna Pardo Millán

Born in 1937, Myrna Pardo's family was from the city of Morón, in Camagüey Province. Because her father was a representative in Cuba's house of representatives, she lived in Havana most of her life and graduated from El Sagrado Corazón, *the Sacred Heart School, in Havana. She currently resides in Miami*

Left: Myrna Pardo Millán with husband, José "Pepe" Millán. José died in the infamous *rastra.* Photograph by permission of Myrna Pardo Millán.
Above: Myrna Pardo Millán, at her Miami Beach home, 1999. Photograph by author.

Beach, Florida, and has never missed the annual ceremony held on April 17 at the Bay of Pigs memorial.

My husband, Jose "Pepe" Millán Velasco, moved next door when I was fourteen. He was seven years older than me, and I viewed him as the older man next door. We met and started going out when I was sixteen, and I married him when I was eighteen. He was a law student at Villanueva and a professional jai alai player. His family helped us build a small house in the Biltmore area of Havana, and we were very happy.

My father's political party was one that had supported Batista; that is, he supported the last elections held in Cuba so that there would be a way out of the coup d'état, which he had *never* supported. Neither my husband nor his family were involved in any politics. My family wasn't harshly attacked during the first days after the revolution, when they were burning people's houses and doing other horrible things. But they would come and surround the house asking for my father. My husband had many Spanish friends who had told him from the beginning, "This is Communism." So we forced my father to go to a

Carmelite convent where we had friends, but he didn't want to leave Cuba under any circumstances as he felt he had no reason to do so. From there, Father José Luis, the convent's superior, got him into the Nicaraguan embassy. He left Cuba in February of 1959. My family later endured many home searches; those were terrible times.

My father went to Miami, where my mother would come visit him. My husband and I went to see him in mid-1959. We loaded up our car and came on a ferry with the children, who were then one and two years of age. I was pregnant with my third child. While we were in Miami, Pepe went back to Cuba after a while to see if he could get some money from his father, as we didn't even have a penny beyond what we brought with us and my parents had nothing. The Castro government had confiscated all their properties and assets. In any case, we thought our stay would be only for a few months.

When Pepe returned to Miami a month or so later, he started to work and we sold his old Porsche. With the little bit of money we made, we put a down payment on a duplex, and we were extremely happy. The duplex was so empty—we didn't even have a refrigerator. Yet we felt as if we lived in a palace. We were so happy. The thrill of the century was to go out and get some ice cream; it was a great expense, but it was like a celebration for us. Yet those were hard days because of the problems back in Cuba. We never turned off the radio, anxious to see what was going on there. In 1960 friends of ours began arriving in Miami, and we would go to the airport almost every day to see who would come in. We all started gathering around Corpus Christi Church. It was such a strange life, so difficult.

Pepe was playing jai alai in West Palm Beach during the season, but he never stopped talking and thinking about Cuba and all that was happening there. He started to attend meetings with friends, as there was the hope that something could be done. But, most of all, my husband was very religious, very Catholic. I am also very Catholic. At the time, the church gave us a feeling that we had to do something to fight Communism and not just stand by with our arms crossed. That feeling of duty to defend our faith was what motivated my husband to involve himself in something to remedy the situation. What made me give my blessing to his activities were my own feelings of duty: God asked it of me, the church was indicating it was the correct path. Nowadays I question that a little, but that's how it was, and I let him go to the camps. He left on January 6, 1961, and we were both convinced it was our duty.

Our children were one, three, and four years of age. I was twenty-three years old.

My father and uncle took him the day he left and didn't let me go. It was the darkest day of my life. My husband and I were deeply in love with one another. The months between the time he left and the invasion were horrible. For one thing, our children were young, and we had very little money. We received letters from him, and the return address was always somewhere in the United States. He was in the Heavy Weapons Battalion, and he would write to us about how much he was learning and how they had promoted him and about the great physical condition he was in.

When Kennedy took power, I thought it was marvelous—a Catholic president! I was fascinated. We thought his statements were a little bit contradictory, but perhaps we chose not to believe what we heard. We listened to Radio Swan the whole time.

One night I was sleeping, and I dreamed that Pepe had called me on the telephone. I picked up the receiver—I still remember the cold sensation from the telephone—and it was Pepe. I said, "Pepe, how is it that you are calling me?" He said, "Yes, yes, I'm calling you. Listen, do not worry about anything you hear. Be calm." I said, "Did we win?" He said, "We have neither lost nor won. But be calm. Whatever you hear . . . be calm, be calm." I could still hear the words now. It was April 17. I woke up to screams below: "The invasion has started!" I couldn't believe it. My heart was leaping through my chest.

We were glued to the radio, trying to find out what happened. All the early reports were magnificent, and it was all euphoria. Then there was an impasse, and we heard nothing. News came the next day that they had taken prisoners, that they had landed wrong and had landed in the swamp, and that they were drowning. So many horrible things. I was home almost the whole time listening to the radio. We went to Corpus Christi with friends of mine whose husbands were in the Brigade. They also gave a mass at Gesu Church, and we went. The news got worse and worse—I don't even want to remember the things they said. They tried to hide things from those of us who had someone there.

Later the lists of prisoners came. Everyone who read their husband's or son's name was thrilled because they knew he was alive. One day, it was announced that the Frente had received letters from the prisoners for their families. My husband's name had appeared on a list, so I was at least breathing by then. We all went to the Biscayne Boulevard office, and they began to pass out the letters from underneath a tree. When I saw there was no letter for me, I said, "There is something strange here. Pepe would write me at least a small note." I began feeling something very strange. But I was consoled by my father-in-law, who was a super anti-Communist and anti-Fidelista. He would say, "I knew Pepito would not lower himself to write."

A little while later, the prisoners' representatives came for the negotiations. A group of us who had husbands in prison went to see them. When I asked one of them about Pepe, he lowered his head and kept going, saying nothing. It seemed very strange to me. The next day I went to the Frente office to see if there was any news, and friends of my husband who had not disembarked were there. They also evaded me.

The following day I was at my house, cleaning out the children's closets—all the nervousness made me want to fix up the closets. Someone came to the door [she weeps]. My father came in and said, "Myrna, there is very sad news about Pepe." A note had been written by a boy on the *rastra* and sent by a boyfriend of my sister who was in the Brigade. It said, "Tell Myrna I have died praying and thinking of our children and that I love her."

It was horrible, but God gave me the strength to control myself for the children. Every day my children had prayed that their father could take the Communists out of Cuba. We tried hard not to make them suffer. It was horrible. My in-laws were destroyed: My mother-in-law died within two years, and my father-in-law died five years later.

What hurts me the most is that when they first started talking about the *rastra* in which all those men asphyxiated, I thought it was a lie. I thought they were making things up to move public opinion. As bad as the Communists and Fidel were, I thought it was impossible that they would do that. When I learned Pepe had been one of the ones who had died in the *rastra*, it was as if I had been completely smashed. It hurt so much to think that I thought it wasn't true. I learned later that Pepe had forgiven those who were killing him before he died. He was praying the rosary when he died.

During the months the Brigade was in prison, I remained in contact with my friends; the group of us who had lost our husbands, we looked like witches dressed in black. I remember being with Cuca Pino, Ia Freyre, Margarita Oteiza, and Dulce Carrera Jústiz, whose boyfriend had been executed. We would also get together with other women who had lost their men, like the pilots' wives. We helped each other a great deal. We would go all around, here and there and to the church, with our little children. We had been friends before, but now we had an even stronger bond. My faith sustained me enormously. When Pepe died, I really believed in eternal life and that life did not end. I really understood that for the first time—because Pepe's body died, but he did not.

When the Brigade was released, we were all thrilled. We had so many friends there, and we were so happy. We were in pain, of course, but we shared in the joy. The Orange Bowl, though, was painful. We had such illusions and faith—well, we chose to believe because we had to believe in something. We knew Kennedy had betrayed us, but we were sure we would win with the Americans' support. Yet I also felt proud at the Orange Bowl: The boys were there, and Kennedy recognized their bravery. It was terribly painful that our loved ones could not be there and that Cuba's freedom had not yet been achieved, but we thought it was something that we would gain in the end.

After that, I had to live. I had to try so that the children would not suffer. They were so small. We would tell them, "Daddy is in heaven. He was so good and brave, and God took him to heaven." Debbie, the little one, asked, "Can't we call him on the telephone? Can't he at least write to us like before?" Myrna Mari, the eldest, always wanted to mail her drawings to her father as she did when he went to the training camps. It was an emotional bombardment. You have no idea. We went through a great deal with my son, who was three and a half when his father died. When he was seven or eight, someone asked him what he was going to do when he grew up, and he said, "go to heaven with Daddy." He was a very quiet child and was serious most of the time. Thank God all the children turned out to be so wonderful.

None of Pepe's friends who were in the *rastra* ever came to speak to me, because it had been so horrible. But three and a half years ago I received a call from California. It was a man from the Brigade. He said, "I nearly died of a heart attack a few weeks ago. I told my wife 'I can't die without speaking to Millán's widow. He asked me before he died that I talk to her'. So, I would like to see you and speak to you." Last year, that man came to Miami with his son. I called my children so they could be there to hear about their father. The man came to my home and sat with my children and his son. He told us of his experience. When he spoke of the *rastra*, his son could not believe it. The son said his father had never before spoken to him about it. The man said it was such a horrible thing that he had never told his children about it. It was truly a terrible crime. He told us that in the *rastra* he began screaming desperately, and that Pepe had told him: "Calm down. You are not going to die. I am the one who is going to die, and I am going to ask you to speak to my wife and my children and tell them that I love them." He said they prayed together.

Rosa Maria "Ia" Freyre

Born in 1941, Rosa Maria Freyre was a graduate of Havana's Sacred Heard School. She married Alfredo "Cuco" Cervantes, a twenty-seven-year-old executive at Standard Oil in Cuba, a few days after her eighteenth birthday. Rosa Maria's father, Ernesto Freyre, was a labor lawyer in Cuba and later, along with Alvaro Sánchez, was one the central figures on the Cuban Families Committee. She currently resides in Miami and is part owner of Express Travel, one of Miami's best-known travel agencies.

Cuco began working against Batista at around the time we began dating. He wasn't part of any specific group, but at Standard Oil he was with a group of young men who were very involved in distributing pamphlets and things like that. Although we had all been anti-Batista, we realized after the pilots' trial what was really going on with Castro. My father talked a great deal about what a true dictatorship and Communism meant and how it would be worse than what we had before—no matter how terrible it had seemed. What impressed my father most, and what influenced us the most, was that the government was reversing court decisions. So Cuco started doing the same sort of propaganda against Castro as he had done against Batista.

We left Cuba in October 1960. We were able to take $150 per person, plus the jewelry we wore—we looked like show horses with all our jewelry on. I came with my month-and-a-half-old baby. We rented a wood-framed house in Miami, where nineteen of us lived. Whenever a family member came to Miami, they would join us there. We were very tightly squeezed, and we didn't know how to cook or do housework, but we learned. We believed that we would return soon, because the Americans were going to support us since it was impossible for them to have Communism ninety miles away.

When my brother Tito arrived in Miami, he and Cuco enlisted in the Brigade. The two of them had gone down, signed up, and gave us the news later. We all supported them. Tito was only eighteen, and Mother was a little worried because he was so young—but she was supportive. I'll tell you, I thought it was very heroic and beautiful. Although we knew it would be risky, we never thought it would end up like it did: We of course believed the

Americans were going in with them. Tito and Cuco left for the camps in early January.

On April 17, I remember we found out that the invasion had started. We thought it was with American planes, and the news was good. Then for a time nobody knew anything. The next day it all changed. Everyone was around the radio, waiting to hear what names were announced, and whose voices were heard. They then began announcing the names of those who had been imprisoned. We thought that those whose names were not announced would return. I believed Cuco was among those who had escaped and that he would soon show up in Miami. I was—and still am—a hopeless optimist, so it was a great surprise to me when I learned that he had died. In fact, I thought it was a lie at first. He died in the *rastra*; he was an asthmatic. His parents were in Cuba, and they had to identify his body.

Days later I was with my sister Conchita on the shoreline close to where we were living. She told me, "You have been given a cross and a hardship. Today you must choose between being admired or pitied. It is in your hands." I never forgot that. I thought it was the end of my life. I had just turned twenty years of age. I see my children today, and I cannot think of something like that happening to them.

My father, along with Alvaro Sánchez, Berta Barreto, and others, then dedicated himself to gain the release of the prisoners. Mother and I would go to meet with the university students, who were good friends of mine but were ideologically opposed to the prisoner exchange. We would go with the other widows to see them and to show them it was only an exchange for medicine and food.

My father was my hero. He was a labor lawyer, and all I ever heard from him was about justice for the workers. From exile, he modernized Cuba's labor laws for the future. Father always worked in one way or another in exile for Cuba.

We were very relieved when the prisoners were released. I waited for my brother at home and didn't go to Dinner Key Auditorium. If I would have been there, I would have taken some of the joy away from Mother. She was receiving hers, but mine was not returning. I did go to the Orange Bowl ceremony. I truly detested John Kennedy. I didn't believe anything he was saying, and I blame him. Bobby Kennedy accepted that they had made a mistake, and he was the Kennedy who tried to fix things somehow.

María Leonor Portela

María Leonor Portela was born in Oriente Province and raised in Camagüey. A stewardess for Cubana Airlines, she married air force pilot and cadet school graduate José Alberto Crespo. Crespo left Cuba in December 1958, shortly before Batista's fall, because of problems he experienced with the air force leadership. Crespo and Portela returned to Cuba the following month, a few weeks after Batista's fall. During the invasion, Crespo's B-26 went down in the ocean while returning to Nicaragua after having supported the Second Battalion on the road between Playa Larga and Jagüey Grande on April 17. His remains were never found. Portela currently resides in Guatemala, where she operates an orphanage.

We went back to Cuba at the end of January 1959. I didn't want him to go back, because I was afraid. I knew those people in the revolutionary movement, and I knew it wasn't going to be easy. The new chief of the air force had called my husband while we were in Miami and told him, "We need you here. Come back." My husband told me there was no problem and that he wanted to go back. He returned to Cuba and went to the air force the following day. When he got there, they put him in jail at the Columbia military base.

María Leonor Portela poses with children at her Guatemala orphanage, 1999. By permission of María Leonor Portela.

No one was your friend if you had been involved with the military. So I went to see Haydée Santamaria, Castro's right hand. I had met her earlier in Miami. She was a Communist, but she was an idealist, a fair woman. I was desperate, and I didn't know who else to see. When I went to see her, there were a bunch of women dressed in military outfits looking for jobs. It was sickening—all those people who had not done anything for the revolution. Santamaria looked at me and said, "What do you want from me? What have you come here to ask me for?" I said, "I have not come here to ask. I have come here to demand, because my husband is in jail. If this is what the 26th of July Movement is, and if this is what Castro is, both are dirt. Look, if you are going to execute my husband, then I am going to ask you for a big favor: that you let me watch. I have the strength to do that and more. If his life depends on me begging one of you, then you can kill him tomorrow—but let me watch." She looked at me, smiled, and said, "When a woman defends a man the way you defend your husband, he must be very good, and he deserves to live. Where is he?" I said, "In Columbia." She said, "Tomorrow at two o'clock, meet me there."

She went to Columbia and demanded that my husband be freed. She then gave him to me. After that, I called her when the pilots went on trial and were sentenced to thirty years. I said, "I need a pass so that my husband can get out of the country." She said, "Look, I had a problem with Castro because of your husband. I cannot do any more for you. Tell your husband not to look for a job, not to go around the city too much. Get out of the country as soon as you can."

I knew we were on our own. Since I was still flying, I noticed that U.S. citizens didn't need a passport to go to Cuba; they just filled out a small form they would turn in with a seal. With that, they could get out. So I stole one of those forms and put an immigration stamp on it. I had friends who worked there, and while they were distracted I put the stamp on it. On the fifth of April, I got him out through the airport as an American citizen. I left the following day.

We came back to Miami and started working. The first job he got was in a window factory. It was horrible. One time he was caught in Fort Lauderdale trying to load a bomb onto a P-51. He was going to fly to Cuba and drop it where Castro and his ministers were getting together, but the FBI caught him. They told him, in front of me, that "the relations between the United States and Cuba are good. We don't want any problems, and if you do something to harm Castro we will find you wherever you go in the world. We are not going to allow this."

I was eight months pregnant when my husband went to the camps in August 1960. I always had the feeling that if he went back to Cuba, he was going to die. But he suffered a lot for his friends in jail. He said, "I'll never be happy if I sit here and don't do anything for my friends who are in jail. I have to do this." I told him, "You know, this is suicide." He said, "You're probably right, but I have to do it." My son was born on October 12, 1960. We were able to write to each other, but the letters were censored and delivery was very irregular.

On the fifteenth of April, I heard on the radio—like everyone else—that something was going on. When the plane came to Miami and the pilot said he had defected and all that, we knew it was all part of a hoax, since we knew the pilot. What I didn't know then was that my husband had taken part in the bombing of the Columbia military base.

During the invasion, they would send two B-26s at a time to the beaches. My husband went at around 2:00 or 3:00 in the afternoon. He was flying with Chirrino Piedra. They were very close and had always been together. He loved him like a brother. So they went and did the mission, and they were coming out. I had a cousin on the beach who heard the conversation between Piedra and my husband on the radio. My husband said, "Let's go. The fighters are about to get here." Piedra told him, "Wait. I still have some ammunition, and I am going to Central Australia," which was a little bit inland. So my husband went over the ocean and started to circle around, waiting for him. When he communicated with my husband, he said, "I have a Sea Fury after me, and I can't shake him," and they blew him up.

So my husband took off. By then, three planes were after him. He got very low, close to the ocean, and zigzagged, as it was the only way he could possibly escape the fighters. My husband was over international waters, and they still went after him. Two American airplanes showed up and flew over my husband, and those guys (the Castro pilots) took off. One of the Castro pilots, Del Pino, wrote in his book that he said, "Let him go because the airplane is badly hurt." And it was: They had no instruments, they were losing fuel, everything. So the American airplanes left, and my husband was flying over the ocean. By this time it was almost 6:00 at night. He finally started calling "mayday" and made radio contact with another plane coming from the base. There was a priest, Father Cavero, on that airplane. The priest asked him if they—my husband and the navigator—wanted him to hear their confession before they went down. They did, and they confessed over the radio. After that, it was a matter of about twenty minutes. It went silent, and there was nothing else.

It was cruel. Everyone in Miami was saying the pilots didn't take part in the invasion. We had no news for about four or five days, and the Frente would tell us that all the pilots were fine. It was a bunch of lies and confusion. With two of my friends—both wives of pilots—we went to a mass downtown, and people made fun of us, saying, "Your husband didn't go to the invasion." It was horrible. Nobody notified us officially of anything. A mechanic who had returned from the camps and was a friend of my husband came to see me about a week after the invasion. I asked him, "What happened to José Alberto?" He looked at me, and that's when I realized that he was dead. He said, "We don't know. He disappeared." That was the only thing I was ever told. After three days of not working I called my job and told them I didn't know if my husband was dead or alive. They told me, "Well, that's your problem, not ours." I had to go back to work. I have very little memory of what went on during the next three years.

After my husband's death, I didn't want to hear about God. I didn't want to believe there was a God; I couldn't understand that God would do that to me. That went on for more than ten years. In the end, I had no peace and suffered depression after depression. It was really hell. In 1975 I was invited to a prayer group at the Immaculate Conception Catholic Church in Miami. I finally gave up and said, "Lord, do whatever You want with me, but I can't take it anymore." After that, I had like a reencounter with God, like a conversion. From then on, my life changed.

In 1976, the earthquake came in Guatemala, and they asked me to help coordinate the help they were sending from Miami. In Guatemala, I saw the disaster—more than 20,000 people dead and 100,000 injured. The whole country was devastated. That's when I felt I needed to go there. It was like a calling from God to go there and take care of those children. At that point, I started sending medication and toys during Christmas. Ten years later, I was able to raise close to $3,000 at a luncheon, and I then went to Guatemala and opened the children's home in 1986.

María "Mary" Wilrycx Allen

Born in Havana, Maria Wilrycx married Carlos Allen Dosal at the age of eighteen, after graduating from the Catholic school of Our Lady of Lourdes. Carlos

Above: María "Mary" Wilrycx Allen and
Carlos Allen pose at Valle de Viñales,
Pinar del Río Province, Cuba, 1952.
Carlos, Sixth Battalion, lost his right arm
in the invasion. Photograph by permission
of María Allen.
Left: María Wilrycx Allen, at her Miami
office, 1999. Photograph by author.

*worked for his family's business, one of Cuba's largest tobacco companies, which
had been founded by his grandfather. Carlos saw action at Girón, where he lost
his right arm. He was released with the injured prisoners in April 1962. Carlos
remained active in anti-Castro activities until his death in 1973. Mary currently
resides in Miami, where she owns and operates Allen Financial Services.*

We married very young and had a very happy and normal life. I was dedicated
to my home and our children. At the start of the revolution, we all thought that
Cuba was ridding itself of a dictatorship. But when we saw what happened
with the interventions and all that, we knew it was Communism, and we experienced a 180-degree change in our lives.

We instantly saw the problems that were coming, and my husband began working against the revolution. We lived with great anguish and tension during the time we spent in Cuba while Fidel Castro was in power. Then the government seized *Competidora*, the family's cigarette company. It was a Monday morning. Carlos went to work and found *milicianos* there who told them, "Get out. This is ours now." A couple of days later, they came back for him when they found out they couldn't run the operation. They wanted to force him to show them what to do. He left soon afterward for Miami and became involved in groups dealing with Cuba.

While Carlos was in Miami, I was arrested. *Milicianos* came to my home and turned it upside down looking for guns and documents. The police captain who was there wanted me to sign over to him the title to a small German car that I owned. He told me, "If you give me the car, I'll leave you alone." I said, "No. I don't have to give it to you. It's mine." So they took me to the station in a police car. At the station, they sat me on a bench next to a black man who had just been injured by a blow and was bleeding all over. They did it to try and scare me into signing over my car. I wouldn't do it. Two days later, they released me. I didn't go home again, because I was afraid to be there alone. So I went to stay with my mother. Two or three days later, I sold the car. It was hard. I had my two little daughters, and I was pregnant with my son. I felt very alone and very sad about what was happening in Cuba.

I left Cuba in November 1960, shortly after my son was born. In Miami, I worked in a drape-making factory. My husband worked in a hotel on Miami Beach. The first house we rented came with the condition that the baby did not cry. They told us that if he cried, they would throw us out. Today it makes me laugh, but at the time I was very nervous.

In late March 1961, Carlos left for the camps. At first I was frightened, because it was not going to be easy being alone with three children and no money. But I knew my husband, and when he said "I'm going," I knew it would be better for him to go peacefully than for me to have screamed and cried and all of that.

On April 17 we heard the news of the invasion all over the radio, and I prayed Carlos would live. I went to all the functions during those days at Bayfront Park and Gesu Church. Nobody knew what was happening— whether they were imprisoned, whether they were going to be sent to Russia, whether they were all going to be executed. But we knew early on that they had been betrayed and that this was a war with two enemies.

The first news I received about Carlos was that he was dead. Some friends of ours gave us the news when they came over to offer their condolences. They thought we had heard. Later we practically had a funeral at my house. Everyone came and cried. I looked at all that, and I just couldn't believe it.

What had actually happened was that Carlos had tried to make it to our farm in Cienfuegos with two companions after the invasion. They were trapped by a group of *milicianos* and had to kill many of them. (Carlos had always told me that the worst thing in the world was to kill a person.) Anyway, that's where he was injured. He was taken to the hospital in Cienfuegos, where they amputated his right arm. A nurse there sent us a message that he was alive—his family was well known in those parts because of the farm. When the nurse called, she told me, "A *miliciano* saved his life. He kicked him and noticed he was still breathing. They put him on a stretcher and took him away." The *miliciano* who had picked him up later went to see him at the hospital to tell him that although they had lost, he had to salute him because never in his life would he see men fight for a cause the same way they had fought, that they fought fiercely. He said that he would always wear the belt Carlos had worn; that's what he went to show him at the hospital. Carlos was then taken to a hospital in Matanzas. He had several operations, because they amputated it improperly the first time. He suffered great physical pain.

When he returned from Cuba with the injured prisoners, I went to the airport with my three children. The boy was just over a year old, and my daughters were six and seven. All along I had told them their father was in New York looking for work. Before going to the airport, I spoke to them and told them what had really happened. They understood, but they were very nervous when they saw him without his arm. For me, it was as if I had always known him without it. We were living a miracle. It was a miracle from God. It was the Virgin who got the Brigade out of prison.

Carlos was in bad shape. He was operated on in New York Hospital, where they opened him up from the middle of his head to the middle of his back to remove the sensory nerves that went to the arm he lost, since he was living in excruciating pain. He could not be touched anywhere on his body because of it. Although the operation alleviated it to a certain extent, he was never completely cured and always suffered from terrible pain.

The time we spent working with the Families Committee was difficult because we had very little money. But we had to do all that was humanly possible to get the rest of the Brigade out of prison. It was a hard and traumatic experience. Sometimes people who said they were going to help did not; we would often knock at the doors of Latin American embassies, and they didn't want to receive us. Later, when the Brigade got out, the same diplomats all wanted to come to our homes.

Wherever we would go in New York, we were followed by the CIA, the FBI, Fidel's people. I remember one night we went to eat in the Village. There was one at one table to our right and another at the table to our left. Our phones were tapped; it was as if we were in jail.

When the Brigade was finally released, Carlos went with Harry Ruiz Williams to get them aboard the airplanes. The last plane—the one that carried the leaders—was stopped by Fidel Castro because he wanted the money for the injured prisoners. It was a horrible day for me, because Castro said that whoever was there wasn't going back to Miami—and Carlos was there. In a matter of hours, the problem was solved.

Dinner Key Auditorium was completely full during the reunions. It was such a great thing. We were witnessing a miracle. It was never supposed to happen—but I always had faith. There were many people there who fell ill with all the tension and stress from the months prior. Some days we had all thought everything was solved, and the next day we were told there was nothing. It was completely up and down, up and down. That's Fidel Castro.

I feel very proud of what my husband and his companions did for Cuba. They went there with very clear ideals and fought bravely for their cause. It was very hard on our family, but we were living through interesting times. Carlos never stopped fighting for Cuba until he died.

Josefina Encinosa

Josefina Encinosa is the wife of Pedro Encinosa, whose interview appears earlier in the work. She worked as a hairdresser in Bejucal, Havana Province, and lived in Santiago de las Vegas with her family. She was twenty-seven years old at the time of the invasion.

From the time Pedro left for Miami, my life consisted of traveling between Bejucal and Santiago de las Vegas. I didn't know he had been in the camps or the Brigade until after the invasion. In my town, though, there were some *milicianos* who were telling everyone Pedro had drowned in the swamps. Pedro's mother, the poor thing, was in very bad shape. She would spend all day lying down and refused to eat.

His name appeared on a list fifteen days later, and we started trying to find out where he was being kept. About a week afterward, a youngster showed up at the house who had been a literacy volunteer in the swamp. At first we thought he was a *miliciano* kid who had come to bother us. We said, "No, no, we don't want anything." He said, "Madam, I come on behalf of Pedro Encinosa." So, I told him, "Oh, my son, come in, come in." Pedro's mother was thrilled. He was wearing a cap Pedro had given him, and he showed me the watch Pedro had given him. The boy told us my husband was okay and that he had turned himself in at a house. We gave him something to drink and some sweets. I asked him to leave me Pedro's cap, but he told me, "Oh, madam, I would like for you to let me keep it. Now I can go back to San Antonio and tell them that one of the mercenaries gave it to me." He was only thirteen—poor thing, he was so dirty.

In my town, I was harassed a great deal. They would follow me and tell me that Pedro would never be allowed out of prison and that he was going to die. They would tell me that I was a young woman and that I should start my life over. During that time people would come and shout in front of my home, "Down with the worms! Down with the worm bed!" One day a group that had been quartered in the swamp at the Bay of Pigs came through in a truck. My son, who was small, wanted to go out. So he went with a neighbor, as I rarely left the house. Everyone was screaming, "Down with the worms! To the execution wall with the mercenaries!" I was looking out a window, and my little son—in his own tangled way—told them, "I am an invader of Playa Girón, and with great pride." He even swore at them because it angered him that they were saying those things about his father.

The harassment was constant. If I was sitting on the front porch or if I would go out, cars or trucks with *milicianos* would pass by and, when they recognized me, they would shout things. I would ignore them. They never beat me or arrested me, it was all just done to harass me.

I had so many problems in Cuba. As a hairdresser, people would come to my house to have their hair done. When someone would come in dressed as a *miliciana* [a female member of the Castro militia], my son would stare at her. She would ask, "Do you want to be a *miliciano*?" He would say, "No. I am an invader of Playa Girón, and with great pride, just like my father." We thought he would get us all thrown in prison. A *miliciana* once told me, "Do not worry. It's natural—mine say they are *milicianos* and that they are proud. It's natural that he wants to be like his father."

When we visited the prison, we would have to arrive at 7:00 in the morning. The searches were very embarrassing, as they would strip off all our clothes in order to humiliate us. We would all turn, not to look at one another. One time, there was a woman who was missing one of her breasts because of a previous cancer. When the female guard took out the false breast, she joked to the other, "Hey, what do we do with this?" The woman said, "Listen, don't make fun. This is something you shouldn't play with. If I have to live through this moment a thousand times, I will, because I have my sons in there. God willing you won't ever have to live through a moment like this."

One day I took my son to the prison. We bought some candy so that he could give it to his father. When he went in, they searched him, and a *miliciana* took the candy away. During the search, they also touched his private parts, and he told them, "I don't want you touching my private parts, because my father says nobody can touch that." He was naked when he came to me crying. Another woman told the guard, "Let him have the candy." She said no.

During the trial, it was terrible. We were watching the prison day and night in case they moved the men. Next to the prison there was a street that divided into two with an area in the middle that had trees. We went there with an image of Our Lady of Charity, Cuba's patron. Because they didn't want us there praying and all that, they sent a group from the Cuban Federation of Women, who went after us with sticks and hoses. Some people were hit hard. I wasn't hit, because I ran. When the *Federadas* [members of the Cuban Federation of Women] threw the image of the Virgin Mary to the ground, the woman and man who had brought Her jumped on top of Her to protect Her. The *Federadas* hit them a great deal. It was terrible. I knew one of the *Federadas* because she was from Santiago de las Vegas; she later swore to me she was not there. I carry that inside because her family was close to Pedro.

Dulce Carrera Jústiz

Born in Havana, Dulce Carrera Jústiz graduated from Havana's Sacred Heart School in 1957, whereupon she dedicated herself to social charities. Her father was a lawyer and statesman, and her grandfather was a highly renowned professor and diplomat. She met Rogelio González Corzo—who was to become the famed Francisco—in 1958 and was later engaged to him. Although he was executed before they married, she is considered a widow of the invasion. She lives

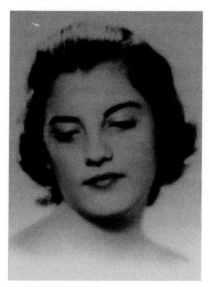

Dulce Carrera Jústiz, fiancée of Rogelio González Corzo, ca. 1960. Photograph permission of Dulce Carrera Jústiz.

in Miami. Her sister Elvira, who passed away a year after the interview was conducted and who was involved with the anti-Castro movement of the early 1960s, is also quoted.

I saw Rogelio for the first time in 1957, at St. Anthony of Padua Church. Later, the *Agrupación Católica* gave a play at the University. I went, and when I sat down, he was next to me. I still get goose bumps when I think of it. When the intermission came, we were introduced. Rogelio, who was an agricultural engineer, went to Baton Rouge, Louisiana, soon after that to take courses in rice cultivation. We began dating when he returned from Louisiana in 1958.

Rogelio was a very straight, serious man. He was strongly Catholic and took daily communion; religion for him was the most important thing in his life. He had established numerous cooperatives throughout Cuba that would loan money to the poor. When Castro came to power, Rogelio became the director of agriculture and Sorí Marín was the minister; they were both later executed on the same day. In any case, once Rogelio was on the inside he saw how quickly things were marching toward Communism.

[Her sister Elvira interjects:] My father had told him so. At our house, Father said, "Listen, Rogelio, all the people they are naming on television (to government positions) are part of the Communist Party, and they are not going to go. So be careful." Rogelio said, "We're going to remove them little by little." Father said, "They are not going to go, and they are going to take over the country.

[Dulce resumes:] After that, Rogelio began attending meetings. He then entered the underground. He was in the MRR and coordinated all the activities inside of Cuba. He had sent his parents and siblings to Spain, and he wanted me to leave the country, too. I refused.

One day, we spoke for eight hours, and he told me we had to pretend that we had broken up. He would later call me under a different name, and he would send flowers the same way. We saw each other several times while he was underground. I do not know where I saw him, because they would pick me up and take me to see him in safe houses, usually for less than half an hour. He sometimes hid in several homes that belonged to my family. One time he called me and said, "Hello, how are you? Fine. Oh, I'm sorry I have the wrong number." It was just so that I would hear his voice. He once called me from the United States. Another time he came back from the United States aboard a submarine, and he brought me a number of souvenirs.

[Elvira:] I learned on March 19 that they had captured Rogelio. I reacted strongly. I knew they were going to find out who he was, in spite of his false identifications and all of that. I told the *Directorio Estudiantil* [Student Directorate], "The Russians, the Chinese, and the Czechs are the ones who run this country. They are going to find out who he is right away." I spent two weeks without telling Dulce. I was dying inside.

[Dulce:] When my sister came into the garage crying one day, I said immediately, "They caught Rogelio." Father Llorente called me and told me there would be no problem and that they were going to get him out. Later I was in front of my house, and we saw two military cars pass. When I looked, Rogelio was looking at me from one of them. It was the last time I saw him. They eventually took him to La Cabaña (a Havana prison), and he was executed on April 20. I wasn't allowed to go to the funeral. I was twenty-two years old. The last time we spoke, he said we would be married on such and such a day. I said "great," and I had everything prepared for our wedding.

Esperanza Díaz Suárez

Born in 1906 in Santiago de Cuba, Oriente Province, Esperanza Díaz went to Havana at the age of seven to attend school. Later she became a school teacher and the mother of Tulio Díaz Suárez, whose testimony appears earlier. She and her husband worked closely with the Cuban Families Committee to gain the release of the Brigade from prison.

My husband was a highly educated and perceptive person. He saw what was behind the Castro regime. He said, "We have to be careful, because this is going to be a revolution that won't take us anywhere; what it will do is drown us and the country." We left Cuba in early 1960.

Tulio came to us at the table one day and told us of his decision to join the Brigade. Because he was an adult, we accepted his decision, although it was with great pain. I took him myself to the office on Twenty-seventh Avenue. After we arrived there, they didn't let us see him or speak to him. It was all very secretive. The last time I saw him was through a gate. He told me, "Mom, when they call me to go, I'll light a cigarette so you know it's me."

When we learned of the invasion, we tried to find out who had survived. We went to the Frente office, and my brother asked a man there if Tulio's name was on the list. He said it was. Later they told us it was not and that what they had told us earlier was an error. You can imagine our condition, with such insecurity. We later learned he was imprisoned. We felt terrible because we did not know what their fate would be. There were rumors that they were going to take the prisoners to Siberia, and about bombs planted underneath the prison at the Isle of Pines.

Isabel Quiñones

Isabel Quiñones, at her Hialeah home, 1999. Photograph by author.

Isabel Quiñones was the cousin of Antonio Sánchez, who remained missing in action after the invasion. They were from the town of Morón, in Camagüey Province.

Antonio had been studying in Havana. His father sent him to the United States to study, which was when he joined the Brigade. His parents knew nothing, and learned of his participation only during the invasion.

It was terrifying during the invasion. My husband told me, "Someone from the army stopped me and told me to go home and stay there, that things were ugly." We later learned who had been in the invasion when they announced the names.

I thought Antonio's mother was going to die when she heard the news. In fact, she died only a short time afterward, grieving. His parents were destroyed; their son was all they had. None of us had known that he was going to war. He was only about nineteen. We thought it was for older people, but they were all so young. I have always said that the best boys of Cuba joined the Bay of Pigs, and there they remained.

7 THE AFTERMATH

The men of Brigade 2506 returned to the United States filled with hope for a free Cuba. Some had to deal with emotional and psychological difficulties;[1] others continued fighting however they could. Even before the release of the Brigade in December 1962, some of those who had escaped were already working with the CIA and running commando missions against Castro.[2] More joined upon their arrival. The agency opened a branch south of Miami called JM WAVE, which soon became one of the largest CIA stations in the world. It had 2,000 Cuban nationals on its payroll, including many Brigade veterans. The station carried out multiple tasks, all aimed at ousting Castro.[3]

Numerous Brigade members also joined the U.S. military within months of their release from prison.[4] Some had successful careers as officers. Erneido Oliva, for instance, retired as deputy commanding general of the District of Columbia Army National Guard in January 1993.[5] However, according to Harold Feeney, Kennedy had arranged for commissions primarily to break up the Brigade in light of his promise to the USSR not to intervene in Cuba and because the Brigade had become a "political embarassment."[6] Most Bay of Pigs veterans' tenure in the U.S. military was short-lived: Many had expected to be part of a force that would invade Cuba, and they were dismayed to realize that no action was forthcoming. A U.S. invasion of Cuba, using Bay of Pigs

The eternal flame honoring the
fallen of Brigade 2506, Miami,
Florida. Photograph by author.

veterans and other exiles, had seemed a logical progression from Kennedy's
promise at the Orange Bowl. Joan Didion explains: "Like other such ad hoc
attempts to neutralize the 2506, the recruitment program involved, if not outright deception, a certain encouragement of self-deception, an apparent willingness to allow those Cubans who 'were quietly entering the American
armed forces' [quote from Sorensen's *Kennedy*] to do so under the misappre-

hension that the United States was in fact preparing to invade Cuba."[7] Although half were discharged from the U.S. military after a few years, sixty-three went on to serve with distinction in Vietnam. Four were killed, and three were wounded in that conflict.[8]

Many Brigade veterans also served in anti-Communist covert missions around the world in the years following their release. Forty-two were part of the CIA's effort to help Congolese president Joseph Kasavubu against a "communist incursion" from Tanzania.[9] Another Brigade veteran was part of the effort that captured Ché Guevara in Bolivia. Throughout the years, many were also part of independent exile commando groups that, drawing on their CIA training, ran operations against Cuba. In time, some became involved in Cuban exile efforts against Castro interventions in many parts of the world, including Africa and, most notably, Nicaragua during the 1980s.[10] The most important anti-Castro political lobby, the Cuban American National Foundation, was founded and led by Brigade veteran Jorge Mas Canosa—whom many considered the most influential Cuban exile leader until his death in the late 1990s. Fellow Brigade member Francisco "Pepe" Hernández, interviewed for this book, was also a powerful member of the group. José Basulto, also interviewed, founded and leads the exile organization Brothers to the Rescue.

Memorial grave of Cuban fighters, Miami, Florida. Photograph by author.

Official Brigade 2506 flag. By permission of Bay of Pigs Veterans' Association.

Most Brigade veterans, however, settled down to normal family life. Many furthered their university studies and entered successful careers, and others did well in business and politics. Some entered the work force as blue-collar workers. Extremely proud of their service, most are members of the Bay of Pigs Veterans Association. The group, which requested the return of their flag from the Kennedy family, has a museum in Miami's Little Havana which is frequented daily by visitors as well as retired Brigade veterans. The men of the Brigade have always enjoyed the status of being the most distinguished and respected group among Cuban exiles. In their community, they are held in perhaps even higher regard than American veterans in the United States following World War II. Each year they gather at the Bay of Pigs monument, just blocks from the museum, for a ceremony to commemorate their fallen comrades. The names of those who died during the invasion are inscribed on the stand that holds the monument's eternal flame. A roll call of the fallen is read, and after each name their comrades call out in unison "¡Presente!" [Present!].[11]

In the decades following the invasion, Kennedy's role and decision making during the Bay of Pigs continued to be judged harshly by Brigade veterans and

Brigade 2506 emblem. By permission of Bay of Pigs Veterans' Association.

Cuban exiles. As time went by and Castro remained in power, the exile community realized that the one true chance they had to overthrow the dictator and ensure democracy in Cuba had been on the beaches of the Bay of Pigs in April 1961. The image of the betrayed freedom fighter faithfully awaiting promised air support remains very powerful and poignant among Cuban Americans. Consequently, President Kennedy was blamed both for abandoning the Brigade and for delivering Cuba to the Soviet Union—the final act being the Cuban Missile Crisis. Many veterans, as well as their families and other exiles, harbor feelings of deep resentment and even hatred for John F. Kennedy. The more sympathetic still place the blame for the invasion's failure squarely on the shoulders of the president but believe it was his inexperience and lack of resolve, rather than cowardice or malice, that were responsible for his poor decisions. Few, if any, blame the CIA and the Joint Chiefs of Staff, as some scholars and writers have done over the years to try to exonerate President Kennedy. The veterans, like most of the era's exiles, nevertheless maintained their faith in the United States as well as their deep love for their native Cuba. They saw no more inherent contradiction in these loyalties as years went by than they had in 1961.

APPENDIX

The Hymn of Assault Brigade 2506

Del fondo de la tierra [From the depths of the earth]
surge nuestro grito, [surges our cry,]
de allí donde los muertos [from the place where the dead]
esperan nuesta acción. [await our action.]
Es un himno que cantan [It is a hymn that is sung]
los árboles y el viento, [by the trees and the wind,]
es un canto de guerra [it is a song of war]
es sangre de Girón [it is the blood of Girón]
Brigade de Asalto [Assault Brigade]
veinticinco cero seis, [twenty-five zero six]
Brigade de Asalto [Assault Brigade]
veinticinco cero seis [twenty-five zero six]
Que nada ya detenga [Nothing will hold back]
esta guerra nuestra, [this war of ours,]
si es una guerra santa [for it is a holy war]
y vamos con la cruz [and we go with the Cross]
Rompamos las cadenas [Let us break the chains]
La Patria nos espera, [the Fatherland awaits us,]

Que rujan los fusiles [may the rifles roar]
Que el fuego se haga luz [may their fire become light]
Brigada de Asalto [Assault Brigade]
veinticinco cero seis, [twenty-five zero six]
Brigade de Asalto [Assault Brigade]
veinticinco cero seis [twenty-five zero six]

NOTES

A Revolution Betrayed

1. H. Thomas, *Cuba*, 1202.
2. Triay, *Fleeing Castro*, 5–11.
3. Schlesinger, *Thousand Days*, 221.
4. Meyer and Szulc, *Cuban Invasion*, 41.
5. H. Thomas, *Cuba*, 1263.
6. Ibid., 1271.
7. Schlesinger, *Thousand Days*, 222.

1. A Call to Arms

1. Gleijeses, "Ships in the Night," 4; Wyden, *Bay of Pigs*, 24.
2. Lynch, *Decision for Disaster*, 14.
3. Wyden, *Bay of Pigs*, 24–25; Gleijeses, "Ships in the Night," 4.
4. Gleijeses, "Ships in the Night," 5.
5. Wyden, *Bay of Pigs*, 25.
6. Gleijeses, "Ships in the Night," 5.
7. Bissell, *Reflections of a Cold Warrior*, 153.
8. Gleijeses, "Ships in the Night," 9, 10; Wyden, *Bay of Pigs*, 30; Schlesinger, *Thousand Days*, 226.
9. Bissell, *Reflections of a Cold Warrior*, 153.
10. H. Thomas, *Cuba*, 1283; Meyer and Szulc, *Cuban Invasion*, 80.
11. H. Thomas, *Cuba*, 1283.

12. Ibid., 1307.

13. Ibid.

14. Wyden, *Bay of Pigs*, 166.

15. Carbonell, *And the Russians Stayed*, 90.

16. Ibid.

17. Johnson, *Bay of Pigs*, 30, 32–34.

18. Sueiro interview.

19. Johnson, *Bay of Pigs*, 36–38.

20. Meyer and Szulc, *Cuban Invasion*, 55–56.

21. H. Thomas, *Cuba*, 1275.

22. Flores interview.

23. Wyden, *Bay of Pigs*, 35; Johnson, *Bay of Pigs*, 44.

24. Wyden, *Bay of Pigs*, 65.

25. Higgins, *The Perfect Failure*, citing John F. Kennedy, 59

26. Gleijeses, "Ships in the Night," 10–12; Schlesinger, *Thousand Days*, 228; Johnson, *Bay of Pigs*, 53; Bissell, *Reflections of a Cold Warrior*, 154–56; Higgins, *Perfect Failure*, 62; Lynch, *Decision for Disaster*, 23.

27. Gleijeses, "Ships in the Night," 15–16; Bissell, *Reflections of a Cold Warrior*, 158–59.

28. Sueiro interview.

29. Johnson, *Bay of Pigs*, 98–99; Schlesinger, *Thousand Days*, 251.

30. Wyden, *Bay of Pigs*, 292; H. Thomas, *Cuba*, 1360.

31. Johnson, *Bay of Pigs*, 98–99; H. Thomas, *Cuba*, 1360; Schlesinger, *Thousand Days*, 251.

32. Kornbluh, *Bay of Pigs Declassified* (citing Artime's "Ideario: Puntos Basicos"), 268.

33. Blight and Kornbluh, *Politics of Illusion*, 71.

2. Training and Preparation

1. Gleijeses, "Ships in the Night," 20–25.

2. H. Thomas, *Cuba*, 1306; Schlesinger, *Thousand Days*, 227.

3. Lynch, *Decision for Disaster*, 29–35.

4. Gleijeses, "Ships in the Night," 34.

5. Hawkins, "Classified Disaster," 36–38.

6. Johnson, *Bay of Pigs*, 82–83; Lynch, *Decision for Disaster*, 41.

7. Mets, *Land-based Air Power*, 69.

8. Ibid., 67.

9. Lynch, *Decision for Disaster*, 41.

10. Lazo, *Dagger in the Heart*, 274–76; Lynch, *Decision for Disaster*, 42–43.

11. Gleijeses, "Ships in the Night," 30–31.

12. Lynch, *Decision for Disaster*, 33.

13. Blight and Kornbluh, *Politics of Illusion* (citing Rafael Quintero), 22–23 (also citing Enrique A. Baloyra), 29; Gleijeses, "Ships in the Night," 29–34.

14. Johnson, *Bay of Pigs*, 85; Lynch, *Decision for Disaster*, 26.
15. Lynch, *Decision for Disaster*, 43; Lazo, *Dagger in the Heart*, 269.
16. Bissell, *Reflections of a Cold Warrior*, 172.
17. Vandenbroucke, "'Confessions' of Allen Dulles," 372–73.
18. Lynch, *Decision for Disaster*, 42; Mets, *Land-based Air Power*, 68.
19. Johnson, *Bay of Pigs*, 55–56.
20. Wyden, *Bay of Pigs*, 59–64.
21. Lynch, *Decision for Disaster*, 158.
22. Wyden, *Bay of Pigs*, 81–83; Zayas-Bazán interview.
23. Wyden, *Bay of Pigs*, 125–27.
24. Ibid., 84.
25. Ibid., 57–59.
26. Johnson, *Bay of Pigs*, 60–62; Wyden, *Bay of Pigs*, 57–59.
27. Sueiro interview.
28. Kornbluh, *Bay of Pigs Declassified*, 288–89.
29. Johnson, *Bay of Pigs*, 122; Wyden, *Bay of Pigs*, 112.
30. Schlesinger, *Thousand Days*, 241.
31. Wyden, *Bay of Pigs*, 56–57.
32. Carbonell, *And the Russians Stayed*, 152.
33. Ibid.
34. Ibid., 154.
35. Sánchez interview.
36. Zayas-Bazán interview.
37. Johnson, *Bay of Pigs*, 79.
38. Ibid., 77.

3. The Battle

1. Bissell, *Reflections of a Cold Warrior*, 183; Lynch, *Decision for Disaster*, 44.
2. Persons, *Bay of Pigs*, 80; Johnson, *Bay of Pigs*, 94; Lazo, *Dagger in the Heart*, 286.
3. Persons, *Bay of Pigs*, 80.
4. Lynch, *Decision for Disaster*, 70.
5. Montalvo interview.
6. Wyden, *Bay of Pigs*, 170–72; Flores interview.
7. Lazo, *Dagger in the Heart*, 22–28; H. Thomas, *Cuba*, 1365, 1358.
8. Bissell, *Reflections of a Cold Warrior*, 196; Hawkins, "Obsession."
9. Wyden, *Bay of Pigs*, 198–99.
10. Bissell, *Reflections of a Cold Warrior*, 184.
11. Beschloss, *Crisis Years*, 144–45.
12. Wyden, *Bay of Pigs*, 204.
13. Ibid., 205
14. Ibid., 205–6; Lazo, *Dagger in the Heart*, 294.
15. Lynch, *Decision for Disaster*, 72; Johnson, *Bay of Pigs*, 100.
16. Wyden, *Bay of Pigs*, 216–17; Lynch, *Decision for Disaster*, 73.

17. Lynch, *Decision for Disaster*, 83–86; Wyden, *Bay of Pigs*, 217–20; Zayas-Bazán interview; Lynch interview.

18. Johnson, *Bay of Pigs*, 105; Lynch, *Decision for Disaster*, 88.

19. Lynch, *Decision for Decision*, 88; Wyden, *Bay of Pigs*, 221.

20. Lynch, *Decision for Disaster*, 88; Wyden, *Bay of Pigs*, 221.

21. Lynch, *Decision for Disaster*, 89.

22. H. Thomas, *Cuba*, 1364.

23. Lynch, *Decision for Disaster*, 93–94; Johnson, *Bay of Pigs*, 105–7.

24. Johnson, *Bay of Pigs*, 106–7; Wyden, *Bay of Pigs*, 222; Lynch, *Decision for Disaster*, 93–94.

25. Lynch, *Decision for Disaster*, 94.

26. Johnson, *Bay of Pigs*, 112–13.

27. Lynch, *Bay of Pigs*, 97.

28. Ibid., 98.

29. Ibid., 109.

30. Johnson, *Bay of Pigs*, 111; Díaz Suárez interview.

31. Johnson, *Bay of Pigs*, 114–15; Lynch, *Decision for Disaster*, 100, 112–14; H. Thomas, *Cuba*, 1364.

32. Lynch, *Decision for Disaster*, 160.

33. Ibid., 113.

34. Johnson, *Bay of Pigs*, 113.

35. Lynch, *Decision for Disaster*, 113–17.

36. Johnson, *Bay of Pigs*, 110.

37. Wyden, *Bay of Pigs*, 228; Johnson, *Bay of Pigs*, 123; Lynch, *Decision for Disaster*, 100–101.

38. Johnson, *Bay of Pigs*, 123.

39. Mets, *Land-based Air Power*, 75; Wyden, *Bay of Pigs*, 228; Johnson, *Bay of Pigs*, 124–25; Lynch, *Decision for Disaster*, 101–2.

40. Lynch, *Decision for Disaster*, 101–2.

41. Wyden, *Bay of Pigs*, 234–35.

42. Lynch, *Decision for Disaster*, 102; Johnson, *Bay of Pigs*, 126.

43. Johnson, *Bay of Pigs*, 126–27; Sánchez interview.

44. Lynch, *Decision for Disaster*, 159–60.

45. Johnson, *Bay of Pigs*, 134; Wyden, *Bay of Pigs*, 272; Lynch, *Decision for Disaster*, 102–3.

46. Lynch, *Decision for Disaster*, 103.

47. Wyden, *The Bay of Pigs*, 273.

48. Johnson, *Bay of Pigs*, 138; Lynch, *Decision for Disaster*, 104.

49. Lynch, *Decision for Disaster*, 104.

50. Johnson, *Bay of Pigs*, 129–30.

51. Lynch, *Decision for Disaster*, 116–22.

52. Lynch, *Decision for Disaster*, 123–24; Johnson, *Bay of Pigs*, 143, 147–48.

53. Lynch, *Decision for Disaster*, 124; Wyden, *Bay of Pigs*, 243–45.

54. Johnson, *Bay of Pigs*, 138–39.

55. Johnson, *Bay of Pigs*, 144–45, 148–49.

56. Wyden, *Bay of Pigs*, 235–36; Mets, *Land-based Air Power*, 79.

57. Johnson, *Bay of Pigs*, 145–46, 149–50.

58. Lynch, *Decision for Disaster*, 127.

59. Wyden, *Bay of Pigs*, 267.

60. Johnson, *Bay of Pigs*, 151–52.

61. Wyden, *Bay of Pigs*, 270–71.

62. Wyden, *Bay of Pigs*, 271; Johnson, *Bay of Pigs*, 153; Lynch, *Decision for Disaster*, 128–29.

63. Lynch, *Decision for Disaster*, 128–29; Johnson, *Bay of Pigs*, 154–55.

64. Johnson, *Bay of Pigs*, 157–58.

65. Ibid., 163–64.

66. Wyden, *Bay of Pigs*, 282; Johnson, *Bay of Pigs*, 165–66.

67. Johnson, *Bay of Pigs*, 166.

68. Lynch, *Decision for Disaster*, 130–31.

69. Johnson, *Bay of Pigs*, 168; Wyden, *Bay of Pigs*, 285.

70. Wyden, *Bay of Pigs*, 291–93.

71. Johnson, *Bay of Pigs*, 178–79; Lazo, *Dagger in the Heart*, 296; H. Thomas, *Cuba*, 1370.

72. Lynch, *Decision for Disaster*, 135.

73. Chapman, "View From PriFly," 50.

74. Wyden, *Bay of Pigs*, 300.

75. Chapman, "View From PriFly," 49.

76. Johnson, *Bay of Pigs*, 175–76.

77. "Histórica Carta de 'Francisco,'" Diario las Americas.

4. Retreat and Capture

1. Johnson, *Bay of Pigs*, 192–202.

2. H. Thomas, *Cuba*, 1370.

3. P. Encinosa interview.

4. Johnson, *Bay of Pigs*, 184–85.

5. Prison and Liberation

1. Johnson, *Bay of Pigs*, 188.

2. Johnson, *Bay of Pigs*, 188; Lynch, *Decision for Disaster*, 143; Silveira interview.

3. Herrera interview; Marquet interview; Sánchez interview; Sánchez de Cárdenas interview; Martínez Malo interview.

4. Martínez Malo interview.

5. Johnson, *Bay of Pigs*, 214–17.

6. Johnson, *Bay of Pigs*, 207–11; Lazo, *Dagger in the Heart*, 319–320; Martínez Malo interview.

7. Johnson, *Bay of Pigs*, 206–7; Wyden, *Bay of Pigs*, 303.

8. Lazo, *Dagger in the Heart*, 313–18; Johnson, *Bay of Pigs*, 230–44.

9. Lazo, *Dagger in the Heart*, 320–21.

10. Johnson, *Bay of Pigs*, 251, 255.

11. Johnson, *Bay of Pigs*, 256–57; Carrillo interview.

12. Marquet interview.

13. Carrillo interview; Palmer, *Brigade 2506* (film).

14. Lazo, *Dagger in the Heart*, 322–23.

15. Montalvo interview; Marquet interview.

16. T. Díaz Suárez interview, July 26, 1999; Carrillo interview; Marquet interview.

17. Lazo, *Dagger in the Heart*, 324.

18. Allen interview; Morse interview; Zayas-Bazán interview.

19. Morse interview.

20. Johnson, *Bay of Pigs*, 294–302; Martínez Malo interview; T. Díaz Suárez interview.

21. Lazo, *Dagger in the Heart*, 324–25; Johnson, *Bay of Pigs*, 303–4.

22. Lazo, *Dagger in the Heart*, 324–27.

23. Johnson, *Bay of Pigs*, 321–34   1.

24. Ibid., 334–41.

25. Ibid., 338–41.

7. The Aftermath

1. Johnson, *Bay of Pigs*, 352.

2. Ibid., 261–62.

3. Lynch, *Decision for Disaster*, 169–71.

4. Johnson, *Bay of Pigs*, 353.

5. "Soldier Renews His Battle," A22.

6. Feeney, "No Regrets," 554.

7. Didion, *Miami*, 86.

8. Feeney, "No Regrets," 554.

9. Ibid.

10. Ibid., 554–55.

11. Didion, *Miami*, 19; Palmer, *Brigade 2506* (film).

BIBLIOGRAPHY

Interviews (Tape Recordings)

Abril, Mario. Telephone interview by Roberto N. Allen. Baltimore, Md., to Signal Mountain, Tenn., October 27, 1999.

Basulto, José. Interviewed by author. Coral Gables, Fla., July 22, 1999.

Bovo, Esteban. Interviewed by author. Miami, Fla., July 22, 1999.

Bustamante, Alberto Sánchez de. Interviewed by author. Orlando, Fla., August 6, 1999.

Carbonell, Néstor. Interviewed by author. Greenwich, Conn., August 28, 1999.

Carrera Jústiz, Dulce. Interviewed by author. Coral Gables, Fla., August 13, 1999.

Carrera Jústiz, Elvira. Interviewed by author. Coral Gables, Fla., August 13, 1999.

Carrillo, Father Sergio. Interviewed by author. Miami, Fla., July 7, 1999.

Clark, Juan. Interviewed by author. Miami, Fla., July 8, 1999.

Cortina, Humberto. Interviewed by author. Coconut Grove, Fla., July 15, 1999.

Díaz, Higinio "Nino." Interviewed by author. Key Biscayne, Fla., August 13, 1999.

Díaz Suárez, Esperanza. Interviewed by author. Miami, Fla., July 26, 1999.

Díaz Suárez, Tulio. Interviewed by author. Miami, Fla., July 26, 1999.

Encinosa, Josefina. Interviewed by author. Miami, Fla., July 28, 1999.

Encinosa, Pedro. Interviewed by author. Miami, Fla., July 28, 1999.

Figueras, Juan. Interviewed by author. Coral Gables, Fla., July 12, 1999.

Flores, José. Interviewed by author. Miami, Fla., August 11, 1999.

Freyre Delgado, Rosa María. Interviewed by author. South Miami, Fla., July 27, 1999.

Girbau, Mario. Interviewed by author. Miami, Fla., July 15, 1999

Giró, Jorge. Interviewed by Roberto N. Allen. Baltimore, Md., September 27, 1999.

Gonzalez de León, Antonio. Interviewed by author. Miami, Fla., July 9, 1999.

Hernández, Francisco. Interviewed by author. Miami, Fla., July 20, 1999.

Herrera, Jorge. Interviewed by author. Coral Gables, Fla., July 15, 1999.

León, Luis. Interviewed by author. Newington, Conn., August 24, 1999.

Lynch, Grayston. Interviewed by author. Tampa, Fla., August 6, 1999.

Macho, Father Tomás. Telephone interview by Roberto N. Allen. Baltimore, Md., to Miami, Fla., November 29, 1999.

Manso, Andrés. Interviewed by author. Miami, Fla., July 9, 1999.

Marquet, Jorge. Interviewed by author. Miami, Fla., July 9, 1999.

Martínez, Rolando. Interviewed by author. Miami, Fla., August 9, 1999.

Martínez Malo, Mario. Interviewed by author. Coral Gables, Fla., July 12, 1999.

Martínez Reyna, Fernando. Interviewed by author. Coral Gables, Fla., July 22, 1999.

Molina, Francisco. Interviewed by author. Miami, Fla., June 23, 1999.

Montalvo, Rafael. Interviewed by author. Coral Gables, Fla., August 10, 1999.

Morse, Luís. Interviewed by author. Tallahassee, Fla., August 16, 1999.

Pardo Millán, Myrna. Interviewed by author. Miami Beach, Fla., July 28, 1999.

Ponzoa, Gustavo. Interviewed by author. Miami, Fla., August 12, 1999.

Portela, Leonor. Telephone interview by Roberto N. Allen. Baltimore, Md., to Miami, Fla., December 8, 1999.

Quiñones, Isabel. Interviewed by author. July 26, 1999.

Regalado, José. Interviewed by author. Coral Gables, Fla., July 14, 1999.

Sánchez, Ricardo. Interviewed by author. Hialeah, Fla., July 9, 1999.

Sánchez de Cárdenas, Julio. Interviewed by author. Miami, Fla., August 10, 1999.

Silveira, Jorge. Interviewed by author. Miami, Fla., July 14, 1999.

Sordo, Juan. Interviewed by author. Hialeah, Fla., July 29, 1999.

Souto, Javier. Interviewed by author. Miami, Fla., July 22, 1999.

Sueiro, Hugo. Interviewed by author. West Miami, Fla., July 13, 1999.

Wilrycx Allen, María. Interviewed by author. Coral Gables, Fla., July 13, 1999.

Zayas-Bazán, Eduardo. Interviewed by author. Key Biscayne, Fla., July 7, 1999.

Written Material

"After Cuba: Who Stood for What?" *U.S. News and World Report*, December 17, 1962, 33–35.

"The Air Will Be Ours: Cuban Fighters Tell Why They Expected Air Cover." *U.S. News and World Report*, February 4, 1963, 33–36.

Aguilar, Luis. Introduction to *Operation Zapata: The "Ultrasensitive" Report and Testimony of the Board of Inquiry on the Bay of Pigs*. Frederick, Md.: University Publications of America, 1981.

Beschloss, Michael R., *The Crisis Years: Kennedy and Khrushchev, 1960–1963*. New York: HarperCollins, 1991.

Bissell, Richard M., Jr. *Reflections of a Cold Warrior: From Yalta to the Bay of Pigs*. New Haven and London: Yale University Press, 1996.

Blight, James G., and Peter Kornbluh. *Politics of Illusion: The Bay of Pigs Invasion Reexamined.* Boulder, Colo.: Lynne Rienner, 1998.

Bosnal, Philip. *Castro, Cuba, and the United States.* Pittsburgh: University of Pittsburgh Press, 1971.

Carbonell, Néstor T. *And the Russians Stayed: The Sovietization of Cuba: A Personal Portrait.* New York: Morrow, 1989.

Chapman, William. "A View from PriFly." *U.S. Naval Institute Proceedings* 118 (October 1992): 45–50.

Didion, Joan. *Miami.* New York: Pocket Books, 1987.

Dille, John. "We Who Tried." *Life,* May 10, 1963.

Feeney, Harold. "No Regrets—We'd Do It Again." *The Nation,* April 19, 1986, 550–57.

Ferrer, Eduardo. *Operation Puma: The Air Battle of the Bay of Pigs.* Miami: International Aviation Consultants, 1982.

Flynn, Michael. "A Perfect Failure." *The Bulletin of the Atomic Scientists* 54, no. 3 (May/June 1998): 7–9.

"For the First Time: The Story of How President Kennedy Upset the Cuban Invasion of April 1961." *U.S. News and World Report,* February 4, 1963, 29–33.

Gleijeses, Piero. "Ships in the Night: The CIA, the White House, and the Bay of Pigs." *Journal of Latin American Studies* 27 (1995): 1–42.

Handleman, Howard. "Prisoners Tell—The Real Story of the Bay of Pigs." *U.S. News and World Report,* January 7, 1963, 38–41.

Hawkins, Jack. "Classified Disaster: The Bay of Pigs Operation Was Doomed by Presidential Indecisiveness and Lack of Commitment." *National Review,* December 31, 1996, 36–38.

———. "An Obsession with 'Plausible Deniability' Doomed the 1961 Bay of Pigs Invasion from the Outset." *Military History,* May 1998.

Higgins, Trumbull. *The Perfect Failure: Kennedy, Eisenhower, and the CIA at the Bay of Pigs.* New York: Norton, 1987.

Hunt, Howard. *Give Us This Day.* New Rochelle, N.Y.: Arlington House, 1973.

"The Inside Story—Kennedy's Fateful Decision: The Night the Reds Clinched Cuba." *U.S. News and World Report,* September 17, 1962.

Johnson, Haynes. *The Bay of Pigs: The Leaders' Story of Brigade 2506.* New York: W. Norton, 1964.

Klein, Richard. *Focus on 1960–1964: The Kennedy Years.* ABC Video Enterprises, 1982.

Kornbluh, Peter, ed. *Bay of Pigs Declassified: The Secret CIA Report on the Invasion of Cuba.* New York: The New Press, 1998.

Lazo, Mario. *Dagger in the Heart: American Policy Failures in Cuba.* New York: Twin Circle Publishing Company, 1968.

Lynch, Grayston L. "Bay of Pigs Report Contains No Dark Secret." *New York Times,* April 29, 1996, A26.

———. *Decision for Disaster: Betrayal at the Bay of Pigs.* Washington and London: Brassey's, 1998.

Mets, David R. *Land-based Air Power in Third World Crises*. Maxwell Air Force Base, Ala.: Air University Press, 1986.

Meyer, Karl E., and Tad Szulc, *The Cuban Invasion: The Chronicle of a Disaster*. New York, Washington, and London: Frederick A. Praeger, 1962.

Murphy, Charles J. V. "Cuba: The Record Set Straight." *Fortune*, September 1961.

Palmer, Eduardo, exec. prod. *Brigade 2506* (film).

Penabaz, Manuel. "'We Were Betrayed': A Veteran of the Cuban Invasion Speaks Out." *U.S. News and World Report*, January 14, 1963, 46–49.

Persons, Albert C. *Bay of Pigs: A First Hand Account of the Mission by a U.S. Pilot in Support of the Cuban Invasion Force in 1961*. Jefferson, N.C.: McFarland, 1990.

Peterzell, Jay. "An New Look at an Old Failure." *Time*, June 1, 1987, 29.

Robbins, Carla Anne. "'La Causa' Lives on—25 Years after the Bay of Pigs Invasion." *U.S. News and World Report*, April 21, 1986, 36.

Robinson, Linda. "The Price of Military Folly." *U.S. News and World Report*, April 22, 1996, 53–56.

Ros, Enrique. *Playa Girón: La verdadera historia* (Girón Beach: The true story). Miami: Ediciones Universal, 1994

Sandman, Joshua. "Analyzing Foreign Policy Crisis Situations: The Bay of Pigs." *Presidential Studies Quarterly* 16 (1986): 524–29.

Schlesinger, Arthur M., Jr., *A Thousand Days: John F. Kennedy in the White House*. New York: Houghton Mifflin, 1992.

Smith, Charles B., prod. *American Foreign Policy: Kennedy and Confrontation*. Encyclopedia Britannica Educational Corporation, 1981 (film).

Smith, Thomas. "Negotiating with Fidel Castro: The Bay of Pigs Prisoners and a Lost Opportunity." *Diplomatic History* 19: 59–86.

"Soldier Renews His Battle for Castro's Overthrow." *Miami Herald*, December 27, 1992, A22.

Sorensen, Theodore C. *Kennedy*. New York: Harper and Row, 1965.

Thomas, Evan. "Wayward Spy." *Civilization* (September/October 1995): 36.

Thomas, Hugh, *Cuba: The Pursuit of Freedom*. New York: Harper and Row, 1971.

Triay, Victor Andrés. *Fleeing Castro: Operation Pedro Pan and the Cuban Children's Program*. Gainesville, Fla.: University Press of Florida, 1998.

Turtle, Candace. "A Father's Homecoming." *Reader's Digest*, February 1989, 57–51.

Vandenbroucke, Lucien S. "Anatomy of a Failure: The Decision to Land at the Bay Of Pigs." *Political Science Quarterly* 99, no. 3 (Autumn 1984): 471–91.

———. "The 'Confessions' of Allen Dulles: New Evidence on the Bay of Pigs." *Diplomatic History* 8, no. 4 (1984): 365–75.

Wheeler, Keith. "Hell of a Beating in Cuba." *Life*, April 28, 1961.

Will, George. "The First Contras." *Newsweek*, March 31, 1986, 80.

Wyden, Peter. *Bay of Pigs: The Untold Story*. New York: Simon and Schuster, 1979.

Personal Communications

Corzo, Rogelio Gonzalez, Letter to family. Provided by Dulce Carrera Jústiz.

INDEX

Abril, Mario, 50–51, 151–52
African Pilot, 136–37, 154
Agrupación Católica Universitaria, 10, 19, 46–47, 49. *See also* Roman Catholic Church
Air campaign, Bay of Pigs invasion: pre-invasion missions, 4, 11; original plan, 38–40; early dilutions, 42; coming together of exile air force, 42; D-2 attack, 68–69; phony defector, 69; President Kennedy's cancellation of D-Day strikes, 70; potential of, if executed as planned, 75–76, 79; April 17 campaign, 75–76, 83–85, 167; April 18–19 campaign, 80, 109–10. *See also* Invasion, Bay of Pigs
Alejos, Roberto, 11
Allen Dosal, Carlos, 168–72
Alonso, José, 43
Artime, Manuel, 9, 10, 24, 61, 64, 72, 132
Auténtico (Party) Organization, 13, 66
Aviators' trial, 2, 20, 56

Basulto, José, 110–12, 148, 181
Batista, Fulgencio, 1, 8, 158, 163

Bay of Pigs, geography of, 38–39. *See also* Operation Pluto
Bay of Pigs Veterans' Association, 182
Bender, Frank. *See* Gerry Droller
Berle, Adolf, 45, 81
Bissell, Richard Mervin: as head of Cuba project, 7; background of, 7; silence of, over lack of guerrilla option, 41; plea by, for air support on April 17, 70; April 18 White House meeting, 80
Bovo, Esteban, 26, 109–10
Brigade 2506: original officers of, 10; confidence of, in United States, 10, 13, 45–48; early members of, 10–11; puts down Guatemalan military rebellion, 12; recruitment and enlistment by, 12, 13, 47; transportation to Nicaragua, 13, 50; choice of name, 13–14; diversity in ranks of, 13–14; ideals and spirit of, 14, 15, 44–46, 51, 60, 69; emblem of, 15; development of air and naval component by, 42–43, 56–57; political conflict in camps of, 43–44, 52, 54; in swamps around Bay of Pigs, 114, 115; *rastra* incident, 131, 138–39, 161–64; at the Sports Palace, 131–33,

Brigade 2506—*continued*
138–39, 142, 145–49; at the naval hospital,
133, 139–40, 142, 149, 150; at the *Castillo del
Príncipe*, 133–36, 140–41, 143, 146–48, 151–
52; trial of, 135, 140–41, 146–47, 152–53; injured prisoners' campaign, 135–36; *Isla de
Pinos*, 136, 143–44, 153–54; release of, from
prison and family reunions, 136–37, 141,
143–44, 154–55, 164, 171; Orange Bowl ceremony, 137, 141, 144, 155, 162, 164; breakup
of, 179–80; in U.S. armed forces, 179–81;
post-invasion activities of, 181; Veterans' Association, 182; views of, on John F.
Kennedy, 182–83; hymn of, 185–86. *See also*
Invasion, Bay of Pigs
Bundy, McGeorge, 70, 150
Burke, Admiral Arleigh, 79, 80

Cabell, Charles, 70–71
Carbonell, Néstor, 45, 58–60, 150
Carol, Oscar Alfonso, 11, 24
Carrera Jústiz, Dulce, 174–76
Carrera Jústiz, Elvira, 175–76
Carrillo, Justo, 9
Carrillo, Father Sergio, 48–49, 124, 146–48
Castillo del Príncipe. See Brigade 2506
Catholicism, *See* Roman Catholic Church
Cervantes, Alfredo "Cuco," 163–64
China, 71
Christian Democratic Movement, 31. *See also*
Rasco, José Ignacio
Clark, Juan, 19–21, 149–50
Clay, Lucius, 136
Committees for the Defense of the Revolution, 4
Cortina, Humberto, 60, 115–18, 151
Crespo, José Alberto, 165–68
Cruz, Tomás, 132, 147
Cuban Families Committee. *See* Negotiations
for release of Brigade 2506
Cuban Federation of Women, 174
Cuban Revolutionary Council. *See* Frente
Revolucionario Democratico
Cushing, Cardinal, 136

Del Valle, Alejandro, 24, 74, 79–80, 94, 96
Díaz, Higinio "Nino," 21–23, 41; aborted landing, 69, 85–87

Díaz Suárez, Esperanza, 176–77
Díaz Suárez, Tulio, 91–93, 153, 176–77
Didion, Joan, 180–81
Donovan, James B., 136
Droller, Gerry (a.k.a., Frank Bender), 9–10
Dulles, Allen, 7
Duque, Montero, 73, 105

Eisenhower, Dwight D., 4, 5, 7–8, 71
Elena, Col. Martín, 9
Encinosa, Josefina, 172–74
Encinosa, Pedro, 119–21, 154, 172–74
Escambray war, 4, 11, 45, 62
Esterline, Jack, 7

Feeney, Harold, 179
Figueras, Juan, 105–7
Flores, José, 85–87
Frente Revolucionario Democrático: forma-
tion of, 8, 9, 29; difficulties with CIA, 9–10;
planned role of, 38; U.S. assurances to, 45;
on invasion day, 71–72; meeting with
Kennedy after invasion, 81
Freyre, Ernesto, 134, 164
Freyre, Rosa María "Ia," 163–64

García, Hector, 147, 151
García Line, 42–43
Garrand, 50
Gesu Church, 61, 156, 160, 170
Girbau, Mario, 35–36
Giró, Jorge, 27–28, 130
González Corzo, Rogelio, 11, 35, 45, 62, 64,
111–13, 174–76
González de León, Antonio, 32–33, 152
Guevara, Ché, 2

Hawkins, Jack, 38, 71
Helvetia, 11
Hernandez, Francisco "Pepe," 51–53, 98–99, 181
Herrera, Gonzalo, 80, 84–85
Herrera, Jorge, 90–91, 149
Hunt, Howard, 9–10

Infiltration units, 33–34, 40–41, 44, 61–67, 110–
13, 127
Invasion, Bay of Pigs: air campaign, 68–70,

75–76, 79–80, 83–85, 109–10, 167; aborted Díaz landing, 69, 85–87; Bay of Pigs landings, 72–74, 87–92, 98, 100, 104, 106; paratrooper landings and battles, 74, 76, 79–80, 94–97; ships pull out, 74–75; Playa Larga (Red Beach) battles, 75–78, 98–108; U.S. Navy fighters, 78; Girón defense, 80–81, 102; collapse of, 81, 102; attrition rate in, 81–82; rescue mission, 82; reaction to Kennedy by Navy and CIA immediately following, 82; Brigade immediately after invasion, 114–15. *See also* Air Campaign; Brigade 2506; Operation Pluto
Isla de Pinos, 136, 153–54

Kennedy, John F.: 1960 campaign, 11, 12; apprehensions about invasion, 37–38, 45; dilutes Cuba plan, 42, 68; cancels D-Day strike, 70, 71; April 18 meeting, 80; post-invasion speech, 82; breakup of Brigade 2506, 179. *See also* Brigade 2506
Kennedy, Robert, 136, 151, 155, 164

Lemnitzer, Gen. Lyman, 71, 80
León, Luis, 108–9
Lynch, Grayston, 43, 57, 76, 87–89; during landings, 72–73; battles with Castro planes, 74–75; at sea April 17, 78; attempt to resupply April 19, 81; rescue effort, 82

Maceo, Antonio, 14
Macho, Tomás, S.J., 125–26, 153–54
Manso, Andrés, 28–29, 148, 155
Marquet, Jorge, 29–31, 104–5, 153, 154
Martínez, Rolando, 33–35, 64
Martínez-Malo, Mario A., 18–19, 142–44
Martínez Reyna, Fernando, 121–22, 149, 155
Mas Canosa, Jorge, 181
Matos, Huber, 2, 20
Mets, David, 40
Mikoyan, Anastas, 3, 17
Millán Velasco, José "Pepe," 157–63
Miró Cardona, José, 9, 14, 45, 71–72, 150
Molina, Frank, 53–54
Montalvo, Rafael, 99–103, 148, 152–53
Morgan (William) and Menoyo Conspiracy, 10, 24–25, 27

Morse, Luis, 103–4, 116, 118–19
Movimiento de Recuperación Revolucionaria, 9, 11, 13, 15, 23, 29, 35, 44–45, 56
Movimiento Revolucionario del Pueblo, 9, 66

Naval Hospital, *See* Brigade 2506
Negotiations for release of Brigade 2506 from prison: Tractors for Freedom Committee, 133–34, 140; Cuban Families' Committee, 134–36; involvement of injured prisoners, 135, 150–51, 171–72; Donovan negotiations, 136; release, 136–37
Nixon, Richard M., 11

Oliva, Erneido, 73, 77, 79–80, 116, 119, 135, 147, 153
Operation Forty, 39, 59–60
Operation Pluto: original planning for, 8; shift to conventional invasion, 12; Trinidad Plan, 38, 41; Bay of Pigs plan, 38–42; Kennedy dilutions of plan, 42, 68, 70. *See also* Invasion, Bay of Pigs
Orange Bowl ceremony. *See* Brigade 2506

Panama, 10–11, 46–47
Paratroopers. *See also* Del Valle, Alejandro; Invasion, Bay of Pigs
Pardo Millán, Myrna, 157–63
Pérez, Silvio, 43
Pinar del Río, 41, 74
Ponzoa, Gustavo, 83–85, 110
Portela, María Leonor, 165–68

Quiñones, Isabel, 177–78

Radio Swan, 8
Rasco, José Ignacio, 9. *See also* Christian Democratic Movement
Rastra incident. *See* Brigade 2506
Ray, Manuel, 9. *See also* Movimiento Revolucionario del Pueblo
Regalado, José, 62–67, 127
Rescate, 8, 13
Retalhuleu, 11
Revolution, Cuban: overthrow of Batista, 1; shift to Communism, 2–5

Río Escondido, sinking of, 74, 89
Rivero, Felipe, 132
Robertson, William "Rip," 43, 57, 73
Rodriquez, Carlos Rafael, 132
Roman Catholic Church: Catholic groups and opposition, 4; and Brigade ideology, 15; at camps, 49; in prison, 134, 147–48, 151; importance of, to families, 156–57, 159; during invasion, 167–68. *See also* Agrupación Católica Universitaria
Rotunda, Battle of. *See* Invasion, Bay of Pigs
Rusk, Dean, 70–71, 80

Salvar a Cuba (SAC), 17, 18
Sánchez, Antonio, 177–78
Sánchez, Ricardo, 94–97
Sánchez Arango, Aureliano, 9, 20, 122
Sánchez de Bustamante, Alberto, 127–30, 155
Sánchez de Cardenas, Julio, 122–24, 148–49
San Román, José "Pepe:" recruitment into the Brigade, 25; during political upheaval in Guatemala camps, 43–44, 52; en route to invasion, 72; lands at Bay of Pigs, 72; tries to radio ships, 77, 78; and collapse, 81
San Roman, Roberto, 24
Santamaría, Haydée, 166
Schlesinger, Arthur, 5, 45, 81
Silveira, Jorge, 16–18, 138–41
Sinatra, Frank, 151

Sordo, Juan, M.D., 107–8, 155
Souto, Javier, 61–62
Soviet bloc, 12, 71. *See also*, Mikoyan, Anastas
Sports Palace, *See* Brigade 2506
Sueiro, Hugo, 23–26, 46–48, 73, 77, 116, 150–51
Sullivan, Ed, 101, 135

Today Show, 135, 146
Tractors for Freedom Committee. *See* Negotiations for release
Trax Base, 11
Trial of Brigade 2506. *See* Brigade 2506
Trinidad Plan. *See* Operation Pluto

United Nations, 69–70
Urrutia, Manuel, 2
Useppa Island, 10–11, 25–26, 46, 61–62

Vandenbroucke, Lucien, 41–42
Varona, Manuel Antonio de "Tony," 8, 9, 14, 56, 58, 150
Vieques, 43, 57
Vietnam, 71, 181
Villanueva, University of, 16–17, 62

Wilrycx Allen, María "Mary," 168–72

Zayas-Bazán, Eduardo, 54–58, 144–46

Victor Andres Triay is associate professor of history at Middlesex Community College in Middletown, Connecticut. He is the author of *Fleeing Castro: Operation Pedro Pan and the Cuban Children's Program* (Gainesville: University Press of Florida, 1998).